MW01052818

THE MEDIATIZATION OF CULTURE AND SOCIETY

Mediatization has emerged as a key concept to reconsider old, yet fundamental, questions about the role and influence of media in culture and society. In particular the theory of mediatization has proved fruitful for the analysis of how media spread to, become intertwined with, and influence other social institutions and cultural phenomena like politics, play, and religion.

This book presents a major contribution to the theoretical understanding of the mediatization of culture and society. This is supplemented by in-depth studies of:

- the mediatization of politics: from party press to opinion industry
- the mediatization of religion: from the faith of the church to the enchantment of the media
- the mediatization of play: from bricks to bytes
- the mediatization of habitus: the social character of a new individualism.

Mediatization represents a new social condition in which the media have emerged as an important institution in society at the same time as they have become integrated into the very fabric of social and cultural life. Making use of a broad conception of the media as technologies, institutions, and aesthetic forms, Stig Hjarvard considers how characteristics of both old and new media come to influence human interaction, social institutions, and cultural imaginations.

Stig Hjarvard, Ph.D., is Professor and Vice-Chair at the Department of Media, Cognition and Communication, University of Copenhagen, Denmark. He has published books and articles on journalism, media and globalization, media and religion, media history and mediatization theory. He is editor of the journal *Northern Lights* and of the English language books *News in a Globalized Society* (2001) and *Media in a Globalized Society* (2003).

"Stig Hjarvard has through the last decade been a leading scholar in the emerging research on mediatization of culture and society. In this book he synthesizes his theory and makes his extensive work accessible in one English volume. He refines his institutional approach to changes in the media and in social and cultural areas that more and more take on media forms".

Knut Lundby, *Professor of Media and Communication,*
University of Oslo, Norway

"In this noteworthy book, Stig Hjarvard redirects theories about the power of media. Hjarvard reveals a complex and vital picture of how contemporary societies are transforming themselves under conditions of high modernity."

Gaye Tuchman, *Professor of Sociology, University of Connecticut, USA*

THE MEDIATIZATION OF CULTURE AND SOCIETY

Stig Hjarvard

Routledge
Taylor & Francis Group

LONDON AND NEW YORK

First published 2013
by Routledge
2 Park Square, Milton Park, Abingdon, Oxon OX14 4RN

Simultaneously published in the USA and Canada
by Routledge
711 Third Avenue, New York, NY 10017

Routledge is an imprint of the Taylor & Francis Group, an informa business

© 2013 Stig Hjarvard

British Library Cataloguing in Publication Data
A catalogue record for this book is available from the British Library

Library of Congress Cataloging in Publication Data
Hjarvard, Stig.
The mediatization of culture and society / by Stig Hjarvard.
p. cm.
Includes bibliographical references and index.
1. Mass media–Social aspects. 2. Mass media and culture. I. Title.
HM1206.H54 2013
302.23–dc23
2012031611

ISBN: 978-0-415-69236-6 (hbk)
ISBN: 978-0-415-69237-3 (pbk)
ISBN: 978-0-203-15536-3 (ebk)

Typeset in Bembo
by Taylor & Francis Books

MIX
Paper from
responsible sources
FSC
www.fsc.org   FSC® C018575

Printed and bound in Great Britain by MPG Printgroup

CONTENTS

LIST OF FIGURES

LIST OF TABLES

ACKNOWLEDGMENTS

This book is partly based on a Danish publication "En verden af medier, medialiseringen af politik, sprog, religion og leg," published by the Danish Academic publisher Samfundslitteratur in 2008. Some of the chapters have also been published in English:

Chapter 2 is partly based on the article "The Mediatization of Society. A Theory of the Media as Agents of Social and Cultural Change," *Nordicom Review*, vol. 29, no. 2, 2008, pp. 105–34.

Chapter 4 is partly based on the article "The Mediatization of Religion. A Theory of the Media as Agents of Religious Change," *Northern Lights, Film and Media Studies Yearbook*, vol. 6, no. 1, 2008, pp. 9–26.

Chapter 5 is partly based on the article "From Bricks to Bytes: The Mediatization of a Global Toy Industry," in Ib Bondebjerg and Peter Golding (eds) (2004), *European Culture and the Media*, Changing Media – Changing Europe Series, vol. 1, Bristol: Intellect, pp. 43–63.

Chapter 6 is partly based on the article "Soft Individualism: Media and the Changing Social Character," in Knut Lundby (ed.) (2010), *Mediatization: Concept, Changes, Consequences*, New York: Peter Lang, pp. 159–77.

We thank the publishers and journals for their kind permission to reproduce the articles in this book. In all cases the chapters have been thoroughly revised, updated, and expanded.

The pictures in Chapter 5 from the LEGO 1960 brochure, LEGO 1984 and 1996 catalogs, and LEGO website www.bioniclestory.com are reproduced with the kind permission of the LEGO Group.

On a more personal note, I would like to thank colleagues and friends for providing inspiration and critical comments to the arguments put forward in this book. In particular, I would like to thank my colleagues with whom I have been cooperating in various research networks devoted to the study of mediatization: The Nordic Research

Network on Mediatization of Religion and Culture (financed by NordForsk), the research group on The Mediatization of Culture at University of Copenhagen, the National Research Program on The Mediatization of Culture: The Challenge of New Media (financed by The Danish National Research Council), and the ECREA Temporary Working Group on Mediatization.

1

INTRODUCTION

From mediation to mediatization

Introduction

Mediatization has emerged as a new research agenda to reconsider old, yet fundamental, questions concerning the role and influence of the media in culture and society. In particular, the concept of mediatization has proved useful to the understanding of how the media spread to, become intertwined with, and influence other fields or social institutions, such as politics (Strömbäck 2008), war (Horten 2011), and religion (Hjarvard 2011). This book presents the core elements of mediatization theory and puts the theoretical framework to work in analyses of various social phenomena: politics, religion, play, and habitus formation. Chapter 2 provides a lengthy theoretical discussion of mediatization theory, while Chapters 3, 4, and 5 are concerned with empirical analyses of separate social and cultural domains. Chapter 6 provides a theoretical discussion of the relations between mediatization and a particular general process of modernity: individualization. Chapter 7 summarizes the complex outcomes of mediatization processes and discusses various forms of media policies for the "big" and "small" society. In this introductory chapter we will provide a brief context for the relevance and theoretical underpinnings of mediatization theory as it is developed in this book.

Media *in* culture and society

Our inquiry takes its point of departure in a classical question in the sociology of the media, namely, how the media come to influence the wider culture and society. Answers to the question, however, are sought in a new social condition, which we will label the mediatization of culture and society. Traditionally, media and communication studies have tended to look for the influence of the media by studying the communication process itself. The media have been conceived as separate from culture and society, and either as something that exerted influence *on* culture and society, or that could be used by individuals and organizations as instruments *to serve* various purposes and ends. Two different traditions of media and communication studies may exemplify this. The "effect-paradigm" (Preiss *et al.* 2007) has tended to focus on what the "media do to people", i.e., the effects certain mediated messages have on individuals or groups in society. For example, the news coverage during an election campaign might be thought to exert influence on people's political opinions; advertisements to affect consumers' shopping preferences; and film content to affect the viewers' morals or distract attention from matters of greater urgency or significance. Within this paradigm, the media are considered to be the independent variable that affects the dependent variable: the individual.

Within a very different research tradition, audience research with a cultural studies orientation, the primary interest has, in a sense, been the opposite, namely, to study what "people do with the media." According to this research paradigm, the people using the media are active and competent, if not powerful, and they are able to make use of the media in their own everyday practices, in order to satisfy their own needs. As active and competent media users they do not succumb to the hegemonic discourses of media texts, but may interpret them critically, in accordance with their own cultural and social backgrounds (Liebes and Katz 1990; Lull 1990), and as "textual poachers" they may even challenge the dominant ideologies in society (Jenkins 1992a). Within the uses-and-gratification tradition of media research, the focus has similarly been on what "people do with the media," rather than the opposite (Blumler and Katz 1974). Here, active audiences and users are the primary variable, while the media are the secondary variable.

Mediatization theory differs from both of these traditions. Contemporary culture and society are permeated by the media, to the extent that the media may no longer be conceived as being separate from cultural and social institutions. Under these circumstances, the task before us is instead to seek to gain an understanding of how social institutions and cultural processes have changed character, function, and structure in response to the omnipresence of the media. As the two aforementioned research traditions exemplify, the majority of existing research has been preoccupied with the study of "mediation," i.e., the use of the media for the communication of meaning. The cultural and social influences of the media have accordingly been sought within the communication circuit itself, as the effect of mediated messages on audiences; or the opposite, i.e., the use of mediated messages by active audiences. Mediatization studies move the focus of interest from the particular instances of mediated communication to the structural transformations of the media in contemporary culture and society. The influences of the media are not only to be found within the communication sequence of senders, messages, and receivers, but also in the changing relationship between the media and other cultural and social spheres. While the study of mediation pays attention to specific instances of communication situated in time and space (e.g., the communication of politics in blogs during a presidential campaign), mediatization studies are concerned with the *long-term* structural change in the role of the media in culture and society, in which the media acquire greater authority to define social reality and condition patterns of social interaction. This altered understanding of the media's importance does not imply that traditional questions regarding aspects such as the effects of mediated messages on public opinion, or the purposes to which people use the media, are no longer relevant. But it does mean that an understanding of the importance of the media in modern culture and society can no longer rely on models that conceive of the media as being separate from culture and society, or that solely consider the process of mediation.

The media are not simply technologies that organizations, parties, or individuals can choose to use – or not use – as they see fit. The presence of the media has become a structural condition for social and cultural practices, both within particular cultural spheres and in society as a whole (Livingstone 2009). A significant proportion of the influence that the media exert arises out of the double-sided development in which they have become an *integral part* of other institutions' operations, while also achieving a degree of *self-determination and authority* that forces other institutions, to greater or lesser degrees, to submit to their logic. The media are at once part of the very fabric of particular social and cultural spheres (the family, politics, etc.) and a semi-independent institution that provides a nexus between other cultural and social institutions, as well as interpretative frameworks for our understanding of society as a whole, and that constitutes a common arena for public discussion. The *duality* of this structural relationship – being both inside other institutions and a provider of a common perspective on society – sets a number of preconditions for how the media, in given situations, are used and perceived by senders and receivers, thereby affecting relations between people. Thus, traditional questions about media use and media effects need to take account of the circumstance that culture and society have become mediatized.

A theory of the middle-range

As a concept "mediation" is too narrowly focused on the communication process itself, so we need another term, "mediatization", to denote the long-term, large-scale structural transformation of relationships between media, culture, and society. Via a combination of empirically founded studies and theoretical reflections, mediatization studies seek to generalize findings beyond the particular communicative situation. The aim is to consider whether and how structural changes between the media and various social institutions or cultural phenomena come to influence human imaginations, relationships, and interactions. A key question here concerns the appropriate level of generalization for building a theoretical framework. The ambition is not to build "grand theory" in order to establish universal or definitive answers to the influence of media in every culture at all times, but rather to stipulate general patterns of development within particular social institutions or cultural phenomena, and within specific historical periods in particular social and cultural contexts. Nor is our theoretical ambition satisfied merely with accumulating insights into the endless minor variations of situated interaction. In order to steer

Middle Range is not enough

free of both of these pitfalls, i.e., over-generalization as well as under-theorization, mediatization studies seek to develop a theory of *the middle-range* (Merton 1957). As Boudon (1991) observes, the notion of a middle-range theory is not clearly defined and from it we therefore cannot derive a clear specification of the required level of generality, or other conceptual requirements of such a theory. Nevertheless, the notion of a "middle-range theory" reflects an ambition to develop theories that combine theoretical ambition with an empirical cautiousness, recognizing that "it is hopeless and quixotic to try to determine the overarching independent variable that would operate in all social processes, or to determine the *essential* feature of the social structure" (Boudon 1991: 519, emphasis in original). Accordingly, the analysis of mediatization processes will predominantly focus on the meso level of social and cultural arrangements, i.e., at the level of specific social institutions (politics and religion) and cultural phenomena (play) within a given historical and socio-geographical context. Similar to other major sociological concepts like globalization and urbanization, mediatization may be considered a macro-social process, because its influences are visible in society as a whole, but in order to *study* mediatization processes and systematize findings we will generally apply a meso-level perspective. In this book we develop a meso-level perspective through an *institutional approach* that allows us to make generalizations across individual micro-social encounters within a particular domain of culture and society, but prevents us from making totalizing accounts of universal media influence at the macro level.

Since we think of it as a middle-range theory, mediatization theory is not meant to replace existing theories of media and communication, or sociological theories in general. The aim is not to build another closed theoretical castle in which all hitherto known concepts or processes must be relabeled in order to pass through the gate into a new conceptual kingdom. On the contrary, the study of mediatization is an invitation to make heuristic use of existing theories and methodologies in order to make sense of the changing role of the media in contemporary culture and society. In particular, it is an invitation to undertake cross-disciplinary work in which we must seek to make use of theories and methodologies from a variety of disciplines. Precisely because mediatization as a process involves the influence and changing role of the media in a variety of social and cultural spheres, we should work across disciplines (Hjarvard 2012b). To study the mediatization of politics, we need to draw on analyses and concepts from both media studies and political science; and to study the mediatization of religion we must engage with concepts and research from the sociology of religion, media studies, and cognitive anthropology, etc. The contribution from mediatization theory to this interdisciplinary venture is to provide a *framework* for *analyzing* and building a *theoretical* understanding of how the media may interact with other social and cultural processes, and a *set of assumptions* about the possible outcomes of the growing presence of various media in culture and society.

Look up "Sensitizing Concept"

At the present stage, mediatization may be considered what Blumer (1954) labeled a "sensitizing concept" due to its heuristic value of rephrasing key questions concerning the influence of the media in culture and society, and because it provides a new framework and set of questions for the empirical study of various social

and cultural domains. "Sensitizing concepts" are more loosely defined as explora-
tory tools to guide theoretical and empirical enquiry, whereas "definitive concepts"
are carefully defined and made operational via a particular set of attributes whereby
they may serve as technical instruments for empirical research. Like other broad
concepts of sociology (e.g., institutions, social structures, individualization, etc.),
mediatization is not a "definitive concept," since it does not refer "precisely to
what is common to a class of objects, by the aid of a clear definition in terms of
attributes or fixed bench marks" (Blumer 1954: 7).

[Handwritten margin note: NOT a definitive concept]

As Jensen (forthcoming) argues, the distinction between "sensitizing concepts"
and "definitive concepts" does not represent a dichotomy, but rather a continuum,
and as Blumer (1954: 8) himself suggests "sensitizing concepts can be tested,
improved and refined" and thereby move towards the definitive end of the spectrum. The ambition of this book is precisely to test, improve, and refine the concept of mediatization, but not necessarily with the aim of ending up with – in
Blumer's sense – a definitive concept. The two types of concept serve different
purposes in research, and at the present phase of the research into processes of
mediatization we find the sensitizing aspect of the concept more useful, for the
same reasons that Blumer (1954: 10) also generally preferred it: "it has the virtue of
remaining in close and continuing relations with the natural social world." Precisely
because mediatization may entail different outcomes in various cultural and social
institutions, there is a limit to how far the concept "mediatization" can move
towards the definitive end of the spectrum. Consequently, in order to study actual
processes of mediatization in particular domains of culture and society we also need
other more definitive and context-sensitive concepts.

[Handwritten margin note: In essense "Think Critically" in regards]

Mediatization studies are concerned with the role of the media in the transformation
of social and cultural affairs. The conceptual emphasis on how the media may
influence social and cultural *change* should not, however, lead us to suggest that the
most important outcome of media developments is always change. As Fischer's (1992)
historical study of the introduction and social uses of the telephone in the United
States demonstrates, the telephone was not always an instrument of the modernization
and restructuring of social ties. For many people, the telephone made it easier to
maintain and reinforce existing social relations, allowing some aspects of life to continue against a backdrop of modernization in other parts of life. We should,
therefore, be careful not to confuse the perpetual and highly visible "newness" of
media developments with a continuous transformation of all social and cultural
arrangements. In the end, the question of transformation versus stability is not a
theoretical question, but an empirical one that needs to be substantiated analytically.

[Handwritten margin note: phone was a good change]

A process of high modernity

Mediatization is an important concept in modern sociology, as it relates to the
overriding process of modernization of society and culture. The discipline of
sociology was founded in conjunction with the study of the breakthrough of
modern society. Pioneers in the field such as Max Weber, Karl Marx, Emile

Durkheim, and Georg Simmel were not particularly interested in the role or importance of the mass media, but instead focused on such phenomena as industrialization, urbanization, secularization, and individualization. Later sociologists did not show very much interest in the media either. Only late in his career did Pierre Bourdieu, for example, write about the media, and his critique of television journalism (Bourdieu 1998b) appears rather shallow compared to his earlier published work. Viewed in a historical perspective, the lack of interest in the media among classical sociologists should perhaps not surprise us. Throughout the nineteenth century the "media" were not visible in their own right; they were specific technologies and separate cultural phenomena – books, journals, newspapers, the telegraph, etc. – each of which were instruments in the hands of other institutions, such as literature, science, politics, commerce, etc.

[margin note: Weren't aware it was going to be so influential?]

Only with the expansion of the mass media in the twentieth century did the media begin to be perceived as media in their own right, i.e., as forms of communication that shared certain constitutive characteristics and were of some consequence. North American sociology flourished in the 1930s and onwards, and the study of the mass media – film, radio, and newspapers – played a central role for some brief decades. Prominent figures such as Paul Lazarsfeld, Bernard Berelson, and Robert Merton applied sociological perspectives to the media, but then abandoned the media in favor of other objects of study. In post-war Europe critical theory, e.g., The Frankfurt School and structuralism, inspired critical thinking about the role of mass media in society, but it was predominantly a one-way street going from critical theory to media studies. Instead, in North America, Europe, and elsewhere, specialized disciplines arose – communication research, mass communication research, or media studies – that focused exclusively on the media. As a consequence of this specialization, the study of the media lost contact with broader sociological perspectives, and vice-versa. This should not be taken to imply that media research has been completely isolated from sociology and other core disciplines. On the contrary, media scholars have frequently drawn upon other disciplines in their studies of one phenomenon or the other. For example, political theory has been applied to the study of opinion formation, and anthropological theory to the study of media use. But when it comes to more fundamental sociological issues, such as modernization processes, there has been limited cross-fertilization, so that in sociology, the media has remained a marginal topic. In recent years, and in view of the expansion of various forms of digital media, we have seen certain new steps towards a rapprochement between the two disciplines. Manuel Castells' (2001, 2009) discussion of the Internet and the network society is an attempt to integrate a media perspective into sociological theory. Likewise, from a media studies point of view, studies of globalization have aroused interest in sociological and cultural analysis (Silverstone 2007). The theory of mediatization is an attempt to bring this rapprochement a step further. Mediatization is both an empirical process that calls for mutual research efforts by media scholars, sociologists, and researchers from other disciplines; and a theoretical concept that needs to be developed via interdisciplinary dialog.

[margin note: Media & Sociology have not always been studied]

Mediatization should be viewed as a modernization process on a par with globalization, urbanization, and individualization, whereby the media, in a similar way, contribute to both disembedding social relations from existing contexts and re-embedding them in new social contexts (Giddens 1984, 1990). Compared to these other processes, mediatization only became prominent in a later phase of modernity, high modernity, when the media have both become more differentiated from other institutions (what we label the emergence of a semi-independent media institution) and re-embedded into culture and society (what we label the integration of the media in a variety of social institutions). Mediatization is thus a distinct late-modern process that is, to quote John B. Thompson (1990: 15), "partially constitutive of modern societies, and … partially constitutive of what is 'modern' about the societies in which we live in today." When classical sociology was in its formative years, the media did not receive much attention because they had not become distinct enough from other institutions, nor were they by any means as pervasive and influential as they are today. For contemporary sociological inquiry into late-modern society, a theory of the importance of the media to culture and society is no longer an interesting possibility, but an absolute necessity.

We cannot wait any longer to study this

2

MEDIATIZATION

A new theoretical perspective

Introduction

The term "mediatization" has been used in numerous contexts to characterize the influence that the media exert on a variety of phenomena, but not much work has been done to define the term and develop it into a theoretical concept. Only very recently have media researchers sought to develop the concept towards a more coherent and precise understanding of mediatization as a social and cultural process (Hepp 2012; Hjarvard 2008a; Krotz 2009; Schulz 2004). Therefore, let us start by examining the various meanings the concept has been given in earlier works (for overviews of mediatization research see Lundby [2009a] and Kaun [2011]).

At an early stage, mediatization was applied to the media's impact on political communication and other effects on politics. Swedish media researcher Kent Asp was the first to speak of the mediatization of political life, by which he meant a process whereby "a political system to a high degree is influenced by and adjusted to the demands of the mass media in their coverage of politics" (Asp 1986: 359). One form taken by this adjustment is when politicians phrase their public statements in terms that personalize and polarize the issues, so that the messages have a better chance of gaining media coverage. Asp sees the media's growing independence of political sources as yet another sign of mediatization, in that the media thereby gain even more control over media content. Asp acknowledges a debt to the Norwegian sociologist Gudmund Hernes' expression of the "media-twisted society" (Hernes 1978), although Hernes' perspective is broader. Hernes argued that the media had a fundamental impact on all social institutions and their relations with each other. Although Hernes did not actually use the term mediatization, his concept of a "media-twisted society" and the holistic view of society he applies, is consonant in many respects with the concept of mediatization put forward here. Hernes urges us:

to ask what consequences media have for institutions as well as for individuals: the ways public administration, organizations, parties, schools and business function and how they relate to one another. In what ways do media redistribute power in society? […] In short, from an institutional point of view the key question is, how media change both the inner workings of other social entities and their mutual relationships.

(Hernes 1978: 181; my translation from Norwegian)

We find a contemporary and fairly parallel notion in the work of Altheide and Snow (1979, 1988), who call for an "analysis of social institutions-transformed-through-media" (Altheide and Snow 1979: 7). While traditional sociological approaches to the media seek to isolate certain "variables" for media influence, ignoring how the media affect the overall premises for cultural life, Altheide and Snow wish to show how the logic of the media forms the fund of knowledge that is generated and circulated in society. Although they time and again make reference to "media logic," form and format are their principal concepts, drawing on one of the "classics" of sociology, Georg Simmel. Thus they posit the "primacy of form over content" (Altheide and Snow 1988: 206), whereby media logic for the most part appears to consist of a formatting logic that determines how material is categorized, the choice of mode of presentation, and the selection and portrayal of social experience in the media. In their analyses, they mention other aspects of media logic, including technological and organizational aspects, more or less incidentally, and because Altheide and Snow (1979, 1988) are working with North American material, the logic at play is essentially a commercial one. Their prime interest with regard to these "other aspects" is a desire to explore the extent to which, and how, technology affects communication formats, in particular the format of political communication, so that broader institutional change remains little more than an incidental interest. As Lundby (2009b) has pointed out in a critical examination of Altheide and Snow's argument, they tend to reduce Georg Simmel's notion of social form to a communication format and, therefore, are not able to link media change to a wider theory of social change. Following Simmel, Lundby (ibid.) argues that social form is constituted through continuous patterns of social interaction and, therefore, "mediatization research should put an emphasis on how social and communicative forms are developed when media are taken into use in social interaction" (ibid.: 117).

Like Asp (1986, 1990), Mazzoleni and Schulz (1999) apply the concept of mediatization to the media's influence on politics. Considering the cases of Fernando Collar de Mello's use of television in the Brazilian election campaign of 1989, Silvio Berlusconi's use of the media on his way to power in Italy, and Tony Blair's use of "spin" in the UK, they demonstrate the increasing influence of the mass media on how political power is exercised. They characterize mediatization as "the problematic concomitants or consequences of the development of modern mass media." As to its effects, they comment that "mediatized politics is politics that has lost its autonomy, has become dependent in its central functions on mass media, and is continuously shaped by interactions with mass media" (Mazzoleni and Schulz 1999: 249f). But they also stress that it is not a question of the media having abrogated political power from the political institutions; political institutions such as parliaments, parties, etc. continue in good measure to control politics, but these institutions have become increasingly dependent on the media, and have had to adapt to the logic of the media.

Other important studies concerning the mediatization of politics include the work of Jenssen and Aalberg (2007), Strömbäck (2008), and Cottle (2006a), of whom the latter considers the mediatization of conflicts as the "active *performative* involvement and *constitutive* role" of the media in a variety of political and military conflicts (Cottle 2006a: 9, original emphasis). Strömbäck (2008) suggests a model of four phases of mediatized politics in which each phase is characterized by a qualitative shift in the influence of the media on politics (see Chapter 3).

In other subfields of media studies, the concept of mediatization has been used to describe the media's influence on research. Väliverronen (2001: 159) does not consider mediatization to be "a strict analytic concept, but rather an ambiguous term which refers to the increasing cultural and social significance of the mass media and other forms of technically mediated communication." Seen in this light, the media play an important role in the production and circulation of knowledge and interpretations of science. Consider, for example, the number of people whose knowledge of various phases in the history of evolution has been formed not so much in the classroom as by Steven Spielberg's *Jurassic Park* films, or the BBC documentary series, *Walking with Dinosaurs*. Moreover, the media are also an arena for public discussion and for the legitimization of science. Peter Weingart (1998) sees this as a decisive element in the linkage between media and science:

> It is the basis for the thesis of the *medialization* of science: With the growing importance of the media in shaping public opinion, conscience and perception on the one hand and a growing dependence of science on scarce resources and thus on public acceptance on the other, science will become increasingly media-oriented.
>
> *(Weingart 1998: 872, original emphasis; note that*
> *Weingart spells "mediatization" with an "l")*

Rödder and Schäfer (2010) report that the mediatization of science is an empirical fact, but that it is limited to particular disciplines, scientists, and phases of the research. Accordingly, science may be an institution that, compared to other parts of society, is less mediatized. Another important area of mediatization studies concerns the influence of the media on religious institutions, beliefs, and practices (Hjarvard 2008b, 2011; Lövheim and Lynch 2011; Hjarvard and Lövheim 2012). The overall outcome of the mediatization of religion is not a new kind of religion as such, but rather a new social condition in which the power to define and practice religion has changed (see Chapter 4).

Winfried Schulz (2004) has sought to develop a typology of mediatization processes across individual social institutions or fields. He identifies four types of processes whereby the media change human communication and interaction. First, they *extend* human communication abilities in both time and space; and second, the media *substitute* social activities that previously took place face-to-face. For example, for many, Internet banking has replaced the physical meeting between bank and customer. Third, the media instigate an *amalgamation* of activities, as face-to-face communication combines with mediated communication, and the media infiltrate everyday life. Finally, players in many different sectors have to *adapt* their behavior to accommodate the media's valuations, formats, and routines. For example, politicians learn to express themselves in "sound-bites" in impromptu exchanges with reporters. Not all of these processes may be equally important in all sectors of society, but Schulz' (2004) typology may be a useful analytical tool for the study of mediatization.

Mediatized modernity or civilization?

Beyond using the concept to describe the media's influence over areas such as politics, science, and religion, some researchers have also very explicitly related it to broader theories of modernity or civilization. The sociologist John B. Thompson (1990, 1995) sees mediatization as an integral element of the development of modern society. The invention of the printing press in the mid-fifteenth century saw the birth of a technology that made it possible to circulate information in society on an unprecedented scale. This revolutionary technological event institutionalized the mass media (books, newspapers, magazines, etc.) as a significant force in society and enabled communication and interaction over long distances and among larger numbers of people, while also making it possible, as never before, to store and accumulate information over time. As a consequence, the mass media helped to transform an agrarian and feudal society, and to create modern institutions such as the state, the public sphere, and science. The subsequent development of other media, such as radio, television, and the Internet, have further accentuated this modernization process. Communication, once bound to the physical meeting of individuals, face-to-face, has been succeeded by mediated communication, where the relationship between sender and recipient is altered in decisive respects. In the case of mass communication, senders typically retain control over the content of the message, but have very little influence on how the recipient makes use of it; while in the case of interactive media, both sender and recipient can influence the content of communication, yet the situation is still not equivalent to physical, face-to-face communication. Thompson (1995) sees a strong connection between mediatization and its cultural consequences, and the emergence of very large media organizations at national and global levels. These corporations' production and distribution of symbolic products have changed communication flows in society, both between institutions and between institutions and individuals. Fornäs (1995) builds on Thompson's (1995) notion of mediatization, but in particular considers it in relation to the growing cultural reflexivity of modernity. As more and more media become part of the individual's everyday life, media texts, images, and discourses become part of the individual's identity construction.

Krotz (2007a, 2007b, 2009) too, uses the concept of mediatization to specify the role of the media in social change in a broader sense. He treats mediatization as a *meta-process*, on a par with individualization and globalization, and he defines it as "a historical, ongoing, long-term process in which more and more media emerge and are institutionalized" (Krotz 2009: 24). He refrains from offering a more detailed formal definition, for, he writes, "mediatization, by its very definition, is always bound in time and to cultural context" (Krotz 2007a: 39). Within a specific period or historical phase, mediatization may take on a particular form or specific realization, but it is a meta-process and is therefore not restricted to a particular historical period. Inspired by the sociology of Norbert Elias (1939), Krotz conceives of mediatization as an ongoing process whereby the media change human relations and behavior and thereby change society and culture. This means that he sees it as part of an ongoing civilization process that has followed human activity ever since the dawn of literacy.

Several researchers (e.g., Schulz [2004] and Krotz [2007a]) point out certain similarities between mediatization theory and so-called medium theory (or media ecology as it is sometimes called), of which the well-known proponents include Harold Innis (1951), Walter Ong (1982), Marshall McLuhan (1964), and Joshua Meyrowitz (1986). The two theories both choose to view the impact of the media in an overall perspective and focus on other aspects than media content and media use, which have otherwise occupied so much of media research. Mediatization theory is thus consonant with medium theory with respect to taking note of the different media's particular formatting of communication and the impacts on interpersonal relations to which this gives rise. Krotz (2007a) also points out a number of shortcomings in medium theory, among them a tendency towards technological determinism. Medium theorists typically focus on certain intrinsic logics of the individual media's technology, so that either printing technology or television is seen to be the key factor in bringing about a new kind of society. The interaction between technology and culture, as well as the circumstance that culture also forms technology, are neglected, and the medium is reduced to its technological "nature." Krotz warns against decontextualizing the mediatization concept, as medium theory is seldom interested in specific historical, cultural, or social relations, but is mainly oriented toward changes at the macro level. By contrast, mediatization theory is found to be far more committed to empirical analysis, including the study of specific mediatization processes among different groups within the population, Krotz (2007a) stresses. Despite the tendencies for technological determinism we should, however, be careful not to over-emphasize the differences between medium theory and mediatization theory. Meyrowitz' (1986) analysis of television's influence on human behavior is clearly historically situated and is not infused by the same kind of techno-optimism as McLuhan (1964). Instead, Meyrowitz seeks to consider how the media restructure social interactional spaces, so that in our development of mediatization theory we will seek to integrate Meyrowitz' perspective.

The mediatization concept proposed in this book shares several of Schulz' (2004) and Krotz' (2007a, 2007b) perspectives. Extension, substitution, amalgamation, and accommodation are important processes in mediatization; moreover, empirical validation through historical, cultural, and sociological analysis is required. But the theoretical framework also deviates from these perspectives in two principal respects. First, we apply an *institutional perspective* to the media and their interaction with culture and society. An institutional perspective situates the analysis of mediatization at the meso level of culture and society, i.e., above the level of micro-social interactions and below the macro level of general assertions concerning society as a whole. Furthermore, an institutional perspective makes it possible to specify the elements comprising "media logic" within a particular domain and to better analyze the interplay between the media and other social spheres (institutions). An institutional perspective by no means precludes the consideration of culture, technology, or psychology, but on the contrary provides a framework within which the interplay between these aspects can be studied. Second, the mediatization concept is applied to the *historical* situation of *high modernity* in which the media *at one and the same time* have attained semi-autonomy as a social institution and are crucially interwoven with the functioning of other institutions. Here, we clearly depart from Krotz' (2007a, 2007b) civilizational perspective that tends to include every process by which the media exert influence on society and culture. We find such an all-embracing understanding of mediatization less helpful, since it diminishes the analytical sharpness of the concept. If we wish to use the concept of mediatization to specify a cultural and social condition in which the media come to play a particular and prominent role across societal spheres, the use of the same term to label media influences in Antiquity or the Middle Ages may become confusing.

A historical example may help to clarify the distinction between Krotz' civilizational perspective and our own. The invention of the printing press, and the related development of social and cultural organizations (supply infrastructure, education, etc.) to support the use of printing technology, revolutionized individuals' relationships with the written language and had palpable impacts on both religion and knowledge as social institutions (Eisenstein 1979). We will not, however, consider this an example of the mediatization of either religion or knowledge, because the new print media did not develop into a distinct media institution, but rather came to serve other institutions, helping to solidify their authority (e.g., the spread of the Protestant Church and the rise of the educational system). The content of books and their reception were largely in the control of other institutions in society and were not dominated by a semi-autonomous media institution. The question of control is a matter of degree and not an absolute one, but degrees may certainly also be important. Following our perspective, mediatization is not the only concept through which we may recognize interdependencies between the media, society, and culture. The media may influence culture and society in a variety of ways, but mediatization may not be the keyword to understanding all of these instances. Our notion of mediatization is at the same time more limited and more pronounced. It is used to characterize *a condition or phase* in the overall development of society and culture, in which the media exert a *particularly dominant influence* on other social institutions. Following this, mediatization is on a par with other major processes of modernity such as urbanization and globalization. These concepts similarly do not preclude the importance of urban settlements or international relations in premodern societies, but they are primarily used to designate intensified transformations of culture and society during modern times.

Mediatization in postmodern theory

Some researchers consider mediatization an expression of a particular postmodern condition, in which the media give rise to a new consciousness and cultural order. The most radical linkage between mediatization and postmodernism is found in the work of Baudrillard (1994), who perceives the symbols or signs of media culture – images, sound, advertisements, etc. – to form simulacra, or semblances of reality that not only seem more real than the physical and social reality, but also replace it. This is like a map of the world that has become so vivid, and so detailed and comprehensive, that it appears more real than the world it was created to represent. In Baudrillard's own words, the media constitute a "hyperreality." They are guided by a kind of semiotic logic, and their central influence consists of how they subject all communication and every discourse to one dominant code: "What is mediatized is not what comes off the daily press, out of the tube, or on the radio: it is what is reinterpreted by the sign form, articulated into models, and administered by the 'code'" (Baudrillard 1994: 175f). This simulacrum theory leads Baudrillard to conclude that the symbolic world of the media has replaced the "real" world. He goes so far as to state that the Gulf War of 1990–91 did not take place, but was rather a figment of media simulacra. In Baudrillard's (1995: 40) own words:

> It is a masquerade of information: branded faces delivered over to the prostitution of the image, the image of an unintelligible distress. No images of the field of battle, but images of masks, of blind or defeated faces, and images of falsification.

We should not take Baudrillard's statement or his theory at face value, i.e., as a denial that a physical and social reality exists outside the media, even though some of his formulations may invite such an interpretation. His point is that media representations of reality have assumed such dominance in our society that both our perceptions and constructions of reality, and our behavior, take their point of departure in mediated representations and are steered by the media, so that phenomena such as war are no longer what they once were. Thus, the media-orchestrated Gulf War was not a war as we once knew war to be, since our perception of the war was steered by the images and symbols that the media presented to us. Sheila Brown (2003: 22, original emphasis) seconds Baudrillard's postmodernist view of mediatization and its consequences, describing a new social situation in which a number of traditional distinctions have disintegrated: "Above all, mediatization in the contemporary sense refers to a universe in which the meaning of *ontological divisions* is collapsing: divisions between fact and fiction, nature and culture, global and local, science and art, technology and humanity."

There is no doubt that mediatization has complicated and blurred the distinctions between reality and media representations of reality, and between fact and fiction, but we find the postmodernist understanding of mediatization at once too simple and too grand. Too simple, because it implies one single transformation, whereby mediated reality supplants experiential reality, and traditional distinctions quite simply dissolve. The concept of mediatization proposed in the present book does not embrace the notion that mediated reality reigns supreme, or the contention that conventional ontological distinctions have "collapsed." Mediatization, as conceived of here, rather suggests an *expansion* of the opportunities for interaction in virtual spaces, and a *differentiation* of what people perceive to be real. By the same token, distinctions such as between global and local become far more differentiated, as the media expand our contact with events and phenomena in what were once "faraway places."

The postmodern concept is too grand in that it proclaims the disappearance of reality and the disintegration of distinctions, categorizations, that are fundamental to society and to social cognition. It is difficult to imagine how social institutions could continue to function if fact and fiction, nature and culture, art and science, were no longer distinguishable entities. Furthermore, Baudrillard's reference to an overall and dominant "code" that "administers" the circulation of symbols and signs in society remains unclear. On the whole, his claims regarding media simulacra, hyperreality, and the disappearance of reality seem exaggerated, or at least lack empirical confirmation. Ironically, they seem to rest on an antiquated assumption that, prior to the postmodern epoch, physical and social reality was a straightforward and concrete entity.

The media's construction of a new reality and its relation to the old non-mediated reality is more complicated and nuanced than Baudrillard and Brown suggest, but that does not make it less important to discuss and specify that relationship. One example from the music industry may help. Philip Auslander (1999) traces changes in the relationship between live and mediated musical performance over time. Earlier, mediated versions of music took their starting point in non-mediated performance: radio transmissions of music and recorded music emulated concert performances. Over the years, mediated versions have come into their own, in the sense that film soundtracks, albums, music videos, and so forth have each developed their own forms of expression and assumed positions of their own in the circulation of cultural artifacts. With increasing media influence, the relationship between mediated and live music was gradually reversed: concert performances have come to emulate mediated versions. Many road-show concerts clearly have the character of (re)presentations of newly released albums, and rock concerts are often orchestrated to fit the formats of broadcast transmission and/or make use of large screens to remediate the performance to the audience (Auslander 1999; Middleton 1990). Furthermore, audiences' own recordings of live concerts via mobile media and users' re-editing of official music videos on YouTube provide new layers of mediated reality. Traditionally, the live performance has been considered more authentic than the mediated performance, but as Auslander points out, the increasing interchangeability of the two challenges this perception. The issue of authenticity has not been rendered irrelevant, but authenticity has become conditional on an *interaction* between mediated and live performance:

> The primary experience of the music is as a recording; the function of the live performance is to authenticate the sound on the recording. In rock culture, live performance is a secondary experience of the music but is nevertheless indispensable, since the primary experience cannot be validated without it.
>
> *(Auslander 1999: 160)*

The growing interdependence of mediated and live performance means that one cannot say that one form is more authentic than the other. In a sociological perspective, mediated forms of interaction are neither more nor less real than non-mediated interaction. From a physical or sensual viewpoint, there may be differences in degree in terms of the reality of mediated and face-to-face interaction, in the sense that studio announcers, etc. are not actually physically present in our homes, even though we see and hear them as though they stood before us. Yet from a sociological viewpoint there is no point in seeking to differentiate the reality status of the respective forms of interaction. Non-mediated reality and forms of interaction still exist, but mediatization means that they, too, are affected by the presence of the media. For example, personal, face-to-face communication assumes a new cultural value in a mediatized society since non-mediated interaction tends to be reserved for certain purposes and is assigned special cultural significance. Mediated forms of interaction also tend to simulate aspects of face-to-face interaction: they thus not only represent alternatives to face-to-face interaction, but also extensions of the arena in which face-to-face interaction can take place (Hjarvard 2002a).

Definition

The uses of the concept of "mediatization" in the research cited in the preceding section point to a number of central aspects of the interaction between media and society, which also form part of the definition of "mediatization" proposed here. Previous uses of the concept often lack an articulated or even common definition; in addition, there are a number of aspects that have yet to be spelled out. In some cases (e.g., Väliverronen 2001) "mediatization" has been used more loosely to refer more generally to the successive growth in the media's influence in contemporary society; in other cases, the intention has been to develop a proper theory of how the media relate to politics (e.g., Asp 1986, 1990; Strömbäck 2008). Another fuzzy spot is on what level, or to which spheres, the concept is applied. Some use "mediatization" to describe the developments in a given sector (politics, science, etc.), while others use it as an overarching characteristic of a new situation in society, whether under modernity (Thompson 1995) or postmodernity (Baudrillard 1981).

Here, "mediatization" is used as the central concept in a theory of both the intensified and changing importance of the media in culture and society. By the mediatization of culture and society we understand the process whereby culture and society to an increasing degree become dependent on the media and their logic. This process is characterized by a *duality*, in that the media have become *integrated* into the operations of other social institutions and cultural spheres, while also acquiring the status of social institutions *in their own right*. As a consequence, social interaction – within the respective institutions, between institutions, and in society at large – increasingly takes place via the media. The term "media logic" is used to recognize that the media have particular *modus operandi* and characteristics ("specificities of media") that come to influence other institutions and culture and society in general, as they become dependent on the resources that the media both control and make available to them. "Media logic" does *not* suggest that there is a universal, linear, or single rationality behind all the media. It is to be understood as a conceptual shorthand for the various institutional, aesthetic, and technological *modus operandi* of the media, including the ways in which the media distribute material and symbolic resources, and operate with the help of formal and informal rules. The logic of the media influences the social forms of interaction and communication, such as how political communication is performed in the media (Strömbäck 2008); and media logic also influences the nature and function of social relations, as well as the relationships between sender, content, and recipient of communication. The degree of dependence on the media will vary between institutions and fields of society.

In recent theoretical discussions of mediatization theory, criticism of the notion of "media logic" has often been put forward (e.g., Couldry 2008, 2012; Lundby 2009b; Hepp 2012). A key concern here is how we theoretically come to acknowledge the *specificities* of the media on the one hand, and how these specificities come to influence culture and society *through* human interaction, on the other. Couldry (2008, 2012) has criticized the notion of "media logic" as suggesting a linear development of social change, and a singular logic working behind all media operations. It is, however, very hard to find proponents (if any) of such a narrow understanding of "media logic." Even Altheide and Snow (1979), who are often accused of such a notion of "media logic," are actually seeking to sketch out a series of various *modus operandi* of the media in different social domains. As mentioned previously, Lundby (2009b) seeks to solve the problem by pointing to Simmel's notion of social form, and Couldry (2012) suggests that a Bourdieu-derived notion of "media capital" may provide a key to how the media exert authority on social practices across various domains in society (see the further discussion in this chapter). Hepp's (2012) critique of "media logic" takes its point of departure in Actor-Network-Theory and states that "to the discussion about the *specificity of the media as molding force* … it makes no sense to describe the specifics that a certain medium might have 'on its own.'" Instead, he continues, "media only get 'powerful' in nettings with practices, at this point not understood as a causality or itself as an action but as a 'power' of shaping actions – this constitutes molding" (Hepp 2012: 18, emphasis in original).

These theoretical interventions provide valuable insights on – and an underlining of – how the influences of the media are produced and reproduced through the very practices of social interaction. We will draw on these arguments in our further theorizing and analyses of mediatization processes. However, the critics' dismissal of "media logic" and the one-sided emphasis on social interaction tend to obscure the question of how to grasp the specificities of the media. It is a sociological truism that any kind of cultural and social influence (from politics, media, religion, etc.) must be instantiated by and through social interaction, but that does not answer how we may conceptually recognize that a particular social institution, field, or system (or whatever label we may prefer to use) exhibits a series of internal characteristics that are reproduced across time and space and may influence other institutions. In other words, by denying the media properties and dynamics of their own, the media's specificities are dissolved into the "practice" of situated social interaction and we are left with an enigma, and not an answer to the problem. Following this, the notion of "media logic" also serves as a useful reminder of the necessity of further theoretical work on how to understand the coupling between media characteristics and social practices. By embedding our understanding of media logic in the sociological framework of institutions, we are able to consider the relationship between situated social interaction and the larger units of society. In this chapter, we will address this question later by using the concept of affordances, and in the subsequent chapters we will analytically consider how various types of media (and their different characteristics) may influence other institutions in several ways.

Mediatization is not a universal process that characterizes all societies. It is primarily a development that has accelerated particularly in the *last years of the twentieth century* in *modern, highly industrialized societies*. As globalization progresses, more and more regions and cultures will be affected by mediatization, but there may be considerable differences in the influence mediatization exerts. Globalization is related to mediatization in at least two ways: on the one hand, globalization presumes the existence of the technical means to extend communication and interaction over long distances and, on the other hand, it propels the process of mediatization by institutionalizing mediated communication and interaction in many new contexts.

Mediatization is, in our understanding, a *non-normative* concept. As noted earlier, Mazzoleni and Schulz (1999) associate mediatization directly with more problematic aspects of the media's influence on politics. Indeed, there is a general tendency in both research and public discussion to presume that institutions' dependence on the media is essentially problematic. But to presume a priori that mediatization is negative poses something of a problem, and such a normative judgment can lead to a general narrative of decline, in which media influence becomes synonymous with a decline in the political public sphere, or the disintegration of civil society. Habermas' (1962) theory of structural change in the public sphere is a paradigmatic example of such a normative approach to media influence, and Habermas has since explained that his earlier views on the subject were too pessimistic (Habermas 1990). Whether mediatization has positive or negative consequences cannot be determined in general terms: it is a concrete, analytical question that needs to be addressed in terms of specific contexts, where the influence of specific media over certain institutions is gauged. The question also requires an examination of the normative points of departure if we are to be able to speak of positive or negative consequences.

As noted in the introductory chapter, mediatization is not to be confused with the broader concept of *mediation*. Mediation refers to communication via a medium, the intervention of which can affect both the message and the relationship between sender and recipient. For example, if a politician chooses to use a blog instead of a newspaper to communicate with his constituency, this choice may well influence the form and content of his or her communication, while the communicative relationship between the politician and the electorate will be altered. However, the use of a certain type of media, whether blog or newspaper, will not necessarily have any notable effect on politics as a social institution. Mediation describes the concrete act of communication by means of a type of media in a specific social context. By contrast, mediatization refers to a more long-term process, whereby social and cultural institutions and modes of interaction are changed as a consequence of the growth of the media's influence. It should be noted, however, that some scholars – e.g., Altheide and Snow (1988: 195) and Silverstone (2007) – use the term "mediation" in a somewhat similar sense to the use of "mediatization" here. The different – and at times confusing – labeling seems to originate in different research traditions. In continental European media studies, in particular Scandinavian and German research traditions, there is a longer and more elaborate tradition for using the concept of "mediatization" as distinct from "mediation," whereas Anglo-American scholars have preferred the term "mediation" and consequently used "mediation" in several senses, including to denote specific instances of mediated communication, as well as to label broader influences of the media on society. The British media scholar Nick Couldry (2008) initially defended Silverstone's notion of "mediation" as a more complex and dialectical term, but he has later seconded Krotz' (2009) understanding of the concept of mediatization and stated that "through the concept of mediatization, we acknowledge media as an *irreducible* dimension of all social processes" (Couldry 2012: 137, emphasis in original). Generally, recent debates seem to have settled the terminological discrepancies in favor of the continental distinction.

In sociological theory, meanwhile, one finds a more general use of the term, "medium." Money can, for example, be described as a medium of exchange. Similarly, in linguistic or psychological contexts speech may be considered a medium of expression. In the sociology of religion a medium may refer to a person or object that enables access to a supernatural realm. Although useful in their respective contexts, these meanings of the term "medium" are not relevant here, where the term "media" draws on media and communication studies. By media we understand technologies that expand communication in time, space, and modality. The media are not only technologies, but also acquire social and aesthetic forms that structure how the media come to be used in various contexts.

Furthermore, we use the *plural* form. The media are not a uniform phenomenon since each type of media has its own characteristics, and they vary in both use and content between cultures and societies. The consequences of mediatization, therefore, depend on both the context and the characteristics of the medium or media in question.

Within the process of mediatization, we may distinguish between a *direct* (strong) and an *indirect* (weak) form of mediatization (Hjarvard 2004b). Direct mediatization refers to situations where formerly non-mediated activity converts to a mediated form, i.e., the activity is performed through interaction with a medium. A simple example of direct mediatization is the successive transformation of chess from physical chessboard to computer game. Formerly dependent on the players' physical presence around a chess board, chess is increasingly played with the help of software on a computer. In many ways, the game remains the same: the rules are the same, the chess board has the same appearance, and so forth. But the use of a computer opens up numerous new options: you can play against a computer instead of another person; you can play with distant opponents via the Internet; and you can store and consult earlier matches, etc., and these new options gradually influence the experience of playing chess, as well as the cultural context in which the game is played. A more complicated example of direct mediatization is "on line banking" via the Internet. All kinds of banking tasks and services (payments, loans, trade in currency and stocks, and financial analysis) can be undertaken via interaction with a computer linked to the Internet, and the medium has palpably expanded the options available to both banks and their customers, and meanwhile, the behavior of both parties has changed.

Indirect mediatization is when a given activity is increasingly influenced with respect to its form, content, organization, or context by media symbols or mechanisms. Again, let us consider a simple example: the burgeoning merchandising industry that surrounds hamburger restaurants may be taken as an instance of indirect mediatization. A visit to Burger King or McDonald's is no longer simply an eating experience; it now entails considerable exposure to films and cartoon animations. As much as the opportunity to eat a hamburger, a visit to one of these restaurants may – especially for the youngest guests – mean an opportunity to collect dolls representing the characters in the films they see. Of course, you can still have your meal and not expose yourself to the media entertainment offered, but the cultural context surrounding the burger, much of the attraction of visiting the restaurant, and so forth, have to do with the presence of the media, in both symbolic and economic terms. A more complicated example of indirect mediatization is the development of intertextual discourse between the media and other institutions in society. For example, French people's knowledge of the USA is also indebted to media narratives (fact and fiction) about the country; as a consequence, French political discussions regarding the USA are also interwoven with media representations of American culture, mores, and history.

Direct and indirect forms of mediatization will often operate in combination, so that it is not always easy to distinguish between them. A need to distinguish between the two primarily arises in analytical contexts. Direct mediatization makes visible how a given social activity is substituted, i.e., transformed from a non-mediated activity to a mediated form, and in such cases it is rather easy to establish a "before" and an "after" and examine the differences. Where the media thereafter serve as a necessary interface for the performance of the social activity, we are dealing with a strong form of mediatization. Indirect mediatization does not necessarily affect how people perform a given activity. Consequently, the indirect mediatization of an activity or sphere will be of a more subtle and general character and will relate to the general increase in social institutions' reliance on the media's communication resources and authority. This is not to say that indirect mediatization is any less important, or that it, viewed from a societal perspective, has less impact. Indirect mediatization is at least as important as the direct forms.

The media as a semi-independent institution

Mediatization, as defined here, means not only that the media play a role of their own determination, but that they at one and the same time have attained the status of a semi-independent institution and provide the means by which other social institutions and players communicate. The media intervene with, and influence the activity of, other institutions, such as the family, politics, organized religion, etc., while also providing a "commons" for society as a whole, i.e., virtual shared forums for communication that other institutions and actors increasingly use as arenas for their interaction. In order to treat these social consequences on a theoretical level, we shall first consider mediatization in relation to sociological concepts regarding institutions and interaction. As noted earlier, mediatization itself is characterized by a duality, in that it intervenes in human interaction in many different institutional contexts, while also institutionalizing the media as a semi-autonomous entity. A sociological theory of mediatization must therefore give an account of this duality and describe the linkages between institution and interaction.

Institutions stand for the stable, predictable elements in modern society; they constitute the framework for human communication and action in a given sphere of human life, at a given time and place. Institutions provide for the reproduction of society within the sphere in question, giving it a certain degree of autonomy and a distinct identity in relation to other spheres. As an institution, the family organizes a number of very central aspects of life, such as love, upbringing, rest/recreation, and nutrition. Politics, another institution, creates the framework for collective discussion and decision-making concerning shared resources, norms, and activities. The following more detailed discussion of institutions takes its point of departure in the *structuration theory* proposed by Anthony Giddens (1984), which in contrast to macro-sociological theory (e.g., Parsons' or Luhmann's system theory), or micro-sociological approaches (e.g., symbolic interactionism), makes it possible to describe the dynamic interaction between structure and (inter)action. For Giddens (1984), structure and action are mutually constitutive of each other. Social structure (e.g., an institution such as politics) is constituted (reproduced and/or changed) through the continuous actions of social players. At the same time, social players make use of already existing structures (resources, formal and informal rules, etc.) in order to make sense to each other and pursue their individual goals (e.g., political influence). Overall social structures are not given once and for all, but must be reproduced in social action in order to become real, and since humans do not just "enact" social rules, but have the capability to make use of them in a reflexive way, they can also alter social structures through their particular ways of implementing social rules in given contexts.

According to Giddens, institutions are characterized by two central features: rules and allocations of resources. Together, rules and resource allocations invest the institution with a certain autonomy in relation to the world around it. Rules may be implicit and practical, i.e., outgrowths of so-called tacit knowledge of appropriate behavior in a range of situations within the institution in question. Or they may be explicit and formal; codified in law or taking the form of stated objectives or rules of procedure, such as in a school or firm. Institutions in modern, complex societies distinguish themselves by a high degree of steering by rules, both implicit and explicit. The existence of rules implies, furthermore, that the institutions monitor compliance and can apply sanctions, should the rules be broken. Even the sanctions may be of a more or less explicit or formal character, whereas many rules are internalized by individuals and remain for the most part implicit. The sanctions for violation of rules of the latter kind are generally the withdrawal of recognition from peers, feelings of embarrassment or guilt, or perhaps explicit criticism on the part of colleagues or family members. Informal rules often have the character of norms and are maintained and sanctioned by gossip, ridicule, and scolding.

By virtue of formalization itself, formal rules generally lead to explicit sanctions that are well-defined and known in advance; and in some cases breaking such rules may be prosecuted. Like other institutions, the media, too, are steered by rules. They are subject to numerous laws and regulations, some of which apply to other institutions too, while others are specifically tailored to the activity of the type of media in question. Examples of the latter include legislation on the freedom of the press, built-in features that allow users to report misuse of social networking media (e.g. "report picture"), and laws pertaining to libel. Some media companies have publicly declared their guiding principles and the public role they strive to play. Concrete praxis in media production is mainly steered by informal rules that are expressed in routines, habits, and implicit norms of professionalism. Thus, news journalists obey rules when they select their stories (criteria of newsworthiness) and when they interact with news sources, while they incorporate norms such as objectivity into their news production as a strategic ritual (Tuchman 1972).

As for the other primary characteristic of an institution, the allocation of resources, Giddens distinguishes between two kinds of resources: material resources and authority. Institutions can administer material resources in the form of, for example, raw materials, buildings and facilities, manpower and knowledge; and a delegation of authority also takes place within the institution, so that it is clear who, within the institution, is in charge of the material resources, who may speak on behalf of the institution, who may interact with whom, and so forth. If we consider the family, for example: parents generally control the family's material resources, such as the home and the car, and the law gives parents authority over, and responsibility for, the children (under the legal age of majority) in the household too. (Parental authority may also be regulated by law; certain behavior toward children, such as physical and mental abuse, may be prohibited.) Similarly, the media, too, are characterized by allocations of resources; for production the individual media company will allocate engineering resources, personnel, travel, etc., to the various departments, while on the receiving side, recipients will acquire the necessary hardware and, perhaps not least, devote their time and attention to the media. As will be elaborated further later, mediatization implies that other institutions to an increasing degree become dependent on resources that the media control, so that they will have to submit to some of the rules the media operate by in order to gain access to those resources.

Institutional transformations

The development of the media into semi-independent institutions should be seen as an instance of the increasing differentiation and division of labor that characterize many spheres and aspects of modern society. Premodern, agrarian society was characterized by a low degree of specialization, as most people lived in rural villages and one's family and "birth" mainly determined the course of one's life from the cradle to the grave. As nation states emerged, and with industrialization and urbanization, more and more institutions that accommodated different aspects of life split off from the undifferentiated "whole." Science became divorced from religion, and the labor market developed an ever greater number of specialty occupations and professions. The media played an important role in this early modern era inasmuch as they made it possible to detach an activity from its local context and to create a specialized forum at a national or international level. Books and periodicals helped to lay the foundations for the expansion of science and technology; newspapers helped to create a democratic, political public sphere; and literature and popular magazines contributed to the development of a cultural public sphere.

Yet in this phase of social development the media were still to become semi-independent institutions. Instead, they were chiefly *instruments in the hands of other institutions*. As political parties became formed in many western countries in the nineteenth century, they began to publish newspapers, which gave rise to the system of the party press. Very few of these papers had a journalistic editorial board that operated independently of the party/owner. On the contrary, there were often intimate bonds between parties and newspapers, and indeed, editors were generally part of the political leadership. To consider a Danish example: Viggo Hørup, the nineteenth-century Social Liberal politician and founder of the Copenhagen daily, *Politiken*. Hørup's political work and his work as editor-in-chief of *Politiken* were two faces of the same coin. When he spoke to one group or another one day, the text of the speech was very likely to grace the pages of the paper the following day. Similarly, institutions in the fields of science, the Arts, and jurisprudence all had their own channels of publication, over which they exerted editorial control.

The advent of radio in the 1920s marks the point when the media began to address a generalized and often national public, whereupon they gradually assumed the character of *cultural institutions*. By this we mean that the media are no longer instruments of any particular institution or special interest, but keep an arm's length away from the various social institutions. Radio, and later television, were historically organized very differently in various parts of the world, as either state, commercial, or public entities. In northern Europe, broadcasting was generally institutionalized as a public service institution outside the state itself. Within this framework, radio, and later television, would represent society's common interest vis-à-vis a general public and offer a balanced representation of various interests in the fields of politics, the Arts, science, and so forth. That radio broadcasting was organized in the form of a monopoly had to do with the nature of the technology and the characteristics of the media itself, which, in the 1920s, meant that it was physically impossible to create the same multiplicity of radio channels as characterized the press, for example. But monopoly was also a choice that was well in keeping with other public and national policies; and it was also congenial to requirements that the new media be charged with educating its listeners. At about the same time, the press underwent a development in a similar direction. The decline and ultimate demise of the party press actually extended over most of the twentieth century, but in the present context the point is that the press, once it had adopted the "omnibus" concept ("omnibus" = for all), began its development into a cultural institution. No longer an instrument of particular political interests, the news media began treating various social institutions (politics, the Arts, family, etc.) and special interests from a more general and common perspective. The underlying dynamic in this evolutionary process differed from the dynamic behind the development of the broadcasting media. While European radio and television were established as public institutions and given a "mission" to educate and enlighten, the establishment of the omnibus press was a step in an essentially commercial development, in which advertising revenues were a driving force. Be that as it may, in this concrete historical context the outcome was that newspapers became cultural institutions, appealing to all and offering something for everyone.

Attaining the status of a cultural institution was the first step in the media's further movement towards independence from other institutions. It implied a gradual professionalization of media practices, in which, for instance, the establishment of journalism as a profession in its own right, with professional training and the development of ethical codes, gave the profession a degree of autonomy (Schudson 1978; Kristensen 2000). A key feature of journalists' self-perception is an adversarial stance vis-à-vis political and commercial interests, which is operationalized in the norm of keeping one's news sources at arm's length.

The 1980s witnessed the start of a series of structural changes in both the media sector and society in general in Europe, which presaged the transition from the status of cultural institution to that of media institution. The end of the monopoly of public service radio and television, and the expansion of broadcasting services via satellite and cable, created a more commercial and competitive climate in radio and television, in which market forces challenged television's identity and importance as a cultural institution. The 1990s saw the deregulation of the telecommunications sector, while the rapid expansion of mobile telephony and the Internet suddenly made the media system far more complex. Many of the newer media are only loosely regulated, if at all, in terms of purpose and content. These media developments did not occur in isolation, but were part of a larger neo-liberal "wave" throughout Europe (Preston 2009), but also in many countries outside Europe. The neo-liberal agenda of deregulation was not aimed particularly at the media, but potentially included all public sector institutions. In the case of the media, neo-liberal policies had the profound consequence of diminishing society's (cultural and political) influence on the collective as well as the individual communication in society, at the same time as it allowed a new economic dynamic to accelerate the development and dissemination of new media. Mediatization as a social process is, therefore, not only a result of "internal" media developments, but also a complex outcome of technological, political, and economic changes.

The media are no longer cultural institutions, in the sense of institutions that, in the public interest, represent an entire society to a general public. A stronger market orientation has led the media to focus more sharply on servicing their own audiences and users. This has been described as implying a greater measure of *user steering* of the media, in the sense that attention to audiences and users has taken precedence over deference to other social institutions and cultural obligations (Hjarvard 1999). Newspapers, radio, television, and the Internet still devote space and time to politics, the Arts, and cultural life, but to a lesser degree on those institutions' terms, or from the perspective of "public enlightenment." Other spheres of social life have instead become the raw material for the product that the media serve to their readers, viewers, and listeners. While the media in earlier times were *sender-steered*, e.g., steered by particular interests in the days of the party press, or by the terms of public service broadcasting concessions, as media institutions they are to a great extent driven by a commercial impetus to accommodate to the interests of their audiences and users, and their market demands and purchasing power.

This is not to say that the media have become private enterprises like any manufacturer of, say, furniture or bacon; they continue to perform collective functions in society. The media provide the communicative forums, both private and public, that other institutions depend on for their communication with the public and other institutions, and for their internal communication. The duality of having broken away from other institutions' control, yet still serving collective communication functions in society, gives the media central importance to society as a whole. Therefore, the logic that guides the media cannot be reduced to a logic of the market alone. Yes, the media sell products to consumers, but they also service their audiences and users, both as a general public and as individuals belonging to specific institutional contexts. Families thus use the media to orient themselves concerning norms for their children's upbringing and the practical furnishing of children's rooms, and the media are used for family members' communication with each other. Political parties use various forms of media to communicate with other parties and the general public, and also to communicate within the party.

To be able to serve these collective functions, the media still emphasize the concern for the public interest that imbued them in their roles as cultural institutions, and which continued to imbue the development of journalism as a partly autonomous profession, where the media can claim impartiality, objectivity, and so forth. In the era when the media were cultural institutions, concern for the public interest grew out of the mission to enlighten, a project that engaged the whole of society; while the concern today is primarily internalized as part of the sense of *media professionalism* among media workers such as journalists, television producers, social networking managers, and others in the various media sectors. Professionalism is increasingly being defined as the capacity to act in accordance with the demands of a particular media industry, rather than the ability of a particular work profession to serve the public good (Örnebring 2009). Because the media – and in particular the digital media – have become integrated into the life-world of other institutions, the users have also become media producers. The service of new media is not least to *produce social relations* between people, and users are increasingly prompted to *generate the content by themselves*. Accordingly, contemporary media are steered by a two-sided logic: media professionalism and audience/user involvement.

Table 2.1 summarizes the institutional transformations of the media. It is a highly simplified account and makes no consideration of the variations that the individual media display. Furthermore, it primarily reflects historical developments in the

TABLE 2.1 The institutional development of the media

Dominant period	Institutional character	Dominant logic	Media system	Purposes and objectives
Up to 1920	The media as instruments of other institutions	Steered by particular interests	Party press, scientific journals, religious publications, arts magazines, etc.	Persuasion and agitation on the part of specific interests in the specific institution
1920–80	The media as a cultural institution	Public steering	Public service radio and television (monopoly), omnibus press	Representation of society's common interests in a public arena
1980 onwards	The media as a semi-independent media institution *and* integrated into other institutions	Media professionalism and audience/user involvement	Commercial and competitive media, satellite TV, the Internet, mobile, and interactive media	Servicing of audiences, sales to target groups in a differentiated media system

north-western part of Europe. There are also several exceptions to the general development within a north-western context: In all three periods there have been media that have operated under the superintendence of other institutions (e.g., scientific journals); just as, ever since the 1880s, media offering light entertainment have been primarily market-oriented.

Affordances: structuring interaction

So far, we have defined what mediatization is and how it came to be; while in the following text we shall turn to examining *the ways* in which mediatization comes to influence culture and society. Fundamentally, this is a question of the media intervening in the social interaction between individuals *within* a given institution (e.g., between family members via mobile phones); *between* institutions (e.g., through Internet media that allow one to work from home); and *in society at large* (e.g., by publicizing and observing events of importance to the community, be they festive, threatening, or tragic). First we shall consider interaction at a micro-social level; later, we will turn to the macro-social level.

Social interaction consists of *communication* and *action*. The media, of course, are means of communication, i.e., an exchange of meaning between two or more parties. As linguistic pragmatics (Austin 1962; Searle 1969) have shown, communication may be viewed as a form of action: by communicating, people not only exchange information, but they also influence each another and their mutual relationships by, for example, promising, confirming, rejecting, deciding, and so forth. In addition to acts of communication, the media also permit forms of social action that once required both parties' physical presence: one can buy or sell, work or play.

The ways in which the media intervene into social interaction depend on the concrete characteristics of the media in question, i.e., both material and technical features and social and aesthetic qualities. A medium's characteristics and its relation to social interaction may be illustrated in terms of the perception psychologist James Gibson's (1979) concept of *affordances*. Gibson himself does not apply the concept to the media, but applies it to a general theory of how humans and animals perceive and interact with the world around them. The idea is that neither human beings nor animals sense their surroundings passively; instead, they approach the world and the objects in it in an action-oriented and practical mode. Any given physical object, by virtue of its material characteristics (shape, size, consistency, etc.), lends itself to a set of uses. According to Gibson, the affordances of an object are these potential uses. For some animals a tree represents shade; others may feed on its leaves; and birds may decide to nest in it. Some objects invite certain uses: a flat stone begs to be "skipped" across still water; a closed door is to be opened. Some uses are practically prescribed, whereas others are ruled out. In sum: the affordances of any given object make certain actions possible, exclude others and, structure the interaction between actor and object. Furthermore, whether or not an object's affordances are made use of depends on the characteristics of the human or animal that interacts with the object. With the help of a ladder you can climb up or down, but only if you have the use of your limbs. Thus, affordances are also defined by the extent to which the characteristics of object and user "match." In his study of the human use of technology and other manufactured objects, Norman (1990) points to a third determining factor, besides the material or objective characteristics of object and user. He introduces the concept of "perceived affordance" in order to incorporate the relational aspect of affordance, where the crucial factor is the user's psychological evaluation of the object in relation to his/her objectives. Thus, an object's affordances are influenced by the user's motives/objectives and, in extension, also by the cultural conventions and interpretations that surround the object.

Hutchby (2001, 2003) argues that Gibson's concept of affordance allows us to consider the relationship between media technology and social interaction from a position that transcends the dichotomy between technological determinism on the one side, and radical social constructionism on the other side. Media as technologies do not simply enforce themselves on culture and society, neither are they infinitely malleable. As Hutchby (2001: 453) suggests, technologies "do set limits on what it is *possible* to do with, around, or via the artifact. By the same token, there is not one but a variety of ways of responding to the range of affordances for action and interaction that a technology presents" (emphasis in original). Following Hughes (1994), we also need to differentiate between the period when a media technology is being developed and the period in which it has become fully established and institutionalized in society. In the first phase a media technology is open for a variety of social and cultural influences, but in the second phase it may achieve a momentum of its own. Finally, we need to stress that the affordances of a medium arise from a combination of its material, social, and aesthetic characteristics.

In the light of Gibson's (1979) and Norman's (1990) conceptual work, we recognize the media as technologies, each of which has a set of affordances that *facilitate, limit, and structure communication and action*. For example, radio made it possible for listeners to experience musical performances to an extent that was unprecedented. Before radio, concert music was available almost exclusively to a small, urban élite. But organizational factors in the institution of radio also limited the amount of music and the range of genres that were offered, while program schedules, signal range, and the quality of one's loudspeaker, gave structure to the listening experience: when one listened, where and how one sat to listen, and so forth.

Perhaps most of all, the media make it possible for people to interact across distances, which means without their having to be in the same place at the same time. An examination of the differences between interaction via the media and non-mediated interaction face-to-face reveals the ways in which the media alter the interaction. Thompson (1995) distinguishes three types of interaction: face-to-face interaction, mediated quasi-interaction, and mediated interaction. In the case of face-to-face interaction, both verbal and non-verbal expressions are available to all parties present. The mass media, like newspapers, radio, and television, provide what Thompson calls mediated quasi-interaction, by which he means that the communication addresses an unknown, unspecified group of people who, what is more, are unable to interact with the sender. By contrast, a telephone conversation is an instance of mediated interaction: the conversation takes place between identified individuals, all of whom can interact on an equal footing. Thus, according to Thompson, mediated quasi-interaction is monologic, whereas mediated interaction is dialogic.

This latter distinction is important, but Thompson's choice of the term, "quasi-" is a bit unfortunate in that it allows the interpretation that reading a newspaper article or watching a television program only seem like interaction, whereas talking over the telephone or face-to-face is true interaction. From a sociological point of view, neither the interaction between reader and newspaper article, nor that between viewer and television program, is any less true or meaningful than a conversation about the article or program over the breakfast table. The circumstance that mass communication does not allow the recipient to respond immediately to the sender does not mean that no action or communication on the part of the recipient in relation to an article or program takes place. Exposure to a newspaper or to a television channel in itself represents an act that has social significance for recipient and sender alike. In the latter case, exposure is reflected in circulation statistics or ratings, which have tangible commercial value. Furthermore, the reader or viewer may very well remember the message they have read or seen and relate it to others.

In more general terms: we should bear in mind that social interaction does not necessarily imply that the opportunities to express oneself or to take action are equally distributed among the parties involved. This applies to non-mediated, direct interaction such as that between speaker and participant in a meeting, or between the participants in court proceedings, where the opportunities for expression may be very controlled and, indeed, deliberately unequal. Such inequality does not render either the meeting or the proceedings "quasi"; it simply reflects how in any social interaction, be it mediated or direct, the parties assume social roles that confer different degrees of latitude with regard to personal expression and influence over the course of the interaction or its outcome. The media do, however, have an impact on the social roles in the interaction, in that access to the media itself and the modes of interaction it makes available to the participants, affects the respective participants' ability to communicate and act. Since the media play a greater role in an increasing number of contexts, social roles are also evaluated in terms of the access to media coverage they are able to mobilize.

Finally, we should note that Thompson's differentiation of three forms of interaction was inspired by an earlier, now bygone, media landscape. Traditional mass media like newspapers and radio and television channels have developed, and continue to launch, new means by which recipients can respond to, or even participate in, their communication – e.g., via text message, e-mail, or blogs; while interpersonal media like mobile telephones, text messages (SMS), and e-mail also enable one sender to distribute messages to many recipients in a manner analogous to mass media. Rather than adopting Thompson's terminology, then, it seems more satisfactory generally to distinguish between non-mediated (face-to-face) and mediated communication, and then to specify the subcategories in terms of parameters like one-way/two-way, interpersonal/mass, text/audio/visual, and so forth.

The media alter interaction

Mediated interaction is neither more nor less real than non-mediated interaction, but the circumstance that mediated interaction takes place between individuals who do not share the same physical space and time changes the relations between the participants. If we start with American sociologist Erving Goffman's (1956) description of social interaction between people who are in physical proximity to each another, the differences in situations of mediated interaction become apparent. Goffman uses the metaphor of the theater and describes the interaction that takes place on the stage as a performance. He distinguishes between what takes place on the stage and what goes on backstage, i.e., action and communication that is not open to the participants. In addition to their verbal and non-verbal (facial expressions, gestures, body language, etc.) communication, participants will also use various accessories or "props" (costumes, cigarettes, tables, and chairs) and define territories (physical and symbolic) between them and the other participants, as part of the interaction. Typically, participants collaborate in the interaction, seeking to reach a common definition of the situation at hand, in order to achieve a common goal.

In contrast to face-to-face communication, the media can extend interaction in time and space: the media allow instant communication with individuals anywhere in the world. Mediated interaction does not require the parties to be in the same space at the same time. The media also change the ability of individual players to steer how the social situation is defined, to steer the use of verbal and non-verbal communication and accessories, and to define territorial boundaries in the interaction. This has far-reaching consequences, three of which are of interest here: first, the media make it considerably easier for individuals to "act" on several stages simultaneously; second, participants can more easily optimize the social interaction to their personal advantage; and third, the mutual relations between the participants, including norms of acceptable behavior (deference, tone, etc.) change.

Regarding the first consequence, the media not only enable people to interact over long distances, but they also make it possible for an individual to *keep several social interactions going at the same time:* one can talk to others in the family while watching television, give advice to one's children by phone from the office, and so forth. The Internet has multiplied the options available in this regard; given web access, a person can keep windows open to any number of interactions: work, banking transactions, shopping, communicating online with family and friends, etc. In Goffman's terminology, thanks to the media, we can switch between stage and backstage in several, parallel situations.

The media allow actors to optimize social interaction to their own advantage in two principal ways: they lighten the burden of the actor's social relations, and they permit a greater measure of control over the exchange of information. They lighten the burden by making it possible to take part in social activities, or obtain information, with less personal investment. The popularity of television as an evening and weekend pastime is related to how this media offers entertainment and vicarious company without requiring much in the way of money, attention, or effort to make the situation a success. One might instead invite friends over for the evening, but that would require a lot more effort in the form of preparing food, being sociable, etc. Meeting face-to-face has its perks, of course, but generally television is a much easier and surer way to be entertained. Similarly, sending e-mail messages to one's colleagues at work is often preferable to looking in on them, even though they may be just a few doors away. An e-mail allows you to steer the interaction more than is possible during a conversation, which often takes longer and demands some degree of courtesy, and there is always the risk that your colleague will want to talk about an entirely different matter.

While face-to-face interaction gives everyone involved the opportunity to see and hear everything done and said, the media make it possible *to manage information to and from the participants*. For example, the sender can decide when it suits him to respond to others' messages, and he has more control over the image of himself that he projects to others. As Goffman (1956) points out, there is an essential imbalance between an individual's ability to manage the impression that he makes on other participants, and the others' ability to examine and evaluate the impression conveyed. Goffman makes a distinction between the impression we *give* and the impression we *give off*. Typically, we will seek to give a favorable impression of ourselves when talking to others. But we also give off a number of other impressions, alongside our intended communication, either subconsciously or because we have failed to control our message well enough. Our speech may give one impression, while our body language conveys another, conflicting, impression. Goffman comments that we need to be very skilled performing artists to be able to manage all aspects of our self-representation. Most recipients, by contrast, are fully equipped to analyze and evaluate others' behavior, and to find faults or inconsistencies. It is in this regard that the media can help us manage the impressions we project to the world around us and, generally speaking, the narrower the channel of communication a media offers, the easier it is to manage the communication.

Restructuring of social norms

As for the third area of impact, viz., changes in the relations and norms that prevail in interaction, we first need to consider the norm regulating mechanisms in face-to-face encounters. Goffman points out that during social interaction, participants invest considerable effort in deferring to one another. When people meet face-to-face, they negotiate to establish the kind of social situation they are party to, whereby certain social roles and behaviors are considered relevant and acceptable to the situation, while others are not. In order to avoid embarrassment (due, for example, to having misapprehended the situation and behaving inappropriately, which gives rise to ridicule and/or scolding) the participants engage in a considerable amount of *facework*, which has the purpose of preserving the participants' dignity in the situation at hand. The purpose of facework is to ensure that others avoid losing face, but also, and not least, it is undertaken by individuals to preserve their own dignity. Alternatively phrased, social norms are reproduced in the social situation by participants' helping one another observe them. In face–to–face interactions, then, many actions and reactions only occur under particular circumstances, or are taboo. Thus, in social interaction we seek to avoid blatant violations of a norm that might result in a loss of face through *ridicule, gossip,* or *scolding.* Ridicule is a form of humor that is used to set the bounds of social acceptability and to punish those who transgress those bounds (Billig 2005), but it cannot be exercised without consequences for the cohesion of the group. To gossip about people when they are present in the room is not acceptable, as to gossip in itself is to challenge the dignity of an individual. It is, however, more acceptable to gossip about people who are not physically present (Bergmann 1993). Finally, reproof (scolding in its varying degrees) typically represents a threat to the harmony in a group, and for that reason, reprimands, etc., generally take place behind closed doors, unless, of course, the objective is to set an example, and to imprint a norm on a larger group.

Mediated interaction extends and complicates the use of *territories* in the interaction, including how we define ourselves in relation to the other participants. It also regulates the access to information between different territories in the interaction. The media link different physical localities and social contexts in a single interactive space, but they do not do away with the reality of the separate physical and social contexts. Television, telephones, and the Internet all bridge distances, but the users have not left their sofas or desks to enter into the interactive space. Thus, the media link the participants in the interaction and, at the same time, create a distance between the virtual "stage" of the interactive space and the participants' respective place-bound social contexts, of which they remain a part. This phenomenon is particularly apparent in the case of television, where the sender and recipient situations are distinctly separate, but it is also present in interpersonal communication via Internet or mobile phone, where the lack of access to the fullness of the interpersonal exchange reminds us of the distance between the parties.

The de-linking or distance between place-bound social situations that surround the user and the simultaneous establishment of a mediated situation means that various norm-enforcing mechanisms such as ridicule, gossip, and scolding can assume new forms. Because participants in a mediated interaction lack full access to the other participants' behavior, the individual's place-bound context may assume the character of "backstage" in relation to the ongoing mediated interaction. It is not, however, a backstage in Goffman's original sense since it can just as well be "on stage," i.e., the prime focus of the individual's attention, and actually frame how he or she interacts on the virtual media "stage." Text message communication (texting) between a group of teenagers may, for example, be instigated primarily for the entertainment of some of the participants, who, together with friends in their physical social situations, make fun of others' contributions to the "conversation" behind their backs, without those others knowing that the messages they send are being made the butt of derisive comments. Similarly, television viewers can mimic the dialects or make fun of the appearance of people they see on the screen. Interactive media also lend themselves to more insidious forms of ridicule, and even outright bullying, via websites, text messages, and camera telephones.

The distance or de-linking of interaction when it takes place via media leads to changes, extensions, and complications of the relations between the "stage" and "backstage" of the interaction and, as a consequence, norm-enforcing mechanisms can develop in ways that would be perceived as illegitimate and, possibly, even gross violations of others' integrity, were they applied in a face-to-face situation. While gossip about a participant in an interaction is not voiced openly in face-to-face encounters, it may be spread behind the person's back "backstage" (Bergmann 1993). Several media and media genres publish gossip: magazines, reality television, and blogs shamelessly spread all kinds of gossip, particularly about celebrities. Moreover, in addition to filling these media's columns and air time, the media's gossip is also a legitimate topic in face-to-face situations, where such subjects would not normally be fitting (Hjarvard 2002b). The use of norm-enforcing mechanisms in the media does not make them any less effective, and in some cases they may be even more effective because the media make ridicule, gossip, or scolding publicly accessible. But because of the distance or de-linking that characterizes mediated interaction, the application of the mechanisms in the media seems – from the point of view of media users, that is – less intrusive and less consequential for the individual than if they had been applied in a face-to-face situation.

Virtualization and a new social geography

The growing complexity of territories in mediated interaction bears witness to a general effect of mediatization: the *virtualization* of social institutions. Earlier, institutions were more bound to specific places: politics took place in parliament, city halls, and meeting halls; education took place in schools and universities; and art was presented on the stage and in museums and galleries. As a consequence of the intervention of the media, individuals can take part in and partake of many different social institutions, irrespective of their physical location. Contact with politics occurs by reading the paper at the breakfast table, listening to one's car radio, or via the Internet at the office.

The virtualization of social institutions goes hand-in-hand with a *domestication* of those institutions. Typically, the home and family are increasingly the point around which access to other institutions revolves. Newspapers, radio, and television have brought politics and cultural expression into the home; Internet workstations have brought paid employment into family life; and digital media in general have made it possible to interact with players from both the public and private spheres from the comfort of one's own home. On the one hand, all this implies an enrichment of the home and family as an institution, in that other institutions are now accessible. On the other hand, the new accessibility also changes the home and family, as family members may be physically present in the home, yet mentally attuned to completely other institutions. The virtualization of institutions implies that the home loses some of its ability to regulate family members' behavior, and it is left to the individual to decide in which institution he or she is taking part, and adjust his/her behavior accordingly. Institutional contexts are no longer defined by their locus, but are increasingly a matter of individual choice. This tendency is further accentuated by the mobility of the new media, allowing the individual to carry the access point to institutions around in his or her own pocket. When the Internet is accessed from the home, the office or the school there is at least a potential collective control of the activity. When accessed by individual mobile media, this social control is only possible through the functionality of the virtual interface. Virtualization is seldom total, however, as most institutions still maintain physical-geographical bases as an important framework for social praxis. What is new is that these places and buildings now interact with virtual places and spaces, and the reality and forms of interaction that take place in the virtual world will also have consequences for social praxis in the physical locality.

As described earlier, ever since the nineteenth century, the media have dis-embedded (Giddens 1984) social interaction from the local level and embedded it in a national – and later global – context (Hjarvard 2003). In the last decades of the twentieth century it became increasingly possible for the media to transcend national frontiers, and the media supported the globalization process. Thus, Tomlinson (1999) speaks of the role of the media in *de-territorializing* cultural experience and social interaction. With the Internet, mobile phones, and a growing global market for television series, film, music, advertising, etc. – combined with immigration, tourism, and global commerce – human experience is no longer bound to either the local or national context, but also takes place in a globalized context. By the same token, the media make it possible to interact with others across political and cultural frontiers. As a consequence of the media's growing complexity and encompassing nature, society takes on a *complex connectivity* (Tomlinson 1999). In the era of globalization the media not only provide channels of communication between nations and peoples, but also establish networks across all manner of geographical areas and players. This development in turn leads to greater *cultural reflexivity*. As influxes of media products and communication cross more and more frontiers, virtually no culture will be able to develop in isolation from others. Greater cultural reflexivity does not mean that influences from abroad necessarily increase or become in any way indispensable; indeed, foreign media cultures may well be rejected and castigated, as demonstrated so emphatically by, for instance, fundamentalists of all types. But greater cultural reflexivity has the consequence that cultural development no longer takes place in "naïve" isolation from other cultures, but will develop in an awareness that alternative courses are available.

The great difficulty in attempting to chart the social geography of contemporary media trends is that they do not describe a development in any single direction. Instead, the trends seem to tend in many directions at once, which results in a social geography that is far more complex than what we have known to date. But, as we survey the new geography that the media support, we can distinguish between two sets of opposites: first, homogenization versus differentiation; and, second, centrifugal versus centripetal forces. If, in simplified terms, we might say that the media landscape of the twentieth century has revolved around national public spheres, recent years' developments have remolded the communicative spaces of the media. On the one hand, one may speak of a *centrifugal force* that has broadened national public spheres' contact with the outside world. Transnational media such as satellite-distributed television (CNN, Al-Jazeera, Cartoon Network, etc.) and the Internet have helped to bring about a globalized media environment in which sound, images, and texts flow with ease across national boundaries. With the Internet, foreign newspapers and radio stations are seldom more than a click away, and not least, young people can play games and chat with each other around the world. Meanwhile, a *centripetal* force is also at play: the media environment has more "introverted" communication spaces in the form of neighborhood radio, local newspapers, community websites, family blogs, etc.

In some respects these developments have a *homogenizing* effect; in others, *differences* are accentuated. The ongoing proliferation of radio and television channels means that there will be fewer and fewer programs that we all hear and see "together." Access to several different interactive media allows us to create different contexts in which we can communicate; typically, in small groups, in chat rooms, blogs, online games, and so forth. But, despite this segmentation, we occasionally encounter media phenomena that momentarily revive the great collective "we." Events in the lives of national royal family members have, in many countries like the UK and Denmark, become national media events and broken successive ratings records. Reactions to immigration and globalization in general have also revived a nationalistic culture in many countries, and the media may be more or less explicitly part of this process. There are also examples of homo-genization at global and regional levels. Al-Jazeera and other Arabic-language satellite television services have, for example, created supranational political and cultural *public spheres* in the Arab world (Galal 2002; Galal and Spielhaus 2012) that have played an important part in the political, cultural, and religious transformations before, during, and after the Arab Spring.

Figure 2.1 presents an attempt to summarize the contradictory processes outlined here. The point of this model is to underline the fact that the media environment is expanding and developing in different directions, so that one cannot say that the media are moving society in any particular direction. We are not simply moving from a national public sphere toward a global public sphere. Developments may in some cases entail increasing globalization, often by circulating products of Anglo-American origin, but globalization is also spurred by other regional media centers in Brazil, India, China, and South Korea (Tunstall 2007). The global spread of the Internet may not only foster globalization, but also bring a greater degree of indi-vidualization and segmentation, as in the case of the use of interactive media by small groups. Meanwhile, the media can also facilitate local interaction or call attention to national phenomena. It should be borne in mind that these contra-dictory processes are often at play simultaneously. A Turkish satellite-TV channel beamed toward Europe may help to preserve emigrants' cultural bonds with their

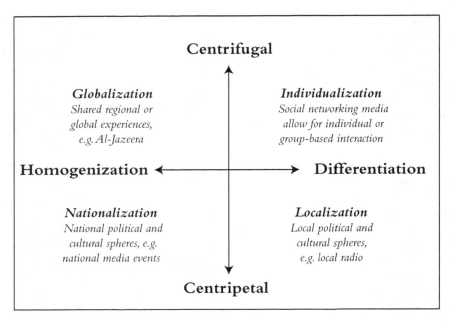

FIGURE 2.1 The media facilitate and structure virtual spaces for communication and action.

homeland, but the channel is also an ingredient in an overall process of globalization whereby Turkish identity, language, and culture are successively transformed and find themselves in a new transnational context (Robins 2003). As indicated in Figure 2.1, mediatization can facilitate highly diverging societal tendencies at both micro and macro levels. These include globalization, individualization, nationalization, and localization. Which tendency predominates will depend on the specific context, i.e., on the institution or social activity in question. The more precise consequences of media intervention will, however, need to be explored empirically, through examination of the interplay of institutions and the media in a historical and cultural context.

The expanding geography to which the media contribute does not have the same degree of cohesion as the national media systems of the past. The links between local, national, individual-/group-oriented, and global are far less stable and bear a resemblance to what in modern governance theory are called *loose couplings* (Orton and Weick 1990). In late-modern, networked societies (Castells 2001), national bureaucratic organizations with well-defined hierarchies and decision-making processes have been replaced in part by network governance, which is of a more fragmentary nature (Bogason 2001). In a similar manner, the different social spaces may be more or less loosely coupled. In the national media systems of yesteryear, the links between the media and political and cultural institutions were generally rather strong. Topics mentioned in the printed and broadcast media often had direct consequences for the political system and in cultural and confessional spheres – and vice-versa. In globalized media systems, the linking mechanism between media representations and social action is less pronounced (Hjarvard 2001). Topics discussed in transnational chat rooms or blogs, on transnational satellite-TV channels, or on local minority radio, generally only have an occasional influence on policy-making in national spaces; conversely, national policies and restrictions can be contradicted and rather easily circumvented by means of foreign websites and radio or television channels. In short, the interplay between mediatization and globalization imposes a more complex social and cultural geography in which individual, local, national, and global entities can be linked in new ways.

A realm of shared experience

Whereas mediatization at the micro-social level is evidenced in the media affordances' structuring impacts on human interaction, at the macro level we find impacts on how institutions relate to each other due to the intervention of the media. In general terms, we can distinguish three functions that the media serve in this regard: they constitute a *realm of shared experience*, which means that they offer a continuous presentation and interpretation of "the way things are," and by doing so, contribute to the development of a sense of identity and of community. Second, the media constitute *an interface in the relations within and between institutions:* television newscasts bring politics into people's sitting rooms, and advertising is an important platform for private firms' communication with potential customers. Finally, the media help to create a *political public sphere*, within which institutions can pursue and defend their own interests and establish their legitimacy. Put another way, the three functions of the media at the macro-social level are to serve as an *interpretive frame* for understanding society, as a *nexus* between institutions, and as an *arena* in which members of a society can discuss and decide matters of common interest.

In a historical perspective, the media's ability to create a common horizon of experience across institutions has mainly served to dissolve local cultures in favor of shared *national* realms of experience. Giddens (1984) describes one aspect of modernity as an ongoing "disembedding" of societal structures: parochial and traditional cultures are broken up, fall into oblivion, and are transformed through contact with the larger, modern world. Viewed in this light, mediatization has been a social force on a par with urbanization and industrialization. Just as electricity and the railroads helped to make people more mobile, the media have contributed to a mental and communicative mobility. Since the mid-1800s, newspapers, and later radio and television, have helped to undermine local, traditional cultures in favor of a national culture and culture of political unity. Julius Bomholt, the first and very influential Minister of Culture in the Danish welfare state, did not mince his words in describing the modernization "mission" of the media when he in 1964 summed up the status of Danish broadcasting media:

> Engrained, parochial cultural habits are, with the help of broadcasting, being sundered. Isolated and backward cultures have been dissolved. A shared

cultural background has put the population on speaking terms. When credit is given for having eradicated the benighted peasantry and ignorant proletariat of yesteryear, Danmark's Radio [Danish public service broadcasting] will have a major share of it.

(Bomholt 1964: 10)

Viewed in this light, then, the creation of a common experiential frame of reference is not just a matter of adding something new and shared; it is also a matter of eroding and doing away with previous experience and culture. The media's creation of a new, shared national or globalized realm of experience may, to use Giddens' terminology, be conceived of as a "re-embedding" of social interaction on a more a general and abstract level than once characterized erstwhile place-bound cultures.

Benedict Anderson (1991) considers national communities as an *imagined community* inasmuch as no one, even in the smallest of nations, can have met of all its other members. The media are the symbolic mortar that makes the individual components appear to be a cohesive social whole. Thus, as Jeffrey Alexander (1981: 18) points out, the media are the symbolic equivalent of the judicial system, as they serve to produce "the symbolic patterns that create the invisible tissues of society on the cultural level, just as the legal system creates the community on a more concrete and 'real' one."

There is more to this than creating common experiential frames of reference. The media create a context that enables the individual to observe and experience the whole of society from a new perspective. As Paddy Scannell (1988: 29, original emphasis) characterizes the accomplishment of radio and television, for example:

Broadcasting brought together for a radically new kind of *general* public the elements of a culture-in-common (national and transnational) for all. In doing so, it redeemed, and continues to redeem, the intelligibility of the world and the communicability of experience in the widest social sense.

The world presents itself at once as a generalized whole (such as "Germany" or "Great Britain") and as something concrete, tangible, and "at hand." With access to the Internet, it has also become possible for individuals to interact with everyone else. Once an abstraction, community has, thanks to the media, become concrete experience.

While Paddy Scannell takes a generally positive view of the media as providers of a common frame of experience, Nick Couldry (2003a) is more critical, not least with regard to this very function. Taking his point of departure in Bourdieu's field theory, Couldry points out that a theory of the roles of the media in society needs to do more than show how the media intervene into and influence various fields, such as cultural life and politics, as it also needs to take account of "the impacts that media might have on all fields simultaneously by legitimating certain categories with not just cognitive, but also social significance" (Couldry 2003a: 665). The influence of the media is, in other words, more than the sum of their influence in the respective fields. In line with Bourdieu's concept of "meta-capital," used to describe the ability of a state to project its power across different fields, Couldry suggests that one may also speak of a "meta-capital" of the media inasmuch as the media are able universally, across all fields, to form the categories that everyone uses to interpret the world. That is to say that the media have an essentially ideological power to describe society in a way that seems the only "natural" way to comprehend it. Couldry (2003b) expands on and exemplifies this idea through a number of analyses, but now using a modified concept of ritual. The media's influence on people's experience consists not least of the media's ability to present themselves as the center of society: they offer an interpretive position that gives the world meaning. Media rituals deliver "formalised actions organised around key media-related categories and boundaries, whose performance frames, and suggests a connection with wider media-related values" (Couldry 2003b: 29). In other words, the media not only describe the world, but also provide basic categorical frameworks through which we apprehend it (see also Couldry 2012).

Couldry makes an important point when he highlights the power inherent in the privilege to define the cognitive, social, and lexical categories that organize people's understanding of the world around them. Yet he seems to have limited appreciation of the potentially positive aspects that the construction of an experiential commons might have. Second, he seems to have a rather monolithic conception of media power, as a power so pervasive that no other institution can challenge the descriptions of reality that the media provide. Third, Couldry's use of ritual as a concept deviates somewhat from standard usage in communication research (Rothenbuhler 1998). Actually, the principal focus of Couldry's (2003b) critique is the ideological impact of the media, although he uses this term only sporadically. Regardless of whether one sides more with Scannell's optimistic interpretation regarding a common world created by the media, or Couldry's more critical views regarding the ideological consequences of this mediatized common world, the most important conclusion for our present purposes is that one of the principal consequences of the mediatization of culture and society is the constitution of a shared experiential world, a world that is influenced by the various *modus operandi* of the media.

The interfaces between institutions

As interfaces, the media are a resource that institutions make use of in their mutual interaction. In order to tap this resource, the institution has to have a degree of participation in a media practice, which is evidenced by the increasing use of journalists, information officers, and PR consultants by private companies, political parties, educational institutions, etc. On a theoretical level, one may assess the importance of the media as a shared resource or interface by viewing the various social institutions, media included, as fields in a Bourdieuan sense (Bourdieu 1993, 2005), i.e., as social areas characterized by a certain autonomy and internal structure, according to which agents occupy specific positions vis-à-vis each other. For example, art is a field that has a certain autonomy in relation to other institutions and is imbued with its own, internally defined norms and hierarchies. No field, however, is totally autonomous; all are influenced to greater or lesser degrees by other fields. Art, for example, is influenced by the market, which is also a field, in that professional artists make their living by dealing in works of art; and by the field of politics, since cultural policy affects artists' ability to show their works and is the source of stipends and scholarships. Art is also dependent on the media as a field, since media exposure is the key to publicity and fame, which may be converted into other forms of value in the art market or in cultural policy contexts. Bourdieu makes a distinction in this regard between autonomous and heteronomous poles, where the former is the site of the field's immanent logic, where actors act in accordance with the field's own values, such as when a work of art is judged on the basis of the genre's criterion of quality. The heteronomous pole, on the other hand, is the site of other fields' influence, such as that of the market, politicians, or the media.

If we examine mediatization in the light of Bourdieu's concepts, we find that the media occupy a prominent place in a growing number of fields' heteronomous poles, thereby challenging those fields' autonomous poles. Thus, the degree of mediatization may be measured according to how much the respective field's autonomous pole has weakened. The media, too, have autonomous and heteronomous poles, where the autonomous pole is the site of aspects such as professionalized journalism and film dramaturgy, and the heteronomous pole is the site of, say, the influence exerted by the advertising market. There is a tension between the poles in the media; in news media, for example, the journalistic criteria of news value and the ideals of good journalism often compete with the demand for the need to sell copies, the influence exerted by news sources, and so forth (Schultz 2006). Inasmuch as the media are influenced by other fields or institutions, we cannot always be certain that observed media impacts imply an influence from media logic alone. Occasionally, mediatization will go hand-in-hand with commercialization or politicization, and whether mediatization is the most dominant process can only be determined by analysis. Any empirical analysis of mediatization should therefore enquire whether, and to what extent, other institutions (conceived of here as fields in the vocabulary of Bourdieu) stand to win or lose autonomy in their interaction with various forms of media.

3

THE MEDIATIZATION OF POLITICS

From party press to opinion industry

Introduction

The media have played a role in the exercise of political power in all major societies. Without print media such as papyrus rolls and letters – and their appurtenant technology and social organization – it would have been difficult to build and maintain political structures such as the Egyptian or Roman Empires. Books, magazines, and newspapers were important instruments in the bourgeois revolutions against absolutist rule in Europe in the eighteenth and nineteenth centuries, while films and posters were important propaganda instruments during World War I, as well as the Russian Revolution. With the rise of modern democracy, the exercise of political power had to be based on popular consent and participation, and the mass media came to play a crucial role in this process – and continue to do so. The media were no longer the sole instruments of the political power élites, but also served democratic functions: the media gradually became bestowed with a duty to provide political information, facilitate political discussion and participation, and exert critical scrutiny of political power. Via this process, the media became important to the public legitimacy of political institutions, actors, and actions.

Many of the changes, opportunities, and problematic outcomes were already diagnosed and discussed by Walter Lippmann in 1922 in his book *Public Opinion*, in which he observed a revolution in democratic practices: "And so, as a result of psychological research, coupled with the modern means of communication, the practice of democracy has turned a corner. A revolution is taking place, infinitely more significant than any shifting of economic power" (Lippmann 1922: 158). By the late nineteenth century, the news media had come to influence the formation of public opinion in significant ways. Among many of the problems, Lippmann pointed to how there may be a considerable difference between the pictures of the world that the news media project into our minds and the actual outside world.

The media not only reflect the world, but also make use of stereotypes to depict the world; and, similarly, the audience's understanding of newspaper stories is influenced by the readers' different viewpoints and prejudices. There is, therefore, no guarantee that the formation of public opinion will be based on a correct description of the world's condition, just as it may be colored by both politicians' and citizens' interests and preconceived ideas. Lippmann's perception of the concept of "stereotype" was not entirely negative, because he also considered stereotypes as unavoidable simplifications in the process of mass communication whereby many people with different experiences are to understand a common message.

In addition to its own merits, Walter Lippmann's writing is an early testimony to the heightened interest in media and communication in the first part of the twentieth century both in the United States and in other western countries. Questions concerning the persuasive power of the media and their general influence on public opinion entered not only the public debate, but also commercial markets, politics, and academia. As methods from advertising, marketing, and public relations spread through the commercial sector in support of a new consumer culture, these techniques also entered the political sphere and were adapted to suit political ends. Furthermore, the experience of war propaganda in the two world wars and the demagogical use of the media in the two totalitarian disasters of the twentieth century, Stalinism and Nazism, provided another important backdrop for the heightened attention paid to the political importance of the media and public communication. Within various scientific disciplines such as psychology, sociology, political science, and marketing research, the study of propaganda, public opinion, and media consumption began to emerge, both in order to critically reflect on the growing influence of the media and with the intention of developing more skilled techniques to exploit these opportunities to influence public opinion. In both Europe (cf. Horkheimer and Adorno 1944) and the United States (cf. Merton 1946) media and communication research had its roots in this double-edged political climate: concern for the fate of mass-mediated democracy walking hand-in-hand with a fascination with the idea of the scientifically based management of public opinion.

This two-edged stance toward the media's influence on politics has continued to inform public debate. During the last decades, the notions of "spin" and "media management" have emerged as key terms to describe how political actors seek to influence public opinion through the media (cf. Palmer 2000; Maarek 2011). The success of British New Labour under Tony Blair back in the 1990s and onward in controlling political communication both within the party and in the public media gave credence to the importance of "spin doctors" in politics. The terms "spin" and "media management" undoubtedly point to more recent and intensified ways in which political actors try to steer political opinion. Yet these terms have also become stereotypes in Lippmann's sense: they may not necessarily be wrong, but they oversimplify the relationship between media and politics, just as they may entail different meanings for various audiences. For some, spin may denote manipulative techniques that deliberately seek to outmaneuver political adversaries, and for others spin may refer to the production of a comprehensive and strategic narrative that links together all the political communications of a party in a persuasive way (Høybye *et al.* 2007).

As a rhetorical figure, spin is indebted to the early research on media and public opinion and the then prevalent idea of the manipulation or seduction of mass audiences. At its simplest, it is the idea of the spin doctor – for instance, Tony Blair's legendary chief spin doctor Alistair Campbell – who, as a political Mephisto, orchestrates the manipulation of both the press and the public. Despite its entertaining qualities, spin is only one small element among many others in the general relationship between the news media and politics. As Kristensen (2006) has rightly pointed out, the perceived importance of spin is also a result of the news media's own framing of modern politics. Via the discourse on spin modern politics comes to be centered on the manipulative struggle between journalists, politicians, and media advisors. Consequently, the task of political journalists and political commentators becomes, among other things, to reveal the "true" story by exposing the political spin behind each story. The notion of spin very often entails a focus on political actors and forms of political communication and, as a consequence, politics often comes to be reduced to its processual aspects, while the structural aspects of the media–politics nexus are neglected.

Back in the early twentieth century, Walter Lippmann was no doubt also very critical of the mass media, but his ambition was to address the media–politics–society relationship in its complexity, not to reduce it to a question of manipulative strategies by social actors. By focusing on the *mediatization* of politics, we will, similarly, develop a holistic view of the media and politics that also considers the duality of structure and agency. Using an institutional perspective, we will consider the changing structural relationship between politics and the media, and study the implications of this for both the role of political actors and the function, form, and content of politics. By the "mediatization of politics" we will understand the process via which the political institution is gradually becoming dependent on the media and their logic. By political institution we mean both formal political organizations and practices such as parliament, parties, and election campaigns, and informal practices such as ordinary citizens' everyday conversations about politics and politicians' daily encounters with political journalists. The process of the mediatization of politics is characterized by a double-sided development. The media become *integrated* into the daily practices of political organizations and serve both internal and external communication tasks for political actors. By using press meetings, websites, blogs, etc. the media come to serve political ends at the same time as political organizations and individual political actors in the process of "internalizing" these media must accommodate the media's logic. At the same time, the media have evolved into a partly *independent institution* in society that controls a vital political resource in a democracy: society's collective attention. As a consequence, the media become partly responsible for various political functions, not least the setting of political agendas and the generation of public consent for political decisions and actions. In order to influence the media's management of this vital resource, other institutions – in particular politics, but also industry and any other interest groups seeking to achieve political influence – must accommodate the logic of the media. By the media's logic we understand their technological, aesthetical, and institutional *modus operandi* by which they allocate material and symbolic resources, and work through formal and informal rules. In actual practice, this means that political actors have to take into consideration such factors as the news values of journalism, generic conventions of expression, and the typical forms of relationship that the various media constitute vis-à-vis their audiences and users.

Dimensions and phases of change

By using the concept "mediatization of politics" and not "mediation of politics" we wish to pay specific attention to the *transformative* influence of the media on politics. In accordance with the previously mentioned distinction between these two concepts (see Chapter 2) we hypothesize that the media have come to play a particularly important role in modern politics compared to earlier times. This is not to say that the media did not influence political communication in earlier and other societies, since this was obviously the case. The argument is, instead, that due to developments in late modern societies the media have become implicated in the practice of politics, in particular, and in intensified ways that transform politics to such an extent that it makes sense to talk about "mediatized" politics and not only "mediated" politics. This entails that politics have been subject to changes of both a quantitative and qualitative nature, i.e., both in terms of degree and along various dimensions of politics.

Several researchers have sought to systematize these transformations in terms of periods, dimensions, or phases in relation to both formal characteristics and empirical contexts (Asp and Esaiasson 1996; Blumler and Kavanagh 1999; Jenssen 2007; Norris 2000). Strömbäck (2008) has put forward a useful model stipulating four dimensions that each point to a particular transformation of politics. The first dimension concerns the degree to which the media have become the most important *source of information* about politics. Do personal experience and inter-personal communication constitute a primary source of information, or have the media acquired the principal role in the dissemination of political information? Second, the media may be *dependent* on political institutions, or they may possess a high degree of *independence* vis-à-vis political institutions. Third, the *content of media* (e.g., news about politics) may be governed by a political logic, or by the logic of the media. Finally, *political actors* may chiefly be governed by a political logic, or mainly governed by a media logic. Each of these dimensions represents a scale on which politics may become more or less mediatized.

On this basis, Strömbäck (2008) suggests a development of mediatization in four phases, in which each phase is characterized by a swaying of influence from politics toward the media along each of the four dimensions. The first dimension reflects that an initial move toward the mediatization of politics is the mediation of politics, because the proliferation of mediated politics – that eventually makes the media the primary source of political information – is a necessary precondition for mediatization along the three other dimensions. In the second phase, the media become more independent of political institutions, and journalists acquire a greater degree of autonomy to select the news according to their own criteria. This process continues in the third phase, but here the political institutions begin to accommodate to the demands of the news media, for instance, by communicating politics in accordance with news criteria or journalistic deadlines. As a result, the content of political news becomes governed more by media logic than by political logic. In the final phase, political institutions not only accommodate the logic of the media, but also internalize the media logic to such an extent that media considerations become part and parcel of everyday political thinking and action, including the development of political ideas and priorities. Strömbäck's four phases are based on a *logical* model and he stresses that, in the real world, the relationship between the media and politics may be much more varied and complex than the model suggests. For instance, different media may exhibit various degrees of independence from political institutions; and in some countries independent media co-exist with a press partly controlled by political actors. Similarly, political organizations and politicians may be more or less dependent on the media. There may also be considerable variation among individual countries regarding the degree of mediatization along each of the four dimensions. The role of the political press in southern Europe has a different history compared to experience in the USA, where a commercial press dominated from an early stage.

Strömbäck's model is useful because it highlights key transformative aspects of mediatization in the realm of politics. Its focus on four distinctive phases in relation to four dimensions provides a heuristic model when studying and comparing empirical processes of mediatization historically and across countries. Yet the model's logical and formal character is also its limitation. Empirical analyses of changing relationships between media and politics not only have to consider variations in a general pattern of mediatization, but the process of mediatization of politics itself may be dependent on systemic characteristics in a particular context, i.e., a country or region's historically developed interrelationships between media, politics, and the wider society. It is important to stress that the logic of politics and the logic of the media may not necessarily be antagonistic, as Strömbäck's model implicitly might suggest, but they may also work in tandem in several ways. For instance, the *raison d'être* of both politics and the media is to seek publicity in order to achieve authority. Considered in this way, the logics of politics and the media may support each other in the co-construction of political realities. Mediatization may also produce different outcomes, depending on the context in question. The logic of the media may have come to influence politics to a larger extent in, for instance, the USA, Denmark, and France, but the implications of this influence may vary considerably from country to country.

In order to understand the *historical* process of the mediatization of politics, we need to confront the insights of a formal model of logical phases with the empirical contexts of various political and media systems. In the following, we will provide a tentative historical outline of the mediatization of politics within the Nordic countries. In Hallin and Mancini's (2004) influential study of media systems, the Nordic countries are the quintessential example of the "democratic corporatist model" to which other northern European countries like Germany and the Netherlands also belong. Key characteristics of this model are the early existence of a mass circulation press and a high level of newspaper readership in the entire population, a professionalization of journalism, a medium degree of political parallelism, and public regulation of the media system, with particular emphasis on public service broadcasting. The "liberal model" of media–politics relationships – of which the United States is the prototype – is also characterized by an early mass circulation press and the professionalization of journalism, but in this model the political parallelism is limited. In the United States the "partisan press" was succeeded by a commercial mass circulation press in the nineteenth century, and public intervention in the media system was kept to a minimum. In southern Europe we find the "polarized pluralist model," with a higher degree of political partisanship and less emphasis on professional journalism. Here, newspaper readership is more restricted to an educated and politically interested élite, whereas broadcasting has traditionally been the primary channel for the wider public. Within the conceptual framework of Hallin and Mancini (2004), the Nordic countries come to represent a hybrid between two extremes: on the one hand the liberal model's commercial and non-partisan mass media, and on the other hand the polarized pluralist model of politicized media with limited experience of professional journalism. The different media models are, however, converging toward the liberal model, due to the growing commercialization of media systems. As a result, Hallin and Mancini (2004) argue, European media models are moving toward the liberal model:

> Commercialization, in the first place, is clearly shifting European media systems away from the world of politics and towards the world of commerce. This changes the social function of journalism, as the journalist's main objective is no longer to disseminate ideas and create social consensus around them, but to produce entertainment and information that can be sold to individual consumers.
>
> *(Hallin and Mancini: 277)*

From this perspective, the specificities of European models may be apt descriptions of historical developments, but less useful to our understanding of their current and future characteristics, since they are moving toward the liberal model. There are, however, some shortcomings in Hallin and Mancini's conceptual models. Commercialization is, no doubt, a very important force behind the current restructuring in the media industry, but it may not necessarily or unambiguously push other media models toward a liberal model similar to the United States' media system. Hallin and Mancini's idea that commercialization will reduce the political functions of journalism rests on the assumption that commercialism, non-partisanship, and journalistic professionalism are logically interconnected, and the particularities of the liberal model therefore come to stand as a developmental path to be followed – eventually – by others. This not only makes the models less sensitive to more complex relationships between political institutions, journalism, and media within the particular countries, but also prevents them from recognizing that commercialization and professionalization may not be at odds with the continuation of political parallelism or partisan media. In other words, due to specific relationships between the media and politics in particular countries or regions, commercialization and professionalization may end up having different consequences than Hallin and Mancini's (2004) framework anticipates.

The political functions of the news media, including patterns of political partisanship and political parallelism, may not be in decline due to increased commercialization, but may co-exist with market-driven forces. In Denmark and Norway, for instance, political parallelism is still an attribute of major newspapers – not only as a rudimentary feature of the past, but as part of both their present media market strategies and their publicist ambition as voices of opinion. A study of newspapers' coverage of local elections in Norway pointed to the continued presence of political parallelism (Allern 2007). Similarly, Hjarvard (2010b) documented a continued political orientation in editorials, opinion pages, and journalism in national Danish newspapers in the first decade of the twenty-first century. Studies conducted in the United States suggest, furthermore, that also within a liberal media model there are many examples of political partisanship in commercial news media, for instance, Fox News, and such opinionated news media have the potential to attract audiences with similar convictions (Lyengar and Hahn 2009). Partisanship in the US media market is not only restricted to a few highly profiled television networks, since analysis of seemingly neutral and mainstream newspapers also reveals a systematic political framing of the news (Kahn and Kenny 2002).

The continued presence of various forms of partisanship and political parallelism in the media in many countries poses a problem within the framework of Hallin and Mancini's media models, because they basically conceive politics and media markets to be at odds with each other: the commercialization and professionalization of the media are generally thought to be antidotes to political partisanship and parallelism. If we, instead, take on the perspective of the ongoing mediatization of politics, we will not only consider the changing relationship between two different institutions or social systems, as is primarily the perspective of Hallin and Mancini, but also how both media and politics are transformed and intertwined in various ways as a consequence of their mutual adaptation to each other. This may allow for a more complex view of regional media developments, where various media considerations, including market objectives and professional ambitions, may work in tandem with various political functions, for instance, in the form of opinionated news media. Due to mediatization processes, the end of the party press is not the end of the political press, but the media have become an industry of opinion that in other – but no less important ways – is implicated in the production of politics.

The rise of journalism

The Nordic region may be used as a case to illustrate both regional specificities and general changes following mediatization (cf. Bastiansen and Dahl 2008; Djerf-Pierre and Weibull 2001; Jensen 2003). In the second half of the nineteenth century, the press in the Nordic countries gradually consolidated itself as the political instruments of political parties and broader social and cultural movements. Newspapers were edited and written by politicians, academics, administrators, teachers, church ministers, novelists, and other political and cultural power brokers, and audiences were divided according to political beliefs and social class. Newspapers also carried general news, advertisements, and other forms of information and entertainment, but these aspects were generally subordinated to the political functions of the newspaper. Journalism was not yet established as an education or profession, but was – to the extent that it existed in a modern sense – a set of practical skills that everyone writing for a newspaper had to learn. From a sociological point of view, it was the political institutions, i.e., parliament, parties, and movements, that could be considered the mass media of those days, since they constituted the infrastructure for dissemination of information, and public discussion. Newspapers were one channel of communication among many (e.g., union meetings, folk high schools, demonstrations, etc.) for the promotion of political interests. As a consequence, the press reflected the political system via the structure of political parallelism: in many towns there was typically a range of newspapers that each represented a major political party and a particular class interest among the audience.

During the twentieth century the media gradually gained more independence and became cultural institutions (see Chapter 2). Accordingly, journalists progressively acquired greater control of the news media and became the main producers of content. News became separated from views, and political opinions were relegated to particular genres such as editorials and op-ed pages. The new ideal of the newspaper became the "omnibus press" providing general news for a general audience, irrespective of their political leanings. A certain degree of political parallelism continued to play a role in many newspapers, but as journalism became attuned to more professional ideals of objectivity and facticity (Tuchman 1972), the formal ties between political parties and newspapers came to an end. What started as a formal and organized relationship between party and press continued in a weaker form as shared political and cultural values between newspaper and readers. Commercial considerations became gradually more important as political interests became relegated, but newspapers in the Nordic countries were for most of the twentieth century not generally dominated by commercial interests. They were half commercial, half publicist ventures, earning money to publish newspapers, rather than the other way around. Many newspapers were not privately owned companies, but were controlled by various foundations.

The growing role of public service radio and television provided a particular context for the development of journalism in the Nordic countries. Similar to many other countries, newspapers feared competition from the electronic media and sought to curb the latter's entry into the domain of news production and distribution in various ways. But when broadcasting finally was allowed to enter the domain of journalism, radio and television quickly became dominant news media, with a strong influence on the national political agenda. Since the broadcast news media were subject to public service obligations, journalism emphasized political news and was committed to a general, educational mission. Broadcast journalism was not to follow in the footsteps of state-controlled radio and television, as in southern or eastern Europe, or of the commercial media, as in the USA, but on the contrary to provide impartial and serious information about public affairs. As a consequence, journalism became influenced by an educational paradigm via which the aim was primarily to report on important political affairs and represent the various political viewpoints as neutrally as possible. In its early phase, broadcast journalism was to facilitate well-informed public discussion, but to leave the controversies to the politicians themselves. In general, the news media did not challenge political parties, but their importance in the field of politics was reflected in how they became the public's primary source of information about political affairs.

The development of journalism was also influenced by the then prevailing corporative structure of democratic politics. In the mid-twentieth century the Nordic countries were characterized by elaborated cooperation between the dominant organized interests (industry and labor organizations, political parties, interest groups, etc.) that influenced policy development and governance in most domains. The combination of strong social democratic influence and the general growth in the western economy made it possible to engage various organized interests in the building of welfare societies. As a consequence, political discussions very often took place as negotiations between these organized interests, allowing them a certain degree of control of the political process. As long as the various corporative interests could dominate the process of developing and negotiating politics, the news media were left to report from the outside, rather than intervening in politics in a more direct way. The combination of journalism's own emerging ideals of objectivity and non-partisanship, the enlightening mission of public service media, and the corporative interests' ability to steer political processes, pushed news media in the Nordic countries toward an informative and educational role. Journalism – like other public service institutions – was to provide a mirror of society, but in such a way that the public would be enlightened, rather than confused or disinterested, by looking in that mirror.

From the late 1960s and onward this division of labor between the news media and politics began to break up. Similar to developments in other parts of the western world, journalism achieved greater autonomy and was no longer content with the predominantly passive role of the factual reporting of politics. Instead, investigative journalism, critical interviews of politicians, and a general culture of questioning authorities began to emerge. In the political realm the corporative structure began to crack and the consensus hitherto about the welfare state began to receive criticism from both left and right. The oil crisis of the 1970s and the USA's withdrawal from Vietnam in 1975 provided an international backdrop to a general feeling that existing political and economic structures and values were about to change. In the political realm, this meant that the combination of corporative democracy and Social Democratic dominance in the Nordic countries gradually gave way to a social-liberal state that combined public welfare services with a stronger emphasis on individual responsibility and market solutions. Political negotiations became more open and indeterminate, as new political parties entered the stage and challenged the existing corporative framework, at the same time as the old parties lost many of their members and voters became less loyal. The transformation of political parties from mass membership organizations based on clear class interests and ideologies to smaller and more professionalized political parties gave the media a more prominent position. The direct links between party and members were to some extent lost, and politicians had to communicate with their constituencies via the news media. Increasingly, political parties became aware of the need to influence the news media, in order to influence the public's agenda. Politicians learned to perform adequately in the media, and various forms of media-related work, such as press meetings, became integrated in political organizations. The political accommodation to the logic of the media was at this stage, however, primarily concerned with the communication of politics, i.e., "selling the message," and not the development of political strategies and programs.

The emergence of neo-liberal politics in the 1980s and onward influenced both the media and politics in a variety of ways. The deregulation of the media sector brought an end to the public service monopoly in broadcasting, while new media such as satellite television, the Internet, and the mobile media were all born as commercial media with few, if any, public obligations. The perceived demands of media users became an overriding concern for most of the media. In public service media and part of the increasingly smaller omnibus press, cultural obligations continued to have a say, but here the media increasingly had to balance public service obligations and publicist ambitions with market demands. The emergence of interactive media further strengthened the media's orientation toward the audience and users, emphasizing audience participation and user-generated content. In the same period as the media changed from cultural institutions to media institutions, politics also became subject to market orientation. Politics increasingly became not entirely market-driven, but market-sensitive, and the citizen was increasingly viewed as a political consumer. Similar to what Negrine (2008) observes from a British context, the professionalization of political parties transformed them into modern, lean, and centralized organizations that increasingly deployed modern PR and marketing techniques in order to win elections.

In a similar vein, the very nature of political governance adapted to market models. With the aid of upcoming theories concerning new public management, public market-like steering logics were implemented in a whole range of public-sector institutions, such as hospitals and schools, at the same time as various other sections of society became increasingly commercialized and globalized. In response to these changes in the media environment and in the very nature of politics, political parties began to integrate media expertise and resources into their everyday practices at many levels. The use of media expertise to manage both internal and external communication in political parties was no longer a simple question of communicating politics, but became an integrated part of "doing politics" in a broad sense. Integral to this transformation was the rise of permanent political campaigning. Earlier, the efforts to "sell politics" were generally confined to election periods, but now political parties increasingly became engaged in various forms of political campaigning all year around. In order to win elections it became important to "prime" voters on various issues on a continuous basis, because this would make them more susceptible to particular agendas and framings in the final election campaign (Lund 2004). The media's use of opinion polls all year round also put pressure on political parties to perform favorably in the polls in relation to everyday political issues. In the shift from a culture of corporative governance to a more external and networked form of political governance in the Nordic countries, the media have come to play a more independent role in the negotiation of political interests and formation of political opinion.

Table 3.1 presents an overview of the historical development in the Nordic countries in terms of the relationship between the media and politics. It follows the

TABLE 3.1 The historical development of mediatized politics in the Nordic countries

Phase	Important media	The political role of journalism	State and politics
Media as instruments of politics up to 1920	Party press	Promotion of political interests	The establishment of parliamentary democracy
Media as a cultural institution – early phase 1920–60	Public-service monopoly of radio and television, the rise of the omnibus press.	Communication and discussion of political agenda. The media become the main source of political information.	The corporative state. Organized interests cooperate on the construction of the welfare society.
Media as a cultural institution – late phase 1960–80	Late public-service monopoly and early competition of radio and television, omnibus press.	Critical coverage of politics. The rise of investigative journalism. Politics must accommodate to the media in order to influence agendas.	The social-liberal state. The welfare society in transition with greater emphasis on individual responsibility.
Media as a media institution – and media integrated into politics 1980 onwards	Intensified competition in radio and television, digital media (Internet, social networking media) become important news providers; omnibus press in decline.	Interpretation of the political "game". Journalism as advocate of the political consumer. News media integrated into the daily routines of politics, including policy development.	The emerging neo-liberal state: market-driven politics and the citizen as political consumer.

three general historical phases of the media: (1) first being in the service of other institutions, (2–3) becoming a cultural institution with varying degrees of autonomy, and finally (4) developing into a media institution (see also Table 2.1 in Chapter 2). However, the particular context of media and politics in the Nordic countries has made it necessary to distinguish between four different phases in the mediatization of politics.

A key outcome of the mediatization of politics is the establishment of the media as an *opinion industry.* By this we mean that the media's contribution to the formation of public opinion becomes institutionalized as a permanent feature of modern politics, and the media no longer solely reflect politics, but become intimately involved in the very production of politics. The media become a steady producer and negotiator of political information and opinions in the form of political journalism and as political contributions from laymen, politicians, and various political stakeholders on a variety of media platforms such as blogs, letters to the editor, and social networking media, etc. The media's industry of opinion is highly oriented toward the realm of politics, but is influenced by a steering logic outside the political institution itself. This is not exclusively a media logic, since the media also become an arena for political intervention in the broadest sense, allowing various media players (editors, commentators, etc.), politicians, and many other stakeholders (industry, labor organizations, individuals, etc.) to take part in the agenda-setting process. Since the media in part exert control over the public agenda and the formation of public consent toward political decisions and actions, it has become important for all political stakeholders to deploy resources in order to influence the media.

In the following text we consider some of the ways that mediatization has transformed political practices. In this discussion we also draw on existing theoretical contributions to the research field of news media and political communication. The ambition of mediatization theory is not necessarily to replace existing theories or analytical approaches, but rather to provide a broader and more integrative perspective on the transformation of politics in media-saturated societies. Following this, we also consider existing theoretical contributions (neo-institutionalism, agenda-setting, etc.) as useful building blocks for our understanding of politics in the new social and cultural environment of mediatization. In particular, we consider the following features:

- the rise of the media as a semi-independent institution and its influence on the agenda-setting and framing of political issues
- the restructuring of the political communication process
- the personalization and conversationalization of politics
- the emergence of a new class of political commentators in the media.

News media – a political institution?

In his analysis of the political role of the American news media Timothy E. Cook (1998) observes that the news media have achieved a higher degree of independence vis-à-vis the political institutions (government, parties, etc.). This is, he argues, not a sign of a de-politicization of news media, but this independence allows the news media to take on a new political role. According to Cook (1998) the news media have themselves become a type of political institution in society, and journalists may be considered as political actors serving an important political function: they not only disseminate politically important information, but also contribute to the construction of the political agenda. As a consequence, traditional political actors and institutions may accommodate the norms and routines that characterize the news media. The paradox is, following Cook (1998), that the political influence of news media is a result of their separation from political institutions:

> the political role of newspersons is that their political influence may emerge not in spite of, but because of, their principled adherence to norms of objectivity, deference to factuality and authority, and a let-the-chips-fall-where-they-may distance from the political and social consequence of their coverage.
>
> *(Cook 1998: 85)*

From this point of view, it is the very apolitical nature of news media that enables their political influence. In particular, news values become an important factor in the construction of political agendas. Cook's (1998) analysis was the beginning of a general "neo-institutional turn" in the study of interrelations between news media and politics (see, e.g., Ryfe and Ørsten 2011), and following this "turn" March and Olsen's (1989) notion of a "logic of appropriateness" has been used to conceptualize how specific norms of appropriate behavior govern human interaction within institutions (Allern and Ørsten 2011). In the case of the news institution, the logic of appropriateness is comprised of a series of norms and rules, such as general ideals of the press as the fourth estate, a temporal logic of news production (deadlines, etc.), news values and news criteria, editorial divisions of labor, and rules and routines for access to and use of news sources. Through the use of these "appropriate" norms of interaction, the news media come to act as a political institution that not only in the USA, but also in other countries like Denmark, "since the beginning of the eighties has become an important actor in political decision making processes that in the end influence the allocation of resources in society" (Ørsten 2005: 19; my translation).

Our general institutional perspective on mediatization is in many ways compatible with the neo-institutional turn in news media studies, but it also differs in certain respects. The various institutional characteristics that Cook (1998) and other neo-institutionalists suggest are quite clearly key features of the news media's *modus operandi* and they undoubtedly influence the news media's coverage of political issues. They are also well-documented in the literature of media and news sociology. Tuchman (1972), for instance, has demonstrated how the ideal of objectivity has been internalized in news production routines, and Schlesinger (1978) has shown how newsrooms are influenced by a "stop-watch culture." However, the fact that the news media are governed by an institutional logic, and may influence politics in various ways, does not imply that the news media may be considered a *political* institution. News media as an institution are *not*, as Cook (1998) also observes, bestowed with an intention to influence society in a political way, although individual newspapers, editors, and journalists may occasionally have their own political ambitions. Other social institutions also exert influence on public opinion, both in individual instances and in terms of long-term development. For instance, the educational institution and the legal institution generate knowledge and rulings, respectively, that may affect public opinion. But we would not label these institutions political, unless they attempted to influence the political system in a more direct and intentional way. Accordingly, we find it more reasonable to say that the media have developed into semi-independent institutions. By virtue of their influence on collective communication in society they influence politics in a variety of ways. The media's political influence is, in other words, a structural, non-intentional effect, rather than the result of intentional political action.

There is an additional reason not to label the *news media* as a political institution. The media and journalism may not necessarily work in tandem. The process of mediatization implies that the media become an institution of which the news media are only one component. Developments during the last decades have put the prerogative in the hands of the media and this has not only been beneficial for journalism, since the developments have occasionally been detrimental to the autonomy of journalism. The logic of journalism, including the norms of the journalistic profession (e.g., the ideal of the press as the fourth estate, etc.), has to some extent been under pressure to accommodate to the demands of the media in general. For instance, media convergence has transformed newsrooms into multi-media production facilities, and journalists are increasingly involved in cross-media production. This media development demands a multi-skilling of journalists, but the result may at times be a de-skilling of journalists (Cottle 1999), because they have to acquire a broad range of elementary technological skills, while downplaying core journalistic skills. In a digital and multi-media newsroom working on a 24/7 rolling deadline with constant pressure for the rewriting and reformatting of existing stories, journalistic work may increasingly appear to be assembly-line production with little room for professional initiative. Furthermore, the commercialization of the media has introduced various marketing tools into the newsroom, making journalists think of the audience not only as citizens, but also as consumers (Willig 2010). Journalism may historically have become more independent of political institutions, but it has also become more attuned to the various demands of the media industries. Journalism has not completely lost its autonomy to the broader media institution, and as such we may think of journalism as a particular profession with partial independence within the broader institution of the media. Instead of designating the news media as a political institution and calling journalists political actors – as the neo-institutionalists do – we may alternatively describe a semi-autonomous profession of journalism within a broader media institution. Together, they have come to assert influence on the political institution.

A dual communication system

The media's influence on politics is first and foremost a result of the media's role as negotiator of public consent for political decisions. In a political democracy, it is important to produce public consent for both political decisions and the political viewpoints motivating political actions. In a representative democracy, the authority to act politically has been delegated to politicians at local, national, or international levels through parliamentary elections, and in most countries the elected politicians are – in principle – free to act as they wish once they are elected. The formal democratic election procedure ensures legitimacy for political actors and there is no formal need to consult the constituency, or the voters, on a daily basis to renew this legitimacy. In a mediatized political reality, however, this formal legitimacy must be supplemented with a continuous consultation process between politicians, media, and the electorate concerning public consent for political action. Although public opinion may have a "phantom" character, as Lippmann (1925) negatively phrased it, the negotiation of public consent for political action has nevertheless become a political reality and an important part of the daily practices of media, politicians, and citizens.

In order to characterize how this negotiation of public consent takes place we will first consider how journalism has come to occupy a prominent position within a *dual circuit of mass political communication*, and second, we will discuss how the proliferation of digital and interactive media has come not to replace, but to *supplement and complexify* the media's role in the production of public consent. The news media take part in a dual circuit of political communication because they both connect political actors to a general audience and political actors to other political actors. Via the journalists' coverage of political affairs the news media become an important connecting node between politicians and audiences. Due to the journalistic research, selection, and framing of political affairs, the news media come to influence which part of political reality receives attention and how that reality is constructed. The news media are also an important channel of communication between political actors, who can both communicate with other political actors via the news media, and read and hear what other political actors are doing. Political actors are not only sources for journalists producing political stories, but are also large-scale consumers of political news, in order to monitor other political actors, be they political opponents, possible alliance partners or fellow party members. In this way, the news media and journalists are centrally placed as middlemen in the communication circuit between political actors (see Figure 3.1).

Public consent for political decisions is created via the continuous discursive negotiations along these two communicative axes. Public opinion is only indirectly represented in the news, but is reflected in, for instance, the salience of topics, the framing of the news story, and the critical questioning of sources. Even though the news is produced by the journalist and is the result of his or her interaction with various sources, the news is interpreted by both political actors and audiences as an indicator of prevalent opinions in society, and thereby guides the construction of consent. There is, however, an important difference between political actors and audiences in the way that they interpret these prevalent opinions in the news.

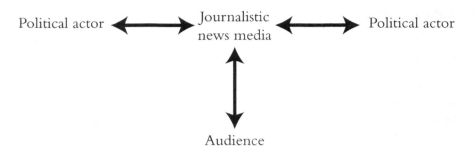

FIGURE 3.1 The dual circuit of political mass communication. The journalist as connecting node and gatekeeper between two communicative axes: between political actors and between politicians and audience.

Because two communication axes are coupled together in a single communication circuit, they can be read from two different viewpoints: the general audience will read the news as a way of "overhearing" the conversation between political actors, with the journalists acting as mediators. The political actors, on the other hand, will read the news as a way of "overhearing" the conversation between journalists and the general public. The coupling of communication circuits creates a common public sphere, but the participants may interpret the textual outcome, the news, as indicators of different phenomena. The audience will generally read the news as an indicator of prevalent opinions among the political élite, i.e., as a reflection of the current agenda and the viewpoints of political actors. The political actors will not only read the news as a source of information about other political actors, but will furthermore interpret the news as an important indicator of what will come to occupy the hearts and minds of the general public. Political actors and the general audience alike will consider the very act of reporting the news as an indicator of the future importance of these topics and viewpoints on the agendas of, respectively, the general audience and the political actors. In other words, the political actors and the general audience will read precisely the same news content as a guide to understanding each other's agendas and viewpoints, and may adjust their own viewpoints and actions on the basis of this perception of public opinion.

In accordance with the "model of influence of presumed influence" (Gunther and Storey 2003; see also Mutz 1989) the influence of media messages may not only be direct, but perhaps more often indirect. Politicians act on their perception of media influence on others, and the more they tend to believe that the media influence other people's perception of politics, the more they will engage in media-related activities to ensure exposure of their own arguments and actions. Cohen *et al.* (2008: 340) report on the basis of a detailed study of Israeli members of the Knesset that

> [P]erceptions of media influences on public opinion, not only perceptions regarding current public opinion climate, are an important force in public opinion dynamics that motivate political actors to act both in the public eye and in the corridors of power.

The very perception of the media's ability to influence the political viewpoints of others is therefore a factor in the political process, irrespective of its possible real influence. In this respect it is interesting to note that politicians often ascribe more power to the media's agenda-setting influence than journalists do. Strömbäck's (2011) study of Swedish politicians' and journalists' perception of various groups' influence on the political agenda demonstrates that both groups ascribe television, radio, and newspapers a high degree of influence, and in the case of members of parliament they consider radio and television more influential than the prime minister. Following this, the perception of the media's influence on political opinion formation may at least partly become a self-fulfilling prophecy, since the politicians may think and act on the basis of this perceived reality.

Within agenda-setting theory it is suggested that we may understand these entwined processes as an interaction between three different political agendas: the agenda of the media, the agenda of politics, and the agenda of the public (Rogers and Dearing 1987; McComb 2004). By an agenda we mean a set of political "issues" that are hierarchically organized according to degree of perceived importance. In itself an agenda does not say anything about the various competing viewpoints or discourses that are prevalent within the particular issues, and the original tenet of agenda-setting theory was that the media's influence on the formation of political opinion concerned the salience of various issues for the public agenda, rather than the persuasion of the public to adopt particular viewpoints. Cohen (1963: 13) famously formulated this key idea of agenda-setting research by stating that the press "may not be successful much of the time in telling people what to think, but it is stunningly successful in telling its readers what to think *about*" (emphasis in original).

In addition to the three agendas, interpersonal communication (face-to-face or mediated through interactive media) and so-called "real world indicators" may influence the formation of public opinion. Interpersonal communication has been recognized as important to the formation of public opinion since the development of the two-step flow of communication model (Lazarsfeld *et al.* 1944). Today, interpersonal communication is not only conducted in situations of co-presence, i.e., face-to-face, but also through various forms of interpersonal media and social networking media (that occasionally may function as broadcast media), and as such the interplay between interpersonal communication and the mass media has become more complex, and the boundaries between them more porous. Interpersonal communication has primarily been ascribed importance in relation to the agenda of the general public, but it may be equally important to the agenda of political actors and the agenda of the mass media, for instance, via journalists' informal discussions with colleagues and sources. The role of real-world indicators is not very well developed in the agenda-setting literature, but here we will understand them typically as statistical descriptions of particular aspects of reality that knowledge-producing institutions publish on a regular basis (e.g., environmental statistics, unemployment statistics, etc.) Such "hard facts" may be active in the very formation of public opinion, since they may inform political actors, media, and

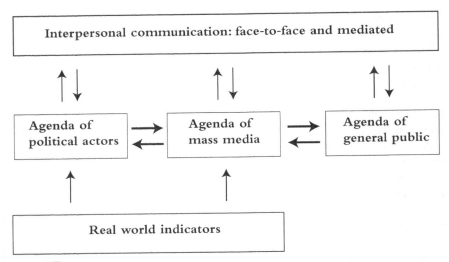

FIGURE 3.2 The agenda-setting process. Interaction between the agendas of political actors, the mass media and the general public, and the roles of interpersonal communication and real-world indicators. The model is partly based on Rogers and Dearing's (1987) model.

audiences about the severity of a particular problem, but they may also be used as an external indicator to measure the extent to which the media's reporting gives too much or too little salience to a particular issue. The model in Figure 3.2 takes its point of departure in Rogers and Dearing's (1987) original model, but is also modified in certain respects. The mass media's agenda is put at the center of the model, because the mass media's agenda works as the transmission point between the agendas of politicians and the general public, respectively, compared with the aforementioned dual communication circuit. Furthermore, there is no direct influence between real-world indicators and the agenda of the general public, since these indicators are typically communicated via the media or political actors, and their wider circulation is therefore dependent on the media's attention to and framing of these indicators.

Early agenda-setting theory focused exclusively on how the agenda of the mass media influenced the agenda of political institutions and the general public (and vice-versa) and refrained from discussion of whether or not the media could influence the particular opinions that people might have about the various issues on the agenda. Newer contributions to agenda-setting theory and analysis have demonstrated that the media may also influence the various opinions on the issues, and not only the salience of the issue itself. This dimension of the media's contribution to the formation of public opinion is often labeled the "second level of agenda-setting" (Ghanem 1997; McCombs 2004) and this strand of research seeks to combine the model of agenda-setting with the concept of "framing." The news media may influence the interpretation of a given issue through its framing of the story. By framing we understand – following Entman's (1993: 52) definition – to "select some aspects of a perceived reality and make them more salient in a communicating text, in such a way as to promote a particular problem definition, causal interpretation, moral evaluation, and/or treatment recommendation." News media not only talk about issues in the world, but also frame the issues in particular ways that may favor or question particular interpretations of a political issue. The media may influence the agendas of political actors and the general public through the salience they give to a particular issue, i.e., *what* the news media report about (first level of agenda-setting); and via the particular framing of issues, i.e., *how* they report on a particular issue (second level of agenda-setting). The distinction between the two levels is a theoretical construction; in practice they are inter-connected, so that how a news story is framed may influence the level of attention the issue receives, and vice-versa.

The political actors may, in a similar vein, influence media agendas, and thereby also the general public, by repeating a particular set of prominent issues and framing political problems in a particular way. In a mediatized environment of continuous political campaigning, it has become important for political parties to seek to "prime" the media's agenda before the actual election campaign starts. By a continuous framing of political issues in ways that are favorable to their own position they may be able to prime the agenda of the news media beforehand (Lund 2004). If they wait until the final election campaign political actors may not have the necessary time to change the news media's agendas on issues where the actors appear weak. In the world of political marketing, attempts to influence the news media's agenda often imply a narrow focus on four to five issues that are consistently repeated throughout the entire campaign. As Maarek (2011: 53) observes, the politician "will have to limit the number of different campaign themes to avoid giving his communication recipients the impression of being too dispersed: modern mass media are even less conducive than the older forms to the transmission of complex messages." Maarek's observations are taken from an American context where Ronald Reagan's presidential campaigns are generally regarded as the first successful examples of this kind of political marketing that condenses a politician's program into a few easily recognizable slogans. But the professionalization of political marketing has spread to many countries. The successful election campaign by Tony Blair's New Labour in Britain in the 1990s inspired many European politicians to adopt similar marketing strategies that in the 2010s have become commonplace.

New media: an extended political communication network

During the last decades politicians have adapted to a mediatized environment in which the news media play a central role in the formation of public opinion. However, the breakthrough of the Internet in the 1990s, and the emergence of various mobile and interactive media during the 2000s, have – also in the realm of political communication – gradually challenged the centrality of journalism and the news media. Deuze (2007: 140) has even proclaimed that "journalism as it is, is coming to an end" because the boundaries between journalism and other forms of public communication are vanishing in the digital era, and older forms of news media are being subsumed by the Internet. Even if we find it premature to write the epitaph of journalism, there is little doubt that journalism has lost some of its authority to influence the formation of public opinion. Politicians have acquired new outlets for political messages and actions, such as websites and social networking media, for instance, blogs, Facebook, and Twitter. As Bruns (2005, 2008) has observed, journalists are no longer the sole gatekeepers of news distribution, because anyone can, in principle, publish news and opinions on the Internet and social networking media. Following Bruns, the role of gatekeeper must give way to the new role of gatewatcher. In a media environment where the problem is not the scarcity of news sources, but the abundance of available information across a range of media platforms, the role of both audiences and journalists becomes to "watch the gate" and redistribute and qualify already existing information. In the realm of political journalism, this development implies that the news media are only one – albeit an important one – among several distributors of political information. The role of the journalist may increasingly be to provide critical interpretation and commentary on information about political developments that is already available.

The reporting of a major news story of international political importance can serve to illustrate the changing role of the journalist from gatekeeper to gatewatcher. The death of Libya's dictator Muammar Gaddafi in October 2011 satisfied almost all journalistic news criteria to become a very important story. It was both a very dramatic event and of tremendous political importance not only for the Libyan revolution, but also for the entire international community. When Gaddafi was captured by rebel Libyan forces and shot soon thereafter, his capture and death were communicated by the rebel forces. In addition, video footage showing both the captured Gaddafi being beaten while still alive, and his dead corpse after he was shot, was quickly distributed via the Internet and all political stakeholders in Libya and the region immediately began to comment on the news on a variety of platforms. In this situation, the role of the news reporter was not primarily to report the news, since the event itself had already been communicated by the people involved in the act, and many political stakeholders had already used the situation to communicate their interpretation of the repercussions of the event. In earlier times, foreign news correspondents or international news agencies would have acted as gatekeepers of such an event; but today, their task is increasingly to verify or repudiate information that is already circulating, and to analyze and comment on the causes and future implications of the event.

The death of Muammar Gaddafi was an exceptional news story in a variety of ways, including how it was communicated to the world. It is important to stress that, when it comes to the mundane life of day-to-day politics, journalists still have some authority left as gatekeeper between political actors and the general audience. The distinction between gatekeeping and gatewatching is, therefore, not an absolute one, but rather one of degree. The media environment has clearly become more diverse, allowing political stakeholders and the general public to bypass the news media in several ways, but journalists have also gained easier access to sources and information via the new media. The spread of digital and interactive media has not generally replaced the traditional mass media, but supplements and interacts with them in various ways. Pew Research Center (2010) reported on the basis of data from the USA that the stories that receive the most attention in the so-called user-driven media often have different priorities to the traditional news media; just as the agendas of various forms of social networking media (e.g., YouTube, Twitter, and blogs) differ from each other. Yet they also observed that blogs, for instance, rely heavily on information from major news media: "despite the unconventional agenda of bloggers, traditional media still provides the vast majority of their information. More than 99 percent of the stories linked to came from legacy outlets like newspapers and broadcast networks" (Pew Research Center 2010).

The various interactive media not only rely on the information produced by traditional mass media, but they very often also strive for public recognition via the mass media. A story may be published by various political actors on social net-working media, but it does not usually come to influence the wider public agenda before it is taken up by the traditional journalistic news media. The rise of the new media has allowed political actors to enter the field of media production and dis-tribution. But in order to make their messages influential beyond their circle of immediate supporters, they need the news media to report them and thereby bestow them with public recognition of both factual validity and societal impor-tance. In general, the spread of the new media has complexified the process of public opinion formation, allowing more political actors to interact with each other, journalists, and the public in more direct ways. The journalistic news media still hold a prominent position in the political communication circuit due to their ability to provide public recognition of political messages, but the role of the journalist may gradually become less that of gatekeeper in the agenda-setting pro-cess and more that of prominent gatewatcher − commentator and qualifier − in the formation of public opinion. A politician may circumvent the journalistic gate-keeper by posting a message on Facebook, thereby reaching his followers directly, but often he or she will try to reach both followers and journalists simultaneously. This is because journalists also monitor social networking media like Facebook and may use them as sources or as background information for stories. In the transforma-tion from a dual circuit of political mass communication to an extended network of mediated political communication the practice of communicating to someone, and at the same time being overheard by others, has become not only a possibility, but also a condition of mediatized politics.

As political actors acquire more professional skills in mastering the media they may occasionally win the battle over the journalists. But they may nevertheless become more dependent on media and media expertise, since they also have to integrate various forms of new media into the inner function of politics, for instance, through communication with party members and constituencies on various social networking media platforms, and by employing various new media

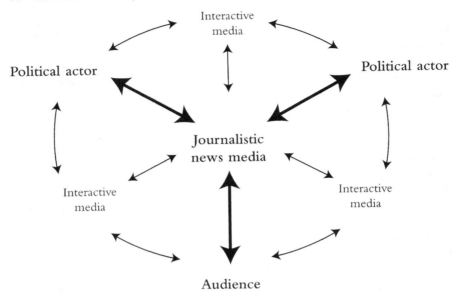

FIGURE 3.3 The extended network of political communication in a new media environment. The journalistic news media play a central role as connecting node and gatekeeper, but their role is supplemented and complexified by interactive media that – potentially – allow all participants to communicate in public and watch or 'overhear' the communication of others.

for fundraising purposes. Figure 3.3 presents a model of the extended political communication network of both the mass and interactive media. In general, interactive media have not completely replaced the gatekeeping role of the journalistic news media, but they expand the field of mediated political communication and also enable all actors to "overhear" the communication of others.

The politics of visibility

As the public political sphere increasingly becomes constituted by various forms of media, political communication has become more and more intertwined with the various *modus operandi* of the media. As mentioned previously, this among other things implies that politicians have to accommodate to the news criteria and deadlines of the news media, and also communicate in particular formats, e.g., soundbites and press releases, in order to get access to the agenda of the news media. However, the accommodation to particular media formats is not the only aspect of mediatization. One particularly important and general development is the *visibility* that the media facilitate for all political actors, and through which the structure of *political persona* and the performative requirements of political actors become altered (Corner 2003). In the following text we will focus on two aspects of this development, the *personalization* of politics and the *conversationalization* of political communication.

One of the pioneers of Danish broadcasting journalism, Poul Trier Pedersen, has described how television changed the access to and conception of politicians. In his childhood between the two world wars he only once caught a glimpse of the famous Danish prime minister Thorvald Stauning at a rally on Constitution Day. With the birth of television after World War II, national politicians and ministers became familiar faces, and almost on a par with family members:

> Just a push on the button brings them into your living room: Jens Otto Krag, Erik Eriksen, Poul Sørensen, Karl Skytte, Aksel Larsen and Iver Poulsen [all well-known Danish politicians]. Here they are, so vividly alive that you almost feel an urge to offer them a cup of coffee. … And now they have entered the living room they have to put up with interruptions from us, a word of recognition or perhaps a rude expression of displeasure. Why should it be any different for them than for Otto Leisner [a popular Danish television entertainment host]?
>
> *(Pedersen 1964: 33; translation from Danish)*

Radio first made the audience familiar with the voices of politicians, and television later made the whole political persona visible: the politician's look, way of dressing, facial expressions, gestures, etc. By bringing politicians into the living room, the electronic media not only created a bridge between the public sphere and the ordinary citizen's private home, but also redefined the relationship between formerly separate social spaces, and brought about changes in the performative requirements of political communication.

By comparing unmediated face-to-face interaction with interaction via electronic media, in particular television, Meyrowitz (1986) suggests that a new kind of mixed – partly public, partly private – form of interaction has emerged as the preferred mode of mediated encounter. Meyrowitz (1986) takes his point of departure in Erving Goffman's (1956) theater model of social interaction, in which the distinction between the social actors' performance "front stage" and their behavior "backstage" plays a crucial role. According to Goffman, social interaction is governed by role-playing in the sense that participants will adjust their performance in relation to the expectations that any given situation suggests in terms of appropriate behavior. In social interaction, participants continuously negotiate how to define the situation at hand (for instance, is a dinner a business dinner, a private dinner, or perhaps a date?), and adjust their social roles accordingly. The use of the term "role-playing" does not suggest that the participants are behaving in a dishonest manner (i.e., different from their "true" selves), although they may naturally do so occasionally. By using the term "role-playing" Goffman wishes to draw attention to the fact that any kind of social interaction requires the participants to perform in certain ways, in order to be recognized by others as making sense of the situation in a particular way.

One of Goffman's examples is the interaction between a waiter and the guests in a restaurant. While attending to the guests, the waiter is performing in the front area and his actions (speech, gestures, facial expressions, etc.) are accessible to the guests, who may judge his performance accordingly. When the waiter withdraws from the guests and, for instance, enters the kitchen, he goes backstage. Here, he may relax from the performative requirements in the serving area (for instance, by having something to eat or drink himself) and make preparations for his re-entry (for instance, by readjusting his clothes). While backstage he may also align himself with other members of staff by, for instance, gossiping about the guests' behavior, and thereby create a common understanding of the situation on the front stage. "Front stage" and "backstage" are always to be understood in relative terms, depending on where the interaction is considered to take place. From another point of view, the kitchen may also be considered a front stage, since it has its own performative requirements of the interaction between staff members (here, for instance, strict formal behavior between co-workers would usually be considered inappropriate), and in relation to this stage the cloakrooms or an outside smoking area may be considered the backstage.

Meyrowitz (1986) considers Goffman's theater model illuminating, but points to the fact that it implicitly presupposes a society in which social interaction takes place face-to-face, and where society is functionally divided into a series of separate localities, each characterized by a clear definition of possible social situations and corresponding social roles. Crudely put, Goffman's interaction model reflects a Victorian society governed by the motto of "everything in its right time and place." In such a society, access to the different types of social localities is socially stratified according to social class, gender, and age. For example, children do not have access to the adult world, and women have only limited access to the world of business and politics, etc. Considered from an informational point of view, a particular locality represents a stage that only few have access to and therefore hold information about. The interactional division of front stage and backstage therefore relies on an ability to deny people access to information, i.e., by performing for a particular audience, without allowing others the insight to either front stage or backstage.

With the advent of electronic media, such locality-bound information systems begin to be eroded. As Meyrowitz (1986) argues, radio and television are used collectively and everything that they convey becomes accessible to the entire household (men, women, and children) and the whole nation (rich and poor, farmers and city dwellers, etc.). Electronic media constitute an open communicative space that cuts across social roles and status. In addition, the content of radio and television is itself a mixed bag of all kinds of social situations that encompass a variety of social spheres and localities: reports on political meetings of heads of states, cooking instructions, and fictional representations of the lives of criminals, soldiers, politicians, lovers, children, etc. In contrast to Goffman's unmediated world of separate social encounters, well-defined social roles and control of informational access, radio and television bring together a variety of formerly distinct social situations into a common communicative circuit. As a consequence, it becomes difficult for all participants to perform the traditional roles bound to particular situations.

Instead of the tight separation of social situations and of backstage and front stage performance, Meyrowitz (1986) suggests that the electronic media foster a modified social scene that combines performative requirements from a variety of social situations, including the private backstage and the public front stage. On this new mediated scene, the "*middle region*," it is no longer possible to adhere to strictly public or formal roles, nor is it acceptable to make use of strictly private or informal patterns of behavior. The media's continuous exposure of this new middle region makes it necessary for political actors, not least, to create a far more secluded social space, a "*deep backstage*," in which they can rest assured that their behavior will not be accessible to anyone apart from their closest allies and friends. At the same time, politicians and other public figures still need to be able to perform formal public duties in which the mixed performance of the middle region would seem inappropriate. For such formal occasions, e.g., the inauguration of a new president, the opening of parliament, etc., the "*forward front stage*" establishes itself as the preferred scene, characterized by a highly ritualized or ceremonial performance that is set clearly apart from the ordinary forms of political interaction. Figure 3.4 provides an

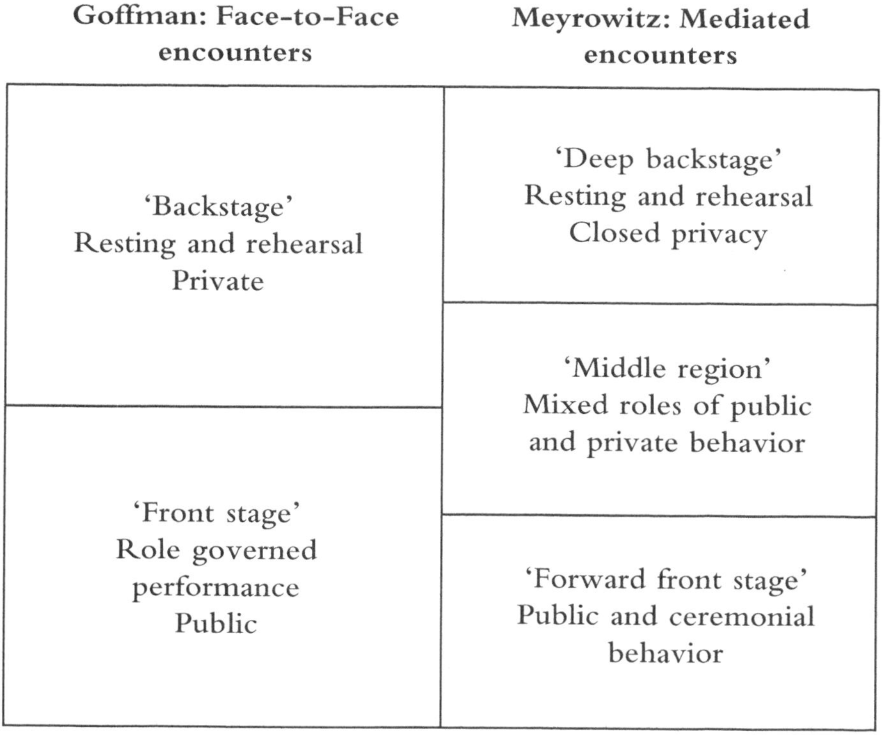

Goffman: Face-to-Face encounters	Meyrowitz: Mediated encounters
'Backstage' Resting and rehearsal Private	'Deep backstage' Resting and rehearsal Closed privacy
	'Middle region' Mixed roles of public and private behavior
'Front stage' Role governed performance Public	'Forward front stage' Public and ceremonial behavior

FIGURE 3.4 Overview of Meyrowitz's (1986) revision of Goffman's theater model of social interaction

overview of Meyrowitz's (1986) reconceptualization of social interaction in the age of the electronic media.

Meyrowitz (1986) primarily explains the emergence of new social role requirements as a result of the new communication circuits established by electronic media. They are, however, also a result of the audiovisual affordances of radio and television that bring the audience in close contact with participants' personal traits such as quality of voice, gestures, facial expressions, dress, etc. In the realm of politics, this makes individual personal traits immediately accessible and part of the political performance. In an audiovisual reality, the balance between the amount and type of information a politician would intentionally like to "give" to an audience, and the information he unintentionally and inevitably "gives off" by exposure in radio and television (Goffman 1956), shifts in favor of the latter. In a political culture of printed media politicians could generally rely on the journalist to focus on the political message, and not the politicians' personal or private appearance. Today's dominance by audiovisual media makes such expectations seem rather naïve. In conclusion, Meyrowitz (1986: 272) argues that the electronic media bring politicians down to the level of their audience: "The personal close-up view forces many politicians to pretend to be less than they would like to be (and, thereby, in a social sense, they actually become less)."

Although the concept of "middle region" behavior as a new and preferred mode of interaction was developed in response to television's influence in particular, the key insights are still valid in the age of networked and digital media. Marwick and Danah (2010) examine users of social networking media like Twitter and their conception of their audiences. Since social networking media are open to a variety of participants and topics, it becomes difficult for users to develop a clear picture of their possible audiences and co-users, and consequently it is more difficult, in the individual communicative encounter, to establish more precise definitions of the social situation at hand and of the corresponding social roles: "Like broadcast television, social media collapse diverse social contexts into one, making it difficult for people to engage in the complex negotiations needed to vary identity presentation, manage impressions, and save face" (Marwick and Danah 2010: 123).

Such "context collapse" in social networking media makes users reach for a "middle region" behavior as a way to balance the half public, half private properties of the interactional space. In many instances, this implies that the preferred mode of interaction bears the imprint of "*sociability*" (Simmel 1971), i.e., a half private, half public mode of interaction where the primary purpose becomes pleasurable conversation and company. In relation to politics, this provides both possibilities and problems. On the one hand, it enables politicians to communicate more directly with their followers in an interactional mode that seems more spontaneous and enjoyable. On the other hand, it may inhibit more serious discussion of political issues. Storsul (2011) has examined the use of Facebook among youth politicians in Norway and reports that Facebook is heavily used as a tool for practical political organization. However, when it comes to willingness to express political viewpoints and engage in political discussion, the sociable, middle-region space of social networking media appears to be counterproductive. Despite their active engagement in party politics, many youth politicians refrain from making very overt political statements and from discussion of controversial political issues, because they consider this to be out of line with the face they are seeking to maintain among their Facebook friends, many of whom may not be politically active.

Personalization of politics

The media's preference for social interaction in the middle region has contributed to the personalization of politics. At the beginning of the twentieth century political parties in many western countries were by and large organized in relation to social class, i.e., a political party had its roots in a particular social class, and the number of "floating voters" crossing the system of class representation remained fairly low. In this system, a politician's authority often relied on his ability to embody the *social role* of his supporters. Thus, a socialist or Social Democrat had to look and talk like a worker, and would often enter politics via an organizational position as trade union representative or similar. A liberal (in economic terms) politician had to not only embody the social role of an industrialist or a land-owning farmer, but also often be recruited from these social classes. In other words, a politician could and had to address his audience in a manner that reflected the particularities of social experience within a social class. In a mediatized society, political authority is to a larger extent constructed via a politician's *personal identity*, i.e., his ability to bestow his career in politics with a personal narrative that may authenticate his political program. It is important to stress that the growing personification of politics by no means suggests that political leaders a hundred years ago were less outstanding personalities compared to those of the present day. Forceful and charismatic political leaders were perhaps more prevalent in the mass political movements before World War II. The construction of political authority via the embodiment of social class by no means implied that a politician could not transcend this social base through individual achievement.

The personification of modern and mediatized politics refers to the way in which politicians perform their public personas. Today, the social role of the politician is typically downplayed in favor of an enactment that mixes political and personal life trajectories. In a longitudinal study of the news media's representation of British prime ministers, Langer (2007, 2010) demonstrates how there has been an increase in focus on the private and personal lives of prime ministers, and as a consequence this has changed the expectations made of top politicians: "The expectation is now for leaders to be more informal, conversational, at ease in confessional mode, and capable of being emotionally reflective and open" (Langer 2010: 68). In particular, Tony Blair was instrumental in sparking the press's focus on the personal traits of politicians, and Langer's study shows that his personal campaign style has had long-term repercussions: "Blair's era should be understood as both a paradigmatic manifestation of the phenomenon and a precipitant of its further intensification" (ibid.: 70).

The Blair phenomena is by no means a particular British experience, since the personalization of politics is also a widespread phenomenon in many European countries, both independently of the British development and in some cases also inspired by it. There are, however, many national and cultural differences in how the political persona becomes constructed. In his analysis of the official websites of four western heads of state, Bondebjerg (2007) points to several such differences. British Tony Blair's website reflected the prime minister's informal personality with a touch of irony and humor. German Angela Merkel's website presented an objective tone, showing her as both a leading political character and a woman of the people. The website of American George W. Bush personalized his presidency with references to his conservative family values, business ideals, and patriotism. French Jacques Chirac's website constructed his public persona as an embodiment of European highbrow culture. How a political persona becomes constructed in the media does not, of course, rely solely on the politician's own efforts to present his or her career via a personal narrative. It relies just as much on the different and often competing portrayals produced and circulated by the media in news bulletins, caricatures, weekly magazines, and biographies, etc., that may vary over time and to a larger or lesser degree challenge the self-image the politician him/herself seeks to project. While the politician tries to construct a harmonious "middle region" identity of him/herself, the media will seek to "go behind" this new political "façade" and provide an allegedly even truer picture of the politician. In this view, the new middle region of personalized politics does not represent a final compromise between the personal and the political; it rather suggests a new condition for the construction of the political persona in which there will be a continuous struggle between politicians and media for the demarcation between the public and the private.

Visibility in the public sphere is an important political resource that the media to some extent administer. They therefore come to influence how politicians project their political personas. The importance of mediated visibility makes politicians vulnerable to *media scandals*. As Thompson (2000) has argued, the fame, reputation, and trustworthiness generated through visibility in the media represent a symbolic capital that politicians are heavily dependent on when building their political careers, and this symbolic capital may be exchanged along the way for "harder" currencies like campaign donations, votes, and subsequently, political office. The value of such symbolic capital is, however, highly volatile, because a single media scandal may put an end to a lifelong political career in just a few days. Mediated scandals have their own media logic in which the politician's initial public response to the accusations becomes extremely important to the future survival of the politician. If a politician denies being involved in a scandalous affair and it later turns out that he was part of it after all, the very denial in the media may become an even more serious transgression than the initial mistake. Politicians' vulnerability to public criticism has made attempts to scandalize political adversaries a recurring element of modern political campaigning. The American political right-wing campaign to scandalize President Bill Clinton's sexual encounter with Monica

Lewinsky is a very prominent example of this trend, but other countries have also experienced the influence of negative media campaigns against individual politicians in which they are criticized for various forms of moral or legal transgressions (Allern and Pollack 2012).

Conversational politics

The transformation of the political scene from "front stage" to "middle region" affects not only the performative requirements of the individual politician, but also the formats and genres of political communication. In her historical analysis of American political speeches, Jamieson (1988) documents how a conversational mode of address gained precedence as a preferred mode of political communication as politicians gradually adapted to the requirements of the electronic mass media. The passionate oratory of a speaker addressing a big crowd progressively gave way to a form of public speech that simulated the calm conversation between people in a small group:

> Electricity transported communication into an intimate environment. Radio and television deliver their messages to family units of twos and threes. By contrast, the torch parade drew hundreds and occasionally thousands to hear a speaker. In the quiet of our living rooms we are less likely to be roused to a frenzy than when we are surrounded by a swarming, sweating mass of partisans.
>
> (Jamieson, 1988: 55)

As Jamieson suggests – and contrary to frequent criticism of the media – the influence of the electronic media has not necessarily made political communication more emotional. Politicians' speeches at political rallies and discussions in village halls were often more prone to make use of rhetorical pathos than the often logos-driven discussions and interviews of modern televised politics. Radio and television may, of course, also convey political feelings, but because the communicative situation and structure is different, the emotional address will usually also be different compared to earlier forms of political communication. A speech at a political rally will often appeal to the "big" collective emotions of nationalism, social class, or race, whereas the political conversation in broadcasting will more likely address individual and personal emotions. The development of a more calm and conversational mode of political communication was not only a result of the "intimate environment" of broadcasting audiences, but was also due to the central role of journalism in broadcasting, and more broadly a result of the affordances of broadcasting as a particular form of social communication. In the case of radio and television, political discussions became moderated by journalists, and the (live) interview became a crucial form of political communication. Here, the politician had to learn to hold a conversation with a journalist, in order to be "overheard" by absent listeners and viewers. The politician had to learn and observe the particular rules of turn-taking in an interview, at the same time as he or she was compelled to learn how to convey an impression of being involved in smooth and informal conversation. The movement towards informal forms of conversation in politics is particularly visible in softer types of factual broadcasting formats such as breakfast television, talk shows, and journalistic entertainment shows, etc. These programs promote ideals of sociable conversation from interpersonal communication, and politicians participating in these programs are expected to address political issues (if at all) in a way that does not interfere with the sociable quality of the program (Hjarvard 2005).

Even though radio and television are mass media, any communication via these media – including political communication – has to consider the particular relationship the media constructs between sender and receiver. A politician has to simulate that he is talking to a small group in such a way that the recipient may perceive himself as a potential partner in a conversation, and not just as an anonymous mass the politician is trying to seduce. Following Scannell (2000), modern broadcasting media are characterized by a particular communicative structure that he labels "for-anyone-as-someone structures." Broadcasting not only addresses "anyone" (like mass media aimed at the masses) or "someone" (like interpersonal media aimed at a particular individual), but constructs a third form of communication that mediates between mass and interpersonal media. Using this "for-anyone-as-someone structure" broadcasting has emerged as a truly social form of communication that, in its very mode of address, bridges the gap between the general and the particular, the impersonal and the personal. The conversational mode that has come to dominate all types of broadcasting genres – including monological genres – is a reflection of this fundamental communicative structure in which "anyone" in the mass audience is recognized as an individual "someone."

From the tradition of discourse analysis Fairclough (1995) has pointed to the same development and refers to the growing "conversationalization" of all forms of public communication. This is linguistically reflected in the growing use of informal language in all social situations, including formal and public situations, and more frequent use of oral forms in written communication. These trends are also very dominant in newer forms of digital media such as texting (SMS), blogs, chatrooms, and social networking media more broadly. Texting usually displays the same spontaneous and informal character as oral communication, and conversational patterns of face-to-face speech are partly replicated in the sequencing of text dialogs. In this way, texting appears as a written form of natural speech or, alternatively, as an oral form of written communication (Crystal 2011). In new media, the sociable forms of communication in broadcasting that bridge the gap between the public and the private, the formal and the informal, are generally taking a step further in the direction of informal and private forms of speech. In politicians' use of blogs, Twitter, and Facebook we see a clear tendency for politicians to seek to communicate through informal, colloquial language that brings him or her at eye level with the recipients of such communication, and invites them to join the conversation.

The conversationalization of political communication is a double-edged sword in relation to democratic participation. Positively speaking, it reflects an egalitarian ethos: all participants are on an equal footing with each another and are – potentially – allocated equal time, space, and opportunities to speak. Furthermore, the conversation seems to be governed by recognizable principles of everyday speech with family and friends. Few, if any, qualifications regarding performance skills or factual knowledge thereby seem to be required of anyone wishing to enter the discussion. This ideal of conversation often rests upon an implicit notion of face-to-face dialog as being superior to (mass-) mediated forms of communication. The democratic merits of new and interactive media are accordingly that they "return" human communication to a more authentic form of dialogical communication. The democratic value of conversation is not only a result of the rise of various forms of (new) media, although the spread of digital and interactive media has certainly intensified the focus on participation and conversation in current discussions about media and democracy (cf. Jenkins and Thorburn 2003; Fenton 2010). There is a long tradition in certain strands of political theory, especially those associated with educational theory, to consider conversation as a cornerstone of democracy that helps to both engage citizens and qualify arguments and leadership. In an American context, John Dewey (1927) represents a significant example of this tradition that in communication scholarship has been critically seconded by James Carey (1989). In a Scandinavian context, the emphasis on conversation has not least been heralded by Hal Koch (1945). From a critical perspective, the apparent equality of conversation may obscure the fact that political communication, at its very heart, is a discursive struggle between often unequal partners who wish to shift the balance of power in their own favor. From this point of view, political communication is part of interest groups' fight for the ideas and the allocation of resources in society. Following this, it would be both objectively incorrect and politically naïve to believe that communication becomes more democratic by following the rules of informal conversation. On the contrary, this would only make communication more open to manipulation and dominance by those who have a superior command of these forms of communication.

Schudson (1997) has put forward a critique of the inherent democratic value of conversation, a critique that has become no less important in view of the last decades' proliferation of interactive media. He stresses the need to distinguish between, on the one hand, *sociable conversation* that is only loosely structured and has no particular purpose, apart from the enjoyment of the conversation and company of others, and on the other hand the *problem-solving* conversation that is rule-governed, oriented toward the public, and often cumbersome or even uncomfortable to participate in. According to Schudson (1997), democratic conversation is best served by keeping to its "unsociable" character and maintaining its focus on public problems, and its formal norms of communicative procedures and decision-making. The ideal of face-to-face conversation as intrinsically democratic is historically wrong, because ideals of conversation have also been heralded by aristocratic regimes in which the power to speak was extremely unevenly distributed. There is nothing inherently democratic about sociable conversation:

> What makes conversation democratic is not free, equal, and spontaneous expression but equal access to the floor, equal participation in setting the ground rules for discussion, and a set of ground rules designed to encourage pertinent speaking, attentive listening, appropriate simplifications, and widely apportioned speaking rights.
>
> *(Schudson 1997: 307)*

Conversation is not, Schudson concludes, the soul of democracy. Democracy arises from democratic institutions and thereby institutionalized public rules and norms of democratic behavior, for – among other things – the conduct of democratic problem-solving conversations. Democratic institutions may ensure the conditions for democratic conversations, not the other way around.

Schudson's critique is well-placed in view of the frequent romanticizing of conversational ideals. The dilemma is, however, that the media nonetheless promote these ideals in social networking media, and radio and television programs, etc. Through their daily practices, the media and their users are institutionalizing sociable conversation as an important ideal of democratic, public discussion. The ideal hereby acquires its own reality and may become the norm by which the performance of politicians is evaluated. Politicians who do not want or do not have the performative skills to engage in such sociable conversations may have less chance of being elected for political office. As such, the sociable norms of conversation may turn out to be a democratic ideal with authoritarian consequences, since they favor one form of political communication over another. Having said this, we also need to recognize that the distinction between sociable conversations and problem-solving conversations need not be an absolute one. There may be different degrees of political seriousness and consequences of various forms of conversations along the spectrum of conversations, from the "purely" sociable to the "purely" problem-solving. As both Habermas' (1962) own historical study of the transformation of the public sphere and newer discussions of this have demonstrated (Plummer 2003; Dahlgren 2006; Gripsrud and Weibull 2010), conversations in the cultural sphere, the private sphere, and the intimate sphere may, under various circumstances, be infused with political meaning, mobilized for political purposes, and have political repercussions. The mediatization of politics implies a push toward conversational modes of political communication, and this is often – also by the media – constructed as an inherently democratic benefit. As Schudson (1997) suggests, we need to maintain a critical distance toward such claims, but we should naturally also remain open to the possibilities of new forms of democratic political communication.

The hybrid role of the media-affiliated political commentator

The final aspect of mediatized politics we will consider is the development and dissemination of various forms of political commentary in the media. The mediatization of politics involves a particular change in the balance of power between several actors taking part in the formation of public opinion. Traditionally, the politician has taken on the role of policy-maker, the political scientist has acted as the expert interpreter, and the journalist was intended to perform the role of critical reporter. One outcome of mediatized politics is a general blurring of boundaries between these roles, and this is reflected in the dissemination of interpretative journalism; a growing interaction between journalists and political media advisors ("spin doctors"); and the rise of a new kind of praxis-oriented media–political expertise. Within this context, the hybrid role of the media-affiliated political commentator has achieved a new political authority.

Political commentary and the influence of a special caste of political pundits are by no means new phenomena, but have played a role since the early opinionated press and later radio and television, and may even have precedents in societies pre-dating mass media, like the Oracle in Delphi (Nimmo and Combs 1992). What is new is the proliferation of political commentary both within various journalistic genres and across other media types and genres such as blogs, broadcast entertainment, and social networking media. As an example, an analysis of the reference to political commentators during the last three elections in Denmark in Internet-based news media showed a tenfold increase in references from 2005 to 2011 (Møller and Kiellberg 2011). Furthermore, contemporary political commentary is not least focused on the relationship between media and politics, for instance, by focusing on the role of media management and spin in the political process. By political commentary we understand a wide range of interpretative practices focused on current politics, ranging from the detached and analytical side of the spectrum, to the opinionated and prescriptive side. Common to this broad spectrum of practices is that political commentary is provided by a group of "political commentators" who are attributed (or attribute themselves) a privileged-speech position as "political experts" that can provide interpretations of political actors and actions from a position at least partly outside the realm of politics itself. The political commentators are, however, not only outside politics, but also partly outside, or on the margins of, other traditional social roles in mediated political communication. Some of them may be (former) journalists by profession, but when commenting on politics they speak in the capacity of a senior editor or correspondent who is allowed to transcend the journalistic role and speak in a more personal voice. Some of them may be (former) academic researchers by profession (e.g., in the field of political science), but when commenting on politics they will speak more freely as individual observers. Several of them may be former politicians or spin doctors, but when providing political commentary they seek to rise above their former political affiliation and speak from an outsider's perspective, but with an insider's knowledge.

The increased prominence of political commentators is part of a broader development in the (news) media in which the interpretation of political events has gained ground. Gulati *et al.* (2004) document an increase in interpretative genres such as news analysis and commentary in both the electronic and the printed media, and Wahl-Jorgensen (2008: 70) observes that "the expression of judgements and opinions [...] increasingly pervades every section of the newspaper." The success of Fox News in the USA also bears witness to the growing influence of opinionated journalism and political commentary, and is furthermore an example of the media adopting an overtly partisan role in politics (Hart and FAIR 2003; Welch 2008). In a Scandinavian context, Djerf-Pierre and Weibull (2001) have demonstrated how, in historical terms, Swedish broadcasting journalism has moved away from the traditional ideal of objective news reporting toward a more interpretative paradigm, and similar trends can be discerned in the development of Danish television news broadcasting (Hjarvard 1999) and newspapers (Hjarvard 2010b).

The development in political commentary is an interesting example of mediatized politics, since it reflects the media's need to develop a particular caste of experts to comment on politics, in view of the growing interconnections between media and politics. As Brian McNair (2000: 82) suggests, "the 'columnary explosion' (and its broadcast equivalent – the proliferation of pundits and specialist correspondents) is an intelligible journalistic adaptation to an environment which is highly competitive, information-rich and intensively manipulated by political actors." From this perspective, the spread of political commentary is not only a media-driven phenomenon allowing the media to take on a more interpretative, analytical, and sometimes overtly opinionated role in relation to politics, but also a reaction to a political development in which mediated communication has become internalized and used by political actors for strategic ends. In this context, the media may feel the need for a particular kind of expertise to explain and expose the political "game," including the strategic use of media management. In summary, the "columnary explosion" is both a reaction to the mediatization of politics and a further step toward its intensification.

In order to understand how this kind of political expertise has gained public authority, an institutional perspective may again prove useful. As Hemmingsen and Sigtenbjerggaard (2008) have demonstrated, the authority of the media-affiliated political commentator is based on his or her ability to mobilize legitimacy from three social roles originating in three different institutions: journalism, politics, and science. In order to be attributed the privileged-speech position as an expert, the commentator needs to perform the role of an "expert." This role originates from academia, i.e., knowledge-producing institutions such as universities, and achieves its legitimacy through its adherence to scientific ideals and practices. The political commentator is, however, seldom a real expert in this sense, since he does not undertake actual research. This may perhaps diminish his expert status, but this potential handicap is compensated for by his ability to speak more freely, including to engage in various forms of instant interpretations, future predictions, and political recommendations that would not usually be allowed for an academic researcher. The extensive freedom to interpret makes political commentators far more suitable for the media compared to traditional experts from the universities. Researchers primarily legitimize themselves among their peers and this will often make them hesitant to engage in public interpretative exercises that their peers would consider scientifically ill-founded or pure guesswork.

Another difference compared to the usual academic expert is the political commentator's communicative skills. In this respect he takes advantage of the performative requirements of the journalist and the legitimacy of the journalistic institution as being separate from and a potential watchdog of the political institution. Equivalent to a seasoned journalist, he will be an imaginative writer or an articulate speaker, but he will not be bound by the same rules as a journalist must obey. A political commentator does not have to be explicit about his use of sources, but on the contrary may often substantiate his analysis with reference to informal and unnamed sources, as a token of his privileged access to the backstage of political life. Similarly, a commentator is not bound by the traditional norms of objectivity and facticity that still govern much journalism, despite developments toward a more interpretative paradigm. Political commentators often write in an essayistic style and focus on motives for actions and possible outcomes, rather than established facts. Although the political commentator may have trained as a journalist, and may work with other journalists in a newsroom, he is not bound by the rules of the journalistic institution to the same degree.

The political commentator also borrows authority from the political institution. In recent years, many commentators have come to this position after previous work experience as media consultants or political advisors for political parties or senior politicians, and this experience from "real politics" serves as a very important credential that is often evoked when commenting on current affairs (McNair 2000). Some commentators may also have their own political agenda by which they brand themselves and become publicly recognized as being politically influential from a leftist or right-wing orientation, for example, a positive stance on immigration or being sympathetic toward the American Tea Party Movement. In contrast to real politicians, political commentators do not have to persuade an electorate to vote for them at the next election. They do not have to defend their political viewpoints toward a constituency, but may comment on political affairs from an arm's length, while demonstrating intimate familiarity with the political process. As a whole, the practice of political commentators makes use of performative characteristics from three institutions: journalism, politics, and academia, but they are free to exploit the benefits of these characteristics without having to conform to the full role expectations originating from these institutions (Figure 3.5). In principle, we would expect such a mixture of various role expectations to create a role conflict (Aubert 1975), but in practice this rarely seems to be the case. In general, political commentators appear in a variety of media formats and move with ease between newspaper essays, television expert interviews, and personal blogs. Precisely because of their eclectic use of various social roles, they have acquired a considerable freedom to maneuver across various genres and media and to speak with authority (Hemmingsen and Sigtenbjerggaard 2008). Furthermore, individual political commentators may position themselves differently in terms of how much they rely on the authority of the three institutions. Commentators working for public service broadcasters usually perform more in line with the role of a senior political editor, whereas independent political bloggers are more often willing to project their own political viewpoints.

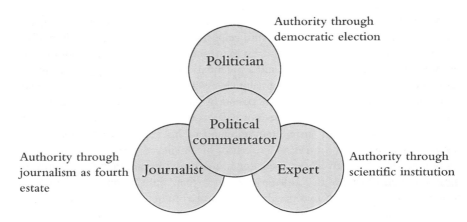

FIGURE 3.5 The hybrid role of the political commentator. By combining performative elements from the role of the journalist, the politician, and the expert, the political commentator has become a new and authoritative voice in contemporary politics.

The influence of political commentators on the political agenda is hard to measure. There is often an ironic contradiction between political commentators' own claims of insignificance, for instance, the British *Daily Mail*'s Peter Oborne stating that "it is hard to see examples of it having any effect at all" (Hobsbawm and Lloyd 2008: 9), and the influence often attributed to them by the public. An indicator of their possible influence may be the fact that, despite still being a numerically small group, they are often more frequently used by the media to comment on politics than other sources such as academic experts. Furthermore, they are usually given an expert status, allowing them to present their analyses and opinions in an authoritative manner, without being challenged by journalists or political actors. A major reason for their growing popularity may also come from their performative merits. In general, contemporary news media are under pressure from a 24/7 rolling deadline and fewer resources to conduct original journalistic research. In such an environment the ability of political commentators to provide often instant, clear-cut, and entertaining analyses of political affairs may be hard to resist. In this way, organizational constraints in the news media walk hand-in-hand with the structural transformation of the media–political nexus, stimulating the further growth of this hybrid form of mediatized political commentary.

Epilog

In this chapter we have focused on the role of the media in the transformation of contemporary politics. It is, however, important to emphasize that developments within political institutions, as well as in society at large, have also played an important role for the ways in which the media and politics become mutually interdependent in today's mediatized society. As briefly described in this chapter, politics has become more market-driven, at the same time as the media have become more commercialized. Political parties have lost some of their former power as mass membership organizations and have instead become professionalized organizations aimed at maximizing election outcomes among an electorate of ever less loyal voters (Negrine 2008). The rise of New Public Management as a strategic political instrument to steer public institutions (from hospitals to universities) has further introduced market-based thinking into political thinking. The break-up of the class-based, party-political structure since World War II has been accompanied by a general shift in beliefs and opinions in modern societies, whereby post-material values have acquired a more prominent place alongside more traditional political questions concerning welfare distribution (Inglehart and Welzel 2005). In this changing organizational and cultural context politics has to a greater extent become dependent on political governance networks that are dependent on political parties, interest groups, media, and other power brokers that, via the media, negotiate the legitimacy of political opinions and decisions. From this perspective, the mediatization of politics is just as much an outcome of the gradual erosion of organized, class-based politics as the result of a new media environment.

Through processes of mediatization, political institutions and actors are increasingly influenced by the *modus operandi* of the media and as such we may consider the mediatization of politics as a shift in the balance of power between two institutions, politics and the media, in favor of the latter. Nonetheless, a political actor – a government, party, or individual politician – may often have the upper hand on the media and be able to influence the media's representation of a particular issue. The extent to which the political actor or the media end up "winning" a particular encounter is an empirical question, and not something to which the theory of mediatization of politics can provide an unequivocal answer. Due to political organizations' professional use of media resources and media management they may be able to steer the political agenda, not least in circumstances in which the news media lack the resources for independent journalistic work. The mediatization of politics primarily concerns the long-term process by which the very *conditions* for political communication are changed and therefore alter the form of political communication and the relationships between the actors involved. Metaphorically speaking, the political actors may occasionally win a battle over the media, but the mediatization of politics implies that the outcome of the war is often decided in the media's arena, and by the ability to communicate strategically within and through the media. In the days of the party press, the relationship between politicians and the editorial desk of a like-minded political newspaper was often close and sometimes personal. Today, the formation of public opinion has become industrialized and the media have become an important producer, distributor, and arbitrator of public opinion.

4

THE MEDIATIZATION OF RELIGION

From the faith of the Church to the enchantment of the media

Introduction

With the help of the most sophisticated media technology, supernatural phenomena have acquired an unmatched presence in modern societies. In blockbuster movies such as *The Lord of the Rings* trilogy, *The Twilight Saga*, and the *Harry Potter* film series; ghosts, elves, vampires, unicorns, monsters possessed by evil, and spirits working for good, are vividly alive and inhabit the world on a par with mortal human beings. The metaphysical realm is no longer something one can only imagine, or occasionally see represented in symbolic forms in fresco paintings or pillars of stone. The media's representation of the supernatural world has acquired a richness of detail, character, and narrative that makes the supernatural appear natural. The salience of the supernatural world is, furthermore, supported by its mundane character in the media. Watching aliens, demons, and vampires in television series such as *The X Files*, *Supernatural*, and *Buffy the Vampire Slayer* week after week, season after season, and spending an hour or two every day fighting supernatural monsters in computer games like *World of Warcraft*, playing a magic character of your own creation, all make the world of the unreal a rather familiar phenomenon.

The supernatural world is not confined to the media genres of fiction. Television reality series such as the Discovery Channel's *Ghosthunters* were among the first in a wave of television programs dealing with the supernatural, the paranormal, and other (quasi-) religious issues. These were followed by the British *Most Haunted* and the American *Ghost Hunters* series. In Denmark, for instance, national television has dealt with ghosts, exorcism, and reincarnation in such programs as *The Power of the Spirits* and *Travelling with the Soul*. On entertainment shows such as *The Sixth Sense*, astrologists and chiromancers appear together with psychologists and fashion specialists. Not only have such popular forms of religion become more prominent in the media in many countries, but the institutionalized religions (Christianity, Islam, and so on) have also drawn greater attention in news and other factual genres. In the Nordic countries, Islam has received far more attention during the last decades (Lundby and Lövheim forthcoming), not least due to immigration's presence on the political agenda. Christianity, too, has received more journalistic attention. Institutional forms of religion not only receive more news coverage, but the treatment also has a stronger focus on opinions and debates, making use of a wider range of journalistic genres than in earlier times. Considering the Danish press in the period from 1985 to 2005, Rosenfeldt (2007) documents a multiplication of stories involving Christian issues (approximately three times as many) and Islamic issues (approximately 11 times as many). The publication of the cartoons portraying the Prophet Mohammed by the Danish daily newspaper *Jyllands-Posten* left no doubt that the media do indeed play a prominent role in the public circulation of religious representations, and in the framing of religious controversy (Kunelius *et al.* 2007; Hjarvard 2010a). Last but not least, the Internet and other digital media have become a prominent platform for the dissemination and discussion of religious issues, allowing many individuals and religious movements to express religious ideas and sentiments outside the traditional framework of the Church, and changing the ways in which religious institutions interact with their communities (Højsgaard and Warburg 2005; Campbell 2010).

The increased presence of religious themes in the media may at first appear to be a negation of the idea that secularization is the hallmark of high modernity, and that the media are agents of enlightenment. Consequently, we could interpret the development as an increased tendency towards the de-secularization (Berger *et al.* 1999) or re-sacralization (Demerath 2003) of modern society, in which secular tendencies are gradually replaced, or at least challenged, by the resurgence of Christianity, Islam, and newer mediatized forms of religion. However, despite the reappearance of religion on the media agenda, there are nevertheless also tendencies towards a secularization of society. Norris and Inglehart (2004) and Inglehart and Welzel (2005) have provided the most comprehensive comparative analyses concerning the relationship between modernization and various dimensions of secularization. Based on the available statistical data from 74 countries, covering the period 1981–2001, Norris and Inglehart (2004) report a clear correlation between the modernization of society and the decline in traditional religious behavior and beliefs. At the same time, Inglehart and Welzel (2005) also point out that the spread of self-expression values in late modern society may increase sensitivity toward various forms of subjectivized spirituality and non-material concerns. Secularization thus does not entail the total disappearance of religion, but denotes a series of structural transformations of religion in the modern world, including a decline in the authority of religious institutions in society, together with the development of more individualized forms of religious beliefs and practices (Bruce 2002; Dobbelaere 2002; Taylor 2007). From this perspective, the mediatization of religion may be considered part of a gradual process of secularization in late modern society: it is the historical process by which the media have adopted many of the social functions that were previously performed by religious institutions.

Rituals, worship, mourning, and celebration are all social activities that used to be part of institutionalized religion, but have now partly been taken over by the media and transformed into more or less secular activities serving other purposes than those of religious institutions. Studying how religion interconnects with the media provides evidence of secularization, as well as re-sacralization, tendencies. It may certainly be possible that both tendencies are at work at the same time – although in different areas and aspects of the interface between religion and the media. For instance, some media genres, like news and documentaries, may generally subscribe to a secular world view, while fantasy and horror genres are more inclined to evoke metaphysical or supernatural imaginations.

For a sociological understanding of the role that the modern media play in religion, it is important to stress that they not only represent or report on religious issues, but also change the very ideas and authority of religious institutions, and affect how people interact with each other when dealing with religious issues. For instance, some strands of faith were previously considered to be superstition and denounced as low culture. The increased presence of such types of faith on international and national television has increased the legitimacy of "superstition" and challenged the cultural prestige of the institutionalized Church. As expressed by a Danish bishop after the screening of the ghost hunter television series *The Power of the Spirits*, "Danish culture will never be the same after this series" (Lindhardt 2004). Similarly, we have witnessed how Dan Brown's bestseller novels and movies *The Da Vinci Code* and *Angels & Demons* acquired a global audience though a mixture of spiritual sensibility, conspiracy theories, and criticism of traditional orthodoxy (Partridge 2008). This success was so immense that the Roman Catholic Church, and other Christian communities, felt threatened by Dan Brown's alternative interpretation of the Gospel and produced numerous media outlets to counter his arguments. As a result, the publication and screening of the Dan Brown novels and films became spectacular media events that spurred news coverage, television debates, and public protests.

The aim of this chapter is to develop a theoretical framework for an under-standing of how the media work as agents of religious change. Through the process of mediatization, the media come to influence and change religion at several levels, including the authority of the religious institution, the symbolic content of religious narratives, and religious faith and practices. A theory of the interface between media and religion must consider the media and religion in the proper cultural and historical contexts, since the mediatization of religion is neither his-torically, culturally, nor geographically a universal phenomenon. As stipulated in Chapter 2, mediatization as a general process is a late modern phenomenon, in which the media have become semi-independent institutions, at the same time as the media have become integrated into various cultural and social institutions. Also, within highly modernized societies, there are many differences in terms of both media and religion, and the theoretical framework and analytical outline presented in this chapter may be more suitable to describe developments in north-western Europe than elsewhere in the world. The studies conducted by Clark (2005) and

Hoover (2006) clearly indicate that the evangelical movement in the United States provides an important cultural context for the interplay between media and religion. This differs from the Nordic experience, which has a far more limited public presence of the Evangelical Lutheran Church, with lower attendance levels. The empirical findings from a Danish context that are presented at the end of this chapter may therefore very well differ from the US experience.

As Lynch (2011) has observed, the mediatization of religion in the Nordic countries may be dependent on four characteristics that dominate the relationship between media and religion: (1) mainstream media institutions have a non-confessional orientation and there is limited use of media with a strong confessional orientation; (2) when the population has little direct engagement with religious institutions mainstream public media become the access point for engagement with religious symbols and narratives; (3) the existence of a clearly identifiable religious institution (e.g., the Evangelical Lutheran Church); and (4) a high degree of secularization at societal, organizational, and individual levels (Lynch 2011: 205). In other words, the mediatization of religion may take different forms and generate different outcomes in, for instance, the USA, Brazil, or India, depending on the religious, social, and media context. Our theoretical framework must also consider the fact that the media are not a unitary phenomenon. The individual media are dependent on their technological features, aesthetic conventions, and institutional frameworks, so that the consequences of the Internet and television for religion may differ somewhat. A thorough understanding of the influence of the media on religion must therefore be sensitive to the differences between the media and the various ways in which they portray religion, transform religious content and symbolic forms, and transfer religious activities from one institutional context to another.

Three metaphors of media

Joshua Meyrowitz (1993) has suggested a useful distinction between three different aspects of communication media: media as conduits, media as languages, and media as environments. In his framework, these metaphors are used to categorize existing strands of research into mediated communication, but here they will be used to specify the various ways in which religion is affected by the media.

(1) The metaphor of *media as conduits* draws attention to how the media transport symbols and messages across distances from senders to receivers. When focused on this aspect, research must deal with the content of the media: what types of messages are transmitted, what topics occupy the media agenda, how much attention one theme receives compared to another, and so on. Following on from this position, the media are distributors of religious representations of various kinds. Most obvious perhaps are the religious key texts such as the Bible, the Koran, hymn books, and so on, which are also media products that are distributed both within religious institutions and via the general media markets. However, the media in the sense of independent media production and distribution companies are only to a very limited extent channels for the distribution of texts originating

from the religious institutions. Newspapers may have columns dedicated to religious announcements, and radio and television usually transmit religious services, but in most western countries this is a marginal activity. Most of the representations concerning religious issues in the media do not originate from the institutionalized religions, but are produced and edited by media professionals, or individual media users, and delivered via such genres as news, documentaries, drama, entertainment, blogs, and so on. Using these genres, the media provide a constant fare of religious representations that mixes institutionalized religion and other spiritual elements in new ways, and the media become an important source of information and experience regarding religion. In general, the media become distributors of three different types of religion: *religious media, journalism on religion*, and *banal religion*. These differ in terms of religious content, control over the communication, and the formatting of religious issues.

(2) Turning to the metaphor of *media as languages*, our attention focuses on the aesthetics of the media, i.e., the various ways that the media may format the messages and construct the communicative relationships between sender, content, and receiver. In particular, the choices of medium and genre influence important features such as the narrative construction, reality status, and the mode of reception of particular messages; and, as a consequence, the media adjust and mold religious representations to the modalities of the specific medium and genre in question. A newspaper story about the papal politics toward Latin America, a horror film like *The Exorcist* and a Facebook site for Asa believers in Scandinavia (da-dk.facebook. com/Asatro) provide very different representations of religious issues and, indeed, involve contrasting assumptions concerning what defines religion and how we should interact with religious issues. In contemporary Europe, but also in many other regions of the world, the media as language first and foremost implies that religion is formatted according to the *genres of popular culture*. Popular culture has always practiced an often contentious representation of religious issues, but the public service obligations of radio and television, and the stricter moral control of commercial media in general, previously meant that the institutionalized religions had a firmer grip on how religion was represented in the public media. Due to the increasingly deregulated and commercialized media systems in most European countries, as well as in other parts of the world, radio and television have become far more integrated into popular culture, and newer media such as computer games, the Internet, and mobile media have, from the very outset, placed the themes and narratives of popular culture at the center of their activity. Through the language of popular culture in the media, religion has become more oriented toward entertainment and the consumer, and the approach to religion is generally more individualized.

(3) Finally, if we consider the metaphor of *media as environments*, our interest concentrates on how media systems and institutions facilitate and structure human interaction and communication. Due to their technical and institutional properties, public service media like the radio and television of the mid-twentieth century generally favored a national, paternalistic, unidirectional (one-to-many) communication pattern, whereas the Internet of the twenty-first century favors a more global,

consumer-oriented, and multidirectional communication pattern. Since environments are far more stable than individual messages, this metaphor encourages studies at a general level, and in particular into long-term historical change. For instance, the printing press stimulated the spread of scientific ideas and weakened the Church's control over the individual's access to religious texts, thereby supporting the individualization of belief and the rise of Protestantism (Eisenstein 1979). In the technologically advanced societies of the twenty-first century, the media have expanded to almost all areas of society and constitute pervasive networks (Castells 1996, 2001) through which most human interaction and communication must be filtered. Consequently, the media also structure feelings of community and belonging (Anderson 1991; Morley 2000). The media ritualize the small transitions of everyday life, as well as the events in the wider society (Dayan and Katz 1992). In earlier societies, social institutions, like family, school, and Church, were the most important providers of information, tradition, and moral orientation for the individual members of society. Today, these institutions have lost some of their former authority, and the media have to some extent taken over their role as providers of information and moral orientation, while at the same time the media have become society's most important storyteller about society itself.

The media's influence on religion may be manifold and at times contradictory, but as a whole the media as conduits, languages, and environments are responsible for the *mediatization of religion*. This process entails a multidimensional transformation of religion that influences religious texts, practices, and institutional relationships, and eventually the very nature of belief in modern societies. The outcome is not a new kind of religion as such, but rather a new social and cultural condition in which the power to define and practice religion has been altered.

Three forms of mediatized religion

As conduits of communication, the media circulate a wide variety of messages that involve the representation of religion. These media representations do not provide a homogenous image of religion, but on the contrary encompass an immense variation in terms of the types of religions represented, attitudes toward religion, and the purpose of the communication in question. Across the various types of media representations of religion we may, however, analytically distinguish between some major clusters of communicative practices, each characterized by a set of dominant genres, institutional control, religious content, and communicative functions. In the following we will briefly characterize three such dominant clusters: *religious media*, *journalism on religion*, and *banal religion*. Table 4.1 provides an overview of these forms of mediatized religion (see also Hjarvard 2012a).

Religious media

By *religious media* we mean media organizations and practices that are primarily controlled and performed by religious actors, either collectively (e.g., a church) or individually. They may encompass mass media (e.g., *God TV*), social networking

TABLE 4.1 Key characteristics of three different forms of mediatized religion

	Religious media	Journalism on religion	Banal religion
Dominant genres	Religious services, preaching, confessions, discussions	News, current affairs, moderated debate	Narrative fiction, entertainment, self-help services, consumer advice
Institution in primary control	Religion	Journalism	Media
Religious content	Interpretations of religious texts and moral advice	Utterances and actions of religious players framed by secular news values	Bricolage of the texts, iconography and liturgy of various institutional and folk religions
Role of religious agents	Owners, producers, performers	Sources	Fictional representations of ministers and believers; in factual genres social counselors, entertainers, etc.
Communicative functions	Persuasion Social rituals Religious community	Information Critical scrutiny Political public sphere	Entertainment Cultural rituals Self-development
Challenge to the Protestant Church	Multiple and individualized religious voices and visual representations	Critical of the religious institution if out of sync with secular values	A bricolage of religious representations provides a backdrop of cultural knowledge about religion

media (e.g., *Catholic Online* on Facebook), and private personal media (e.g., mobile phones) used for communication among religious individuals. From a historical perspective, the media have always been important for the practice and spread of religion, and changes in the media environment have often had an important influence on the development of religion. In the history of Christianity the spread of written texts, and later the invention of printing, were significant processes that restructured and challenged the power of the religious authorities. As Horsfield (forthcoming) argues, the transition of Christianity from an oral to a written culture paved the way for the global spread of Christianity at the expense of a variety of orally based Christian communities (see also Ong 1982). During the latter part of the Roman Empire literate men acquired positions of leadership in Christianity and this clerical class's access to the social and intellectual means of the technology of writing was instrumental in the institutionalization and spread of Catholic Christianity in time and space. Similarly, the invention of printing technology in Europe in around 1450 enabled the mass production and distribution of Christian texts and allowed a more personal relationship between the word of God and Protestant followers to develop (Eisenstein 1979). The establishment of a separate media industry and profession, printers and publishers, outside the Church gave new weight to another authority: the market for religious literature.

More recently, the development of televangelism in USA represents a major example of how religious television has created a new public platform for evangelical movements and allowed many televangelists to become well-known charismatic religious leaders (Peck 1993). Television not only served as a public platform for the spread of religious ideas, but also altered religious movements and organizations. Religious television introduced new forms of religious experiences and feelings of community and influenced the internal power structure of religious organizations. Televangelism as a social phenomenon developed in the USA, but has later spread to other parts of the world. In India, televangelism has developed into a "Masala McGospel" that mixes elements of Hinduism with American media culture (James 2010). In many countries the religious mass media are, however, a limited activity compared to the general output of mass media such as television, radio, and film that are dominated by public or commercial interests and do not generally seek to propagate any particular religious beliefs. This is particularly the case in northern Europe, including the Nordic countries, where religious newspapers and broadcasting only occupy a niche in a predominantly secular media market.

The Internet and other digital media have given religious players new opportunities for communication with their followers, as well as the general public. The interactive potential of new media can enable religious players to strengthen ties with their fellow believers and create a new sense of presence and community. However, most of the existing research does not seem to indicate that the digital media enable religious organizations to reach out to many people beyond their existing faith community. The new media are more often used to communicate among existing members of a religious community, while encouraging members to adapt a more individual stance toward religious institutions (Hoover *et al.* 2004; Lövheim 2008). Meyer and Moors (2006: 11) suggest that the media have "both a destabilizing and an enabling potential" for the religious establishment's control of communication. The media may, for that reason, resemble a "Trojan horse" that, once invited inside and put to use, may challenge the authority of institutionalized religion. Not only does the pluralization of religious voices on the Internet challenge the authority of organized religions, but more individualized and networked forms of religious communication practices, inspired by the general Internet culture, are also developed. Højsgaard's (2005: 62) study of religion on the Internet observes that the "cyber-religious field, moreover, is characterized by such features as role-playing, identity construction, cultural adaptability, fascination with technology, and a sarcastic approach to conformist religiosity." Various online media, such as blogs, provide an opportunity for individuals to express personal religious beliefs and experiences and construct "religious autobiographies" (Lövheim 2005) that may challenge both the orthodoxy of religious institutions and the dominant discourses about religion in secular society. Such online forums are, however, only rarely able to set the public agenda by themselves. In combination with the mass media, blogs may, nevertheless, play a supplementary role in the public discussion of religion, as demonstrated, for instance, by Lövheim and Axner's (2011) study of the Swedish "Halal-TV" debate (see also Lövheim 2012).

Compared to the two other forms of mediatized religion, *journalism on religion* and *banal religion*, *religious media* may be considered a less mediatized form of religion. Due to religious players' control of the media (organizationally or individually), the media serve religious purposes, rather than the other way around. As a consequence, the characteristic *modus operandi* of the media is often instrumentalized in order to serve a religious cause, for instance, in televangelism. The programs on televangelist channels do not make use of all the available genres of television, but on the contrary adapt religious modes of communication to television, in order to preach a particular religious message. Religious media, however, must also accommodate to the demands of the media in a variety of ways, and this may influence not only the form and content of the religious messages, but also change how relationships between religious media and audiences are established, including how religious authority must be exercised. When entering the general public sphere, the religious media are judged according to the same professional criteria as other media, including their ability to make use of media technology and genres in appropriate and interesting ways.

In general, both older and newer forms of religious media are prompted to follow the commercial media's general responsiveness to audiences and users. As Galal (2008) has demonstrated in his study of popular religious genres on Arab satellite television, a more individualized and consumer-based version of Islam is often constructed in these programs. In Koran recitation contests and Koranic healing programs, the "symbolic inventory borrows not only from Islamic tradition, but also from global symbolic resources. The main imperatives in these programs are style and signature or, in other words, performance" (Galal 2008: 177). As a consequence, some of these programs are "thin" on traditional or political religious authority and far more attuned to a wider globalized Islamic culture, "where to be Muslim is to be chic" (Galal 2008: 177). Religious players may use the media for their own purposes, but in the process of serving religious objectives the religious media may end up bringing religion into greater contact with the values and practices of a wider media culture of both secular and multiple religious outlooks. As the experience of the Arab Spring so richly demonstrates, the control and use of new media technologies such as satellite television, the Internet, and social networking media may be used to challenge existing political and religious authorities, as well as to promote competing interpretations of Islam's role in society.

Journalism on religion

During the last few decades religious issues have received more attention in the news media in many countries. Globally, major conflicts such as the war on terror, the Mohammed cartoon crisis, and the more permanent social and cultural repercussions of increasing migration, have put religion, and not least Islam, on the news agenda. The growing attention paid to religion is not only due to such singular conflicts or problems, but represents a more general development. Religion has moved from the fringes of the news media to become a recurring theme or aspect to be dealt with by journalists. Religion is no longer restricted to particular religious columns or newspapers with a specific religious profile, but is regularly covered in mainstream news media reports.

From an institutional perspective, the increased journalistic attention to religion reflects a change in the power to define and frame religion. Religion and journalism may both be considered social institutions, but they are governed by different sets of rationalities and *modus operandi*. Both institutions have communication at the center of their activity and address an audience in order to influence its world views and actions. But the norms and behaviors that govern the two institutions' communicative practices are very different. Journalism developed gradually as a particular craft and semi-profession in the media industry from the late nineteenth century and onward, and journalists gained professional legitimacy via their adherence to the prevailing norms of secular society, in particular the ideals of objectivity from the sciences and the values of democracy from the world of politics. Hence, objectivity and facticity became embedded in the professional language and work routines of journalism (Schudson 1978; Tuchman 1972), at the same time as the news media, as a fourth estate of power, was to strive to make other powerful institutions of society, including religious institutions, publicly accountable for their (mis)use of power.

We should naturally be careful not to take the journalists' self-perception and ideals at face value. In practice, the news media do not restrict themselves to the reporting of objective facts, but have become industries of opinion in society (see Chapter 3). Many studies have demonstrated how the news media *frame* the news in particular ways and thereby come "to promote a particular problem definition, causal interpretation, moral evaluation, and/or treatment recommendation" (Entman 1993: 52). The news media are a vital part of the public agenda-setting process (McCombs 2004), and through their particular framing of various issues they come to produce social facts and opinions – and not only reflect existing ones. Furthermore, journalism is part of the wider domain of popular culture and as a commercial enterprise it is not only a vehicle for public deliberation, but also a source of entertainment and a voice for popular sentiment (Hartley 2009; McManus 1994). The framing of religion in the news media is therefore not only influenced by journalism's professional values, but also by its responsiveness to prevailing discourses in society and by the audience's demand for entertaining stories. Nevertheless, the news media in the western world have generally become professionalized, non-partisan institutions that keep a distance to other – political as well as religious – institutions (Hallin and Mancini 2004). The rise of the news media as a semi-independent institution in society (Cook 1998) has changed the influence of journalism in society. Back in the times of the political press, the news media exerted their influence via their opinionated political reporting. Today, a semi-independent news institution exerts its influence by keeping an arm's-length distance to politics, producing political facts and opinions by adhering to professional values of journalism. In a similar vein, the news media come to influence the representation of religion; not by taking a partisan religious stance, but by keeping a distance and framing religion in accordance with the values and norms of journalism. The news media in general consider themselves to be secular institutions with no ambition of propagating religious values, and no intention of treating religious organizations or actors differently than any other organization or actor.

Journalism and the news media have acquired at least partial control of an important resource in society that other institutions are dependent on: the public representation of political, social, and cultural affairs. If religious organizations and individual actors wish to have access to this resource they have to accommodate to the demands of the news media. In general, this implies that they have to accommodate to at least two dominant logics of journalism: the criteria of *newsworthiness* and the role of *sources*. In order to get into the news, the actions and messages of religious organizations and individual players have to be newsworthy, i.e., comply with the journalistic news values of social significance, topicality, intensity, etc. (Hjarvard 2011). As a consequence, religious issues without a clear conflict of interest will usually not become news, no matter how publicly relevant they may be considered by the religious community itself. Furthermore, in order to gain a voice in the news, religious organizations and interest groups also have to fulfill the role of a relevant and reliable news source. News sources are expected to supply information and opinions concerning the issue at hand, but they will only be quoted inso far as they – in the eyes of the journalist – provide credible (factual and objective) information and opinions that are in line with the framing of the story. Journalists do not, of course, always have the upper hand vis-à-vis news sources (Blumler and Gurevitch 1981) and religious players may also influence the journalist's choice of news topic and framing of the story. Since reporters need sources to produce the news, they are also responsive to the agendas and framings offered by their sources – and in particular those offered by powerful sources. However, religious organizations and individual players cannot use their own communication genres (sermons, prayers, etc.) or norms of credibility (references to holy texts) when negotiating with journalists. They have to comply with the conventions of modern, secular journalism. To gain a voice in the news media's public sphere, you have to understand how to make news and perform as a news source.

Journalism on religion challenges the ability of religious players (organizations and individuals) to define religion and frame religious issues in the public sphere. These players are subsequently far more exposed to criticism based on the general social and political norms of secular society. In his study of the newspaper coverage of religion in the Scandinavian countries, Christensen (2010) demonstrates how the various types of religious authority have a very limited presence in the public sphere of the media and parliaments of the Scandinavian countries. As regards Christianity, more traditional or dogmatic types of religious authority do not exert any particular influence in the public sphere, but in Norway and Sweden, newspaper articles may occasionally represent Christianity as a natural part of public life, for instance, in concert announcements and obituaries (ibid.: 105). Christianity may therefore still exert a type of cultural authority due to its historical legacy in the Nordic countries, but only inso far as the values in question are not considered to be out of sync with the surrounding society. For instance, the journalistic news coverage of questions concerning gender equality and homosexuality typically represent Christianity and the Church as less committed to equality and tolerance than the rest of society (Christensen 2010, 2012).

In view of journalism's commitment to secular values, the news media often become an instrument of "religious modernization," i.e., disclosing and criticizing unacceptable norms and behavior. The Danish media coverage of the scandals concerning the sexual abuse of children and young people in the Roman Catholic Church can serve as an illustration of this critical-secular function (see also Hjarvard 2012a). Since few Danes are members of the Roman Catholic Church, the Danish news media rarely report on Catholicism, and for the most part in relation to foreign affairs. However, these scandals also had repercussions in Denmark, where Roman Catholic priests were also accused of the sexual abuse of minors, and this increased the news coverage of the Roman Catholic Church in Denmark.

Berlingske Tidende – a serious Danish newspaper with a conservative background – covered these issues intensively and dedicated a particular part of its website to news on Roman Catholicism ("Aktuelt emne," www.b.dk/katolsk). This themed collection of 100 news stories from *Berlingske Tidende* in 2010 provides a condensed picture of the newspaper's selection and framing of news about this particular religion. Eighty-seven out of 100 news articles dealt with stories concerning the sexual abuse of children and young people. Apart from focusing on the abuse itself, the coverage was also very critical of the Roman Catholic Church's handling of the accusations. The news stories depicted the leadership of the Roman Catholic Church as either incompetent or eager to cover up the criminal misconduct of its priests. Eight of the remaining news stories reported on the death of a Catholic nun who was mistreated at a convent in Djursland, and here we find a similar critical framing of the Roman Catholic Church's leadership and its handling of the affair. Two further stories dealt with the Roman Catholic Church's policy toward contraception, and one story reported on a German bishop who was removed from office due to accusations of physical violence against children, as well as financial misconduct. Finally, *Berlingske Tidende* carried two news stories dealing with celibacy. Only in this case do we find articles that are not critical of the Roman Catholic Church in one way or another. Yet at least one of the articles could be interpreted as an indirect defense against the criticism voiced elsewhere that celibacy may at least indirectly be a reason for Roman Catholic priests' sexual misconduct.

The news media's coverage of the pedophilia scandal in the Roman Catholic Church was certainly not limited to the pages of *Berlingske Tidende*, but was a global phenomenon. It became an almost textbook example of a media scandal

(Thompson 2000), in which the attempts to deny or explain away the accusations, and the bureaucratic unwillingness to react promptly to the accusations, became a scandal in itself. Nationally, as well as internationally (via the Pope and the Vatican state), the Roman Catholic Church sought to counter the mounting criticism in various ways, including by criticizing the press. This, generally, had the unintended effect of diminishing the moral habitus of the Church even further in the eyes of the public and demonstrated that the Roman Catholic Church had clearly misjudged its ability to define and frame the public representation of itself. Responding to the Vatican state's accusations that the news media were too critical of the Church, the editor-in-chief of *Berlingske Tidende*, Lisbeth Knudsen, re-asserted the right of journalists to criticize the Roman Catholic Church: "the news media's critical stories are not a smear campaign. If the media are to be accused of anything, it is for having paid too much respect for religious feelings and clerical authority" (17 April 2010). In a Danish context the critical framing of the Roman Catholic Church may in part be explained by the fact that Roman Catholicism is considered to be culturally alien, and thus commands less authority in the minds of journalists and the news media. But the absence of the traditional or dogmatic authority of Protestantism in the public sphere points to how the (occasional) cultural authority of Protestantism has been achieved via an accommodation to the secular values that are promoted by *journalism on religion* together with other modern institutions of society, such as schools, science, and politics. Thus, Protestantism has maintained some cultural authority, but this has been achieved by accommodating to the demands of secular society.

Banal religion

If *journalism on religion* brings religion into a political public sphere, a third form of mediatized religion, *banal religion*, brings religious imaginations into the cultural realm. The concept of *banal religion* is derived from Michael Billig's (1995) book on nationalism and cultural identity, in which he develops the concept of "banal nationalism." The study of nationalism is often focused on the explicit and institutionalized manifestations of nationalism, such as nationalistic ideologies (e.g., fascism) or symbols (e.g., the flag). However, nationalism and national identity are not only created and maintained through the use of official and explicit symbols of the nation, but are also to a very great extent based on a series of everyday phenomena that constantly remind the individual of his or her belonging to the nation and the national culture. Billig distinguishes between metaphorically "waved and unwaved flags" (Billig 1995: 39); i.e., between manifest and less noticeable symbols of the nation. Whereas the collective "we" and "them" in specific historical circumstances have evidently served to demarcate the nation against outsiders, such pronouns also live a quiet, everyday existence in other periods, providing natural, yet unnoticeable, references to the members and non-members of the national culture. It is this unnoticed, low-key usage of formerly explicit national symbols that constitutes what Billig calls "banal nationalism."

In continuation of Agger (2005), I take the notion of "banal nationalism" a step further than Billig (1995) and include a whole series of everyday symbols and occurrences that have only a marginal or no prehistory as symbols of the nation or nationalism. Many cultural phenomena and symbols may be familiar symbols of aspects of both culture and society, but they are not necessarily seen as expressions of a national culture or a nationalistic ideology. In a Danish context, phenomena such as pickled or smoked herring and schnapps, the Roskilde rock festival, young people bathing in the North Sea, and the chiming of the bells at Copenhagen's City Hall on New Year's Eve, may for many people be familiar experiences that constitute part of their cultural environment and memories. These experiences and symbols may not be related to nationalism, but can just as well be related to instances of individual history, family events, or class culture. In some circumstances they may, nevertheless, be mobilized for nationalistic purposes, and acquire a whole new set of meanings. A good example of such reinterpretation is the campaign video of the anti-immigration right-wing party in Denmark, the Danish People's Party (Dansk Folkeparti), in the run-up to the 2001 parliamentary election (Dansk Folkeparti 2001). Accompanied only by music, a five-minute-long montage of still pictures of "banal Danishness" was shown. The video conveyed a very powerful and positive picture of Denmark and Danishness, and by using these banal national symbols, it systematically excluded elements of foreign culture from being worthy components of Danishness.

Just as the study of nationalism needs to take the banal elements of national culture into account, the study of religion must consider how both individual faith and collective religious imagination are created and maintained by a series of experiences and representations that may have no, or only a limited, relationship with the institutionalized religions. In continuation of Billig (1995), we label these as *banal religious representations*. They consist of elements usually associated with folk religion, such as trolls, vampires, and black cats crossing the street; items taken from institutionalized religion such as crosses, prayers, and cowls; and representations that do not necessarily have any religious connotations, such as upturned faces, thunder and lightning, and highly emotional music.

From the point of view of human evolution (Barrett 2004; Boyer 2001; Pyssiäinen and Anttonen 2002), it seems reasonable to assume that these banal religious representations provided the first inventory of religious imaginations, and they continue to inform a kind of primary, and to some extent spontaneous, religious imagination. In the course of history, and the subsequent differentiation of society, religion became partly institutionalized, and religious professionals produced progressively more complex and coherent religious narratives that excluded part of the banal elements as superstition and included others as part of the Holy Scripture, while also inventing new ones. Instead of accepting the institutionalized religious texts as the most valid and true sources of religion and belief, and consequently considering folk religion or "superstition" as incomplete, undeveloped, or marginally religious phenomena, it is both theoretically and analytically far more illuminating to consider the banal religious elements as constitutive for religious imagination, and the institutionalized religious texts and symbols as secondary features, and in one sense as rationalization after the fact.

The label "banal" does not imply that these representations are less important or irrelevant. On the contrary, they are primary and fundamental to the production of religious thoughts and emotions, and they are also banal in the sense that their religious meanings may travel unnoticed and can be evoked independently of larger religious texts or institutions. The religious meaning of banal religious elements rests on basic cognitive skills that help ascribe anthropomorphic or animistic agency to supernatural powers, usually by means of counterintuitive categories that arrest attention, support memory, and evoke emotions. Thus, banal religious elements are about the supernatural and intentional force behind a sudden strike of lightning (ascribing agency), or about dead people who still walk about in the night (counterintuitive mix of categories). The holy texts, iconography, and liturgy of institutionalized religions may contribute to the stockpile of banal religious elements, and as such they may circulate and activate meanings that are more or less related to the authorized religious interpretation. The power relationship between banal religious representations and institutionalized religion may, of course, vary historically and geographically, but the increasing role of the media in society seems to make room for more of the banal religious representations.

Re-enchanting media

According to Max Weber (1904), the modern world is characterized by the steady advance of rationality. As social institutions became more and more differentiated and specialized, the bureaucracy, the military, industry, and so on were subsumed into the logic of rationality. Consequently, the modern world became disenchanted: as magical imagination, religion, and emotions – in short, irrationality – lost ground to the all-encompassing logic of modern institutions, modern man gradually became imprisoned in an "iron cage" of rationality. Although Weber's analysis of the role of rationality in modern society may still apply, his diagnosis of a progressive disenchantment is hardly valid. In the muddy reality of modern culture, rationality thrives at close quarters with irrationality. As the two authoritarian catastrophes of the twentieth century, fascism and Stalinism, demonstrate, extreme rationalism may very well go hand-in-hand with rabid irrationalism such as the cultic celebration of a leader, mythological stories and prophecies, and diabolical depictions of the enemy.

Irrationalism may also, in normal social conditions, be rationalism's bedfellow. As Campbell (1987) demonstrates in his analysis of the interconnections between the spread of consumer culture and the rise of a romantic sensibility, the advance of rationality is only one side of the story. Ritzer (1999) has developed Campbell's argument in an analysis of the postmodern consumer culture, in which "cathedrals of consumption," for instance, shopping malls and theme parks, stage consumption in spectacular settings in order to endow the goods of mass production with extraordinary qualities and provide a magical experience. At the same time as both the production and distribution of consumer goods are subject to increasing degrees of "McDonaldization," i.e., more calculation, effectiveness, and technological control, the goods themselves and the process of consumption are bestowed with magical meanings in order to re-enchant an ever more soulless world of identical consumer goods.

In a similar vein, religions may provide a source of re-enchantment in the modern world. In continuation of Gilhus and Mikaelsson (1998), we argue that the advance of new religious movements indicates the return of "enchanting" elements from a premodern world. At the same time, these new religions are a source of identity and meaningfulness for modern, self-reflexive individuals who, increasingly, are left alone with the responsibility of constructing a purpose in life. As secularization relegated institutionalized religion to the periphery of society, less organized and more individualized forms of religion appeared to emerge within various sectors of society, including business and industry, where quasi-religious elements inform management training, branding, and so on. It should be noted, however, that neither the old nor the newer types of religion necessarily imply any re-enchantment in the modern world. The intellectualization of modern Protestantism, and the tight behavioral control within certain Islamic fundamentalist groups, are two very different examples of religious developments that diminish the enchanting potential of religion.

Like the new religious movements, the media may also contribute to the re-enchantment of the modern world (Murdock 1997, 2008; Martin-Barbero 1997). The media are large-scale suppliers of narratives – fictional as well as factual – about adventures, magical occurrences, the fight between good and evil, and so on (Clark 2005). The media are, of course, also a source of information, knowledge, and enlightenment, and as such propagators of reason, but at the same time they are a well of fantasy and emotional experiences. The media have become society's main purveyor of enchanted experiences. When Ritzer (1999) singles out the "cathedrals of consumption" as the re-enchanting institutions *par excellence* in modern society, he is in fact only pointing toward certain specific media industries. A theme park like Disneyland magnificently re-enacts narratives from a single media mogul, and the shopping mall's attempt to induce consumption with extraordinary experiences usually relies on the workings of advertising techniques, licensing of media brands, and physical environments saturated by popular music and television screens. In a similar vein, we argue that a series of new religious movements has achieved a greater resonance among their audiences because the media have published equivalent stories. For instance, there are strong interdependencies between the media's continuous preoccupation with aliens in general and the Roswell mythology in particular, and the proliferation of quasi-religious beliefs in aliens (Rothstein 2000; Lewis 2003).

It may be said that religious messages have always been distributed by the media: the book has been an instrument of religious teaching and a privileged source of key holy texts, and the Church may, from a certain perspective, also be considered a communication medium with a whole series of genres such as the sermon, psalms, and so on. However, both the quantitative and qualitative developments that the media have undergone in society are overlooked in this argument. In the past, the mass media were very much in the service of other social institutions. Books and journals were controlled by religious institutions, the scientific institution, and the cultural public sphere, and newspapers were very much the instruments of political parties and movements. In a northern European context, radio and television were cultural institutions and, through an elaborate scheme of political and cultural control, broadcast a balanced representation of the political and cultural institutions in society.

Moving toward the end of the twentieth century, most media gradually lost their close relationship with specific social institutions, organizations, and parties, and the media themselves became *independent institutions* in society. Consequently, the media no longer see themselves as purveyors of other institutions' agendas; instead, their activities are far more attuned to the service of their audiences – very often incorporating the logic of a commercial market. Phrased differently, the media increasingly organize public and private communication in ways that are adjusted to the individual media's logic and market considerations. Other institutions are still represented in the media, but their function is progressively more as providers of raw material, which the media then use and transform for the purpose of the media themselves. The liturgy and iconography of the institutionalized religions become a stockpile of props for the staging of media narratives. For example, popular action adventure stories about Indiana Jones in *Raiders of the Lost Ark* or a television series like *Lost*, blend and recontextualize many different religious, pagan, and secular symbols in new and unexpected ways. In sum, the media become prominent producers of various religious imaginations, rather than conveyors of the messages of religious institutions.

Community and rituals

Turning to the media as environments, we can take the etymology of the words "medium" and "communication" as a starting point. The word "medium" originates from the Latin *medius*, meaning "in the middle," and the word "communication" derives from the Latin *communicare*, meaning "to share or to make common." Thus, the media are located at the center of, or between people, and through the media, people share experiences that become common knowledge. A part of media studies is concerned with these communal aspects of the media and communication. James Carey (1989) argued that besides transporting information, the significance of the media lies in their *cultural* functions, i.e., in their ability to create and sustain communities and to regulate the relationship and belonging between an individual and society as a whole.

As Dayan and Katz (1992) have demonstrated in empirical studies, the media perform collective *rituals* with a highly social integrative function. The broadcasting media perform a vital role in the ritualization of important societal transitions, such as the funerals of presidents, celebration of national feasts, coronation of a new monarch, and so on. Radio and television's live broadcasts of such events make it possible for an entire community (region, nation, or world) to both witness and participate in the ceremony. Such media events deepen the emotional ties between a community and its members and make the events part of the community's collective memory. The media also become important to the collective mourning process and coping with grief in the case of tragic events, such as the terrorist attack in the United States on 11 September 2001. Kitch (2003) has shown how the news magazines *Time* and *Newsweek*, in their coverage of these events, not only provided information, but also a kind of psychological help, by guiding readers through consecutive stages of grief and providing resilience and closure after a national catastrophe. The treatment of collective emotions is not reserved for the major disasters: it is a recurring feature of the media. The media are not only responsible for emotional guidance, but may also facilitate the actual construction of collective emotions in the first place. A tragic event like the death of Diana, princess of Wales, was turned into an international event by the media (Richards *et al.* 1999), and the media both built up emotional responses and provided examples of how to express grief in a number of ways, for example, by laying flowers at embassies, lighting candles, and so on.

During ritual events, an interesting interplay between the media and the Church can often be noted. Whether it is a tragic disaster like the gunman's attack in Oslo and on the island Utøya (22 July 2011), or a national celebration like the wedding of the Danish Crown Prince Frederik to Mary Donaldson (14 May 2004), the transmission of a religious ceremony plays a minor, yet important role. Most of the media coverage of such events is undertaken by the media themselves, using their traditional genres and formats such as news, interviews, documentaries, live commentaries, and so on. However, ceremonial events are best depicted as direct transmissions: for a moment the media pass the baton to another social institution, making it temporarily responsible for the performance of the ritual. In other words, when the media seek to be at their most solemn, they perform as nakedly as possible: they stage themselves as pure channels of transmission, connecting the community to the religious institution that is conducting the memorial service or performing the wedding ritual. Under these circumstances, the Church and the media interact more directly, and mediatization may be understood as the mutual adaptation to changing social conditions.

As Cottle (2006b) has argued, media rituals are not necessarily consensual or affirmative of a dominant social order. They may occasionally be "politically disruptive or even transformative in their reverberations within civil and wider society" (Cottle 2006b: 411), and despite their festive appearance, celebratory events may serve to exclude particular segments from the imagined community. This may also apply to media rituals and events concerned with religious issues. Thus, the media have not only taken over the performance of affirmative rituals that were previously performed by the Church, but media rituals and events may also serve to challenge and transform religious imaginations and their social status. For instance, the global media coverage of Dan Brown's novel and film *The Da Vinci Code* clearly challenged the Christian Church and suggested an alternative interpretation of key issues in the life of Jesus.

Rothenbuhler (1998) has pointed toward both the habitual and ritual aspects of the use of the media itself. For most people, the use of the media is embedded in everyday routines, and the use of specific media and genres also serves to mark minor and major transitions in the course of the day, the week, the year, and so on. The sound of the morning radio, and reading the newspaper at breakfast, may indicate the beginning of the day in the same way as the final checking of Facebook or email before going to bed at night may ritualize the end of the day. Previously, religious institutions provided such temporal orientation by ringing church bells, conducting morning and evening prayers, and so on. Today, the media mark such nodal points in the temporal flow of everyday life.

A key activity of religious institutions is the worship of symbols, gods, and saints, but they no longer enjoy a monopoly in this field. The media frequently promote worship behavior. A whole section of weekly magazines makes a living out of facilitating parasocial relationships (Horton and Wohl 1956) between the audience of ordinary people and the celebrity world of media personalities, movie stars, royal families, the rich and the famous, and so on. The film, television, and music industries are deliberately seeking to develop cult phenomena, fan clubs, and idolization as an integral element of their marketing efforts, but worship-like behavior may also emerge spontaneously. In a similar vein, modern corporate branding strategies seek to create both a cultural and spiritual relationship between brand, employees, and consumers. Petersen's (2010, 2012) study of young teenage fans' reception of film and television series dealing with supernatural phenomena (e.g., *The Twilight Saga*, *Supernatural*, etc.) demonstrates that the fans' intense emotional engagement in these narratives can be understood as a transformed display of religious emotions or neo-religiosity.

Jenkins (1992a, 1992b) specifies the characteristics of media fan cultures. Among other features, the fans develop a special mode of reception of the key texts, and the fans constitute a kind of interpretative community, as well as an alternative social grouping. Furthermore, fan cultures often take part in the development of an "art world," i.e., special artifacts that in various ways comment on and pay tribute to the worshipped media products. Fan cultures share many of the characteristics of religious groups, although they may differ in the substance of what the adoration is directed toward. The fans do not necessarily believe that the media's heroes and idols possess divine powers, but on the other hand, fans often treat media idols as if they were saints. As Hills (2002) argued, the similarities do not necessarily lead us to equate fan cultures with religious communities. Instead, the parallels bear witness to the fact that, without major changes, a series of religious activities, like worship and idolatry, can be recontextualized in more or less secular settings.

Surveying the media's spiritual function

In order to empirically illustrate the aforementioned arguments concerning the interrelationship between media and religion, a series of questions were posed in consecutive surveys of a representative sample of the Danish adult population (18 years or older) in 2005, 2006, and 2009. One question was intended to chart the

TABLE 4.2 Ways of engaging in spiritual issues. Question: "People may have an interest in spiritual issues, including faith, folk religion, ethics, magical experiences, life and death, and so on. If you are interested in such issues, how did you engage with them during the last couple of months?"

Ways of engaging in spiritual issues	Percent
Discuss with family and close friends	24.3
Watch television programs	22.6
Read non-fiction books (e.g., philosophy and psychology)	10.5
Visit websites/Internet discussions	8.9
Attend church ceremonies	6.7
Read novels	5.8
Attend meetings/public lectures	5.2
Go to the cinema	4.3
Listen to the radio	4.2
Read the Bible (or other holy scripture)	3.9
Other	3.0
Do not engage in such issues	50.4

The respondents were asked to tick a maximum of three possibilities, so that the sum exceeds 100 percent. The question was part of the research institute Zapera's regular Internet-based survey in Denmark (First quarter of 2009). N = 1010.

extent to which Danes use the media to engage in spiritual issues. The questions invited answers that implied a very broad understanding of religion, including "banal religion." As the results in Table 4.2 indicate, discussion with family members and close friends was the most frequent way to engage in spiritual issues. Next, television programs, non-fiction books, and the Internet were frequent ways of engaging in spiritual topics. It is interesting that the institutionalized ways of engaging in spiritual issues – going to church or reading religious texts – were rather marginal activities compared with the use of the media. Reading the Bible (or other religious texts) was the least frequent source mentioned among the possible answers. Reading a novel was just as frequently a way to engage in spiritual issues as going to church. The prominent role played by discussion with family and close friends (rather than talking to the minister or other members of a religious congregation) may reflect how, in a highly modernized society, spiritual issues are considered private and personal, rather than public and social; while at the same time family and friendships have come to serve very emotional functions (Giddens 1992). It should also be noted that many people had not engaged in such matters at all: more than 50 percent had neither used the media nor other sources to explore spiritual issues.

Another question illustrated the extent to which specific media and genres were used as sources concerning the fight between good and evil. As such, the question related to the media as sources of moral orientation, and not necessarily of spiritual guidance, although these aspects may be intertwined. Not surprisingly, as Table 4.3 demonstrates, narrative and fictional media and genres provided most of the stories that made a profound impression on the respondents. Yet factual news was also a frequent source of stories concerning the fight between good and evil and,

TABLE 4.3 Media stories about the fight between good and evil. Question: "The media are full of stories about the fight between good and evil. This may be feature films (e.g., *Star Wars*), novels (e.g., *Harry Potter*), religious books (e.g., the Bible), factual programs (e.g., television news), and so on. Please tick 1–3 media in which you have experienced a story about the fight between good and evil that has made a profound impression on you. If you remember the title, you may specify it."

	Percent
Film	41.1
Television program	25.2
Fiction novel	22.0
Newspaper	14.4
Computer game	11.4
Internet	6.7
Magazine monthly/weekly	6.0
Radio program	6.0
Religious book or text	5.5
Other	3.6
Cannot remember any/don't know	41.4

The respondents were asked to tick a maximum of three possibilities, so that the sum exceeds 100 percent. The question was part of the survey undertaken by the Zapera research institute's quarterly Internet-based survey in Denmark in 2005. N=1005.

accordingly, the two Danish TV newscasts, *Tv-Avisen* and *Nyhederne*, were frequently mentioned as television programs that provided such stories. Religious texts only to a very limited extent made a profound impression on the Danes in this respect. The question invited the respondents to list concrete titles of media products, and the most frequently listed was the *Lord of the Rings* film trilogy. Among the most frequently mentioned films were the *Harry Potter* movies, the Danish *Adams Æbler*, the German *Der Untergang*, and the American *The Passion of the Christ* and *Constantine*. Among fictional novels, Dan Brown's *The Da Vinci Code* and *Angels & Demons* were frequently mentioned together with (again) the *Harry Potter* books and the book *The Lord of the Rings*, as well as the Danish fantasy series, *The Shamer Chronicles*. Among explicit religious writings, the Bible was frequently mentioned.

In order to examine whether the media not only support an existing interest in spiritual issues, but also encourage further interest in such matters, four popular media products were singled out due to their explicit, yet somewhat contrasting, ways of thematizing these issues. The respondents were asked whether these media products increased their interest in "magic and fantasy," "spiritual issues," and/or "religious issues," respectively. This differentiation of possible answers was made in order to distinguish between various aspects of religious issues, since one way of addressing an interest in religion may render other important aspects invisible. "Magic and fantasy" may be said to highlight the supernatural and folk religious aspects; "spiritual issues" may connote existential, philosophical,

TABLE 4.4 The influence of different media stories on an interest in magic and fantasy

The media story has increased my interest in magic and fantasy	Harry Potter *stories (novels, films, and/ or computer games)*	Dan Brown's *novels* (Da Vinci Code *and/or* Angels & Demons)	Lord of the Rings *trilogy (novels, films, and/or computer games)*	World of Warcraft *(computer game)*
Yes	32.3	29.3	35.2	22.5
No	64.6	68.3	62.6	75.5
Don't know	3.1	2.4	2.1	2.0

Tables 4.3, 4.4, and 4.5 indicate the influence of certain media stories on the interest in magic and fantasy, spiritual issues, and religion, as percentages (vertical) of respondents having read, seen, or played at least one version of the media story in question. Among the total number of respondents (N =1007), 588 had read, seen, or played at least one Harry Potter story; 350 had read at least one of the two novels by Dan Brown; 716 had read, seen, or played *Lord of the Rings*; and 133 had played the computer game *World of Warcraft*. The questions were part of the quarterly Internet-based survey undertaken in Denmark in 2005 by the Zapera research institute.

and/or emotional aspects; and "religious issues" may designate an interest in the institutionalized and formal features of religion.

As Table 4.4 shows, for about one-third of the respondents, the *Harry Potter* stories, Dan Brown's novels, and the *Lord of the Rings* trilogy all increased their interest in "magic and fantasy." The computer game *World of Warcraft* increased the respondents' interest in "magic and fantasy" in 22.5 percent of the cases. It should also be noted that most respondents did not report an increased interest in such aspects in all of the four cases. When it comes to the media product's effect on interest in "spiritual issues" (Table 4.5), this was lower in the case of the *Harry Potter* stories, the *Lord of the Rings* trilogy and the computer game *World of Warcraft*. However, more than one out of ten respondents stated that these media products increased their interest in spiritual issues. With regard to an increased interest in "religious issues" (Table 4.6), there was a further decrease in the ratios for these three media products; yet there were still some respondents who felt that the *Harry Potter* series, for instance, made a difference for this topic. Dan Brown's novels

TABLE 4.5 The influence of different media stories on an interest in spiritual issues

The media story has increased my interest in spiritual issues	Harry Potter *stories (novels, films, and/or computer games)*	Dan Brown's *novels* (Da Vinci Code *and/or* Angels & Demons)	Lord of the Rings *(novels, films, and/ or computer games)*	World of Warcraft *(computer game)*
Yes	11.5	38.4	13.4	12.1
No	84.5	58.1	83.7	86.5
Don't know	4.1	3.5	2.9	1.4

TABLE 4.6 The influence of different media stories on an interest in religious issues

The media story has increased my interest in religious issues	Harry Potter stories (novels, films, and/or computer games)	Dan Brown's novels (Da Vinci Code and/or Angels & Demons)	Lord of the Rings (novels, films, and/or computer games)	World of Warcraft (computer game)
Yes	4.5	53.5	7.2	7.1
No	91.7	43.1	90.1	90.0
Don't know	3.7	3.4	2.7	2.8

displayed a rather different pattern compared to the others. His books are more prone to encourage an interest in the spiritual, and even more in the institutionalized bearings of religion, than any of the other three media products. More than half of the respondents reported an increased interest in religious issues after reading these novels. This is not surprising, since Dan Brown's novels deal explicitly with the spiritual and institutionalized aspects of Christianity. It is perhaps far more surprising that media narratives that at first glance seem to have only a remote, if any, relationship with religion, such as *Harry Potter* (Sky 2006), nevertheless stimulate an interest in supernatural and spiritual issues, and even – albeit to a limited extent – encourage interest in more explicit or institutional forms of religion.

An increased interest in such matters is not necessarily equal to an increased belief in magic or religion; on the contrary, it may – as the case of Dan Brown's books demonstrates – go hand-in-hand with a skeptical awareness and critique of dominant forms of religion. In the survey, respondents who had either read the book or seen the movie of *The Da Vinci Code* were asked how far they agreed with Dan Brown's criticism of the Christian Church in the story. It should be noted that, at the time of the survey, the media had already published numerous stories that were highly critical of Dan Brown's historical interpretation in general, and his use of factual details in particular. According to the survey, 50.4 percent of the readers and viewers responded that Dan Brown's critique was either correct or partly correct, and 31.5 percent answered that it was either wrong or partly wrong. The evaluation of the critique differed, furthermore, according to the respondent's type of faith. Only 27.8 percent of respondents with a more traditional belief in a personal god would label Dan Brown's critique correct or partly correct, while 59.7 percent of respondents who believed in a spiritual force would agree or partly agree with his critique (Table 4.7). The receptiveness to Dan Brown's storyline and critique was thus dependent on an already existing and widespread sympathy with individualized forms of religion (see also Partridge 2008), at the same time as the media narrative gave even more credence to such non-institutionalized interest in religiosity. The example of Dan Brown's novels and films illustrates how popular media culture may not only reuse various forms of existing religious stories and imagery, but also stimulate direct criticism of organized religion, while also winning support for alternative religious interpretations.

TABLE 4.7 Readers' and viewers' evaluation of Dan Brown's critique of the Christian Church. Question: "In *The Da Vinci Code* the author Dan Brown criticizes the Christian Church for having suppressed various aspects concerning the lives of Jesus and Mary Magdalene. In general, how do you evaluate the criticism of the Christian Church in *The Da Vinci Code*?"

| | Total | Faith | | | | |
		I believe in a personal god	I believe in a spiritual force	I am in doubt about the existence of a god or a spiritual force	I am not a believer	Other
Wrong	14.5	28.9	9.2	13.0	12.5	14.3
Partly wrong	17.0	22.2	17.2	18.0	12.5	0.0
Partly correct	39.8	21.1	49.4	38.0	42.0	28.6
Correct	10.6	6.7	10.3	10.0	14.3	14.3
Don't know	18.2	21.1	13.8	21.0	18.8	42.9
Total	100.1	100.0	99.9	100.0	100.1	100.1

Among the total number of respondents in the survey (N=1004), 483 people had read the book or seen the movie. Only responses from these actual readers and/or viewers are included in the table. Distribution in percent in total and according to type of faith. The question was part of a special Internet-based survey undertaken in 2006 in Denmark by the Zapera research institute.

Epilog

In this chapter, a framework has been developed to conceptualize how the media may influence religious imaginations, practices, and authority. The developments are complex, and the media do not necessarily have a uniform influence on religion: in some instances, the media may further a re-sacralization of society; in others, they undermine the authority of institutionalized religion and promote secular imaginations, rituals, and modes of worship. At a general level, these processes share a common feature: they are all evidence of the mediatization of religion. Through mediatization, religious imaginations and practices become increasingly dependent upon the media. As conduits of communication, the media have become an important, if not primary source of imagery and texts concerning magic, spiritualism, and religion, as well as means for interaction about such issues. As languages, the media mold religious imagination in accordance with the genres of popular culture, and considered as cultural environments the media have partly taken over many of the social functions of the institutionalized religions, providing both moral and spiritual guidance, and a sense of community. We have, furthermore, identified three forms of mediatized religion, each of which entails a particular cluster of media genres, religious content, communicative functions, and particular challenges to the Protestant Church. Consequently, in high modernity institutionalized religion plays a less prominent role in the communication of religious beliefs and, instead, various forms of mediatized religion move to the fore of society's religious imagination.

5

THE MEDIATIZATION OF PLAY

From bricks to bytes

Introduction

Half a century ago, children's toys were made of *solid materials*: wood, iron, plastic, etc. To play was to some extent synonymous with physical activity, either through the movement of dolls or soldiers, or the running and jumping of the children themselves. Children's toys often resembled the material inventory of the adult world: they were miniatures of mother and father's real worlds. Girls played with small replicas of the inventory of the household, in particular clothes, kitchen utensils, and baby accessories. Boys played with building tools or technical artifacts from the modern world: ships, cars, trains, guns, airplanes, etc.

Today, children's toys are increasingly of an *immaterial* nature. Although the old, solid types of toys are still around, this is increasingly in competition with "softer" kinds of playthings, especially software for computer and video games, although other toys, too, increasingly involve symbolic representations based on film, television, and computer games. To a great extent, play has become a mental activity involving imagination, planning, simulation, communication, role-playing, etc. Furthermore, play has become intertwined with the manipulation of audiovisual representations and narratives. Physical activity, to a limited extent, is still a necessary component of playing, but the manipulation of objects no longer involves the same concrete, sensory-motor action. Objects are visual representations on a screen and they are manipulated via a media interface: the mouse, the joystick, the game pad, etc. Children's toys seldom resemble the inventory of mother and father's worlds. Instead, they are very often part of a fantasy world, situated in a distant past or future, a faraway galaxy, or a supernatural environment. The actors inhabiting these imagined universes are seldom realistic characters. On the contrary, they often possess superhuman strength, power, wealth, or beauty; or they are only partly human, i.e., part-machine part-human (e.g., Transformers), or part-human part-animal (e.g., Spider-Man).

The transformation of children's play and toys, among other factors, has also been stimulated by the proliferation of the media. Play has become mediatized and, through this process, play is increasingly influenced by the logic of the media, including their technology, economic infrastructure, symbolic content, and communicative affordances. Play is subject to direct mediatization (see Chapter 2) in the sense that a considerable proportion of the play activities of children, adolescents, and adults take place via interaction with a media. This is particularly the case with computer and video games, which have not only adapted a multitude of already existing games and forms of play, such as board games, card games, song competitions, guessing games, etc., but also developed their own genres of play and gaming. During the last three decades, computer and video games have achieved enormous success, making computer and video gaming a familiar activity for the majority of children and adolescents, while also spreading rapidly among the adult population. As I will return to later, the sheer number of people and the time dedicated to computer and video gaming provide a strong indicator of how far the direct mediatization of play has evolved.

There is also an indirect mediatization of play taking place, in the sense that more and more forms of play, and in particular the artifacts – toys – they involve, are influenced by the media's symbolic content and business cycle. The interplay between the media and toys has intensified and made toys far more financially dependent on the media (Kline 1993, 1995a, 1995b). As children have developed into an important consumer segment, the advertising industry and toy manufacturers have become close allies; and since the toy business is volatile and sensitive to the changing interests and fashions among children, it is highly dependent on advertising and branding to ensure its market penetration and some degree of predictability. The media are also dependent on advertisement from the toy industry. Commercial broadcasters in both Europe and the United States have generally argued against too many restrictions on television commercials for children, since this would make it less attractive to produce and broadcast children's television. Public service television in Europe has traditionally provided a barrier between children's television and commercial interests, but as the deregulation policies gathered momentum in the 1980s, children's television in Europe has also become more and more dependent on advertising directed at children.

The economic link between toys and the media is not only strong in the case of advertising, but is also equally visible in the areas of sponsorship and merchandising. Furthermore, the borderline between the toy and media industries is becoming blurred. The global expansion of Disney with theme parks and Disney stores is a prominent example of the media industry running commercial "playgrounds" and branded toyshops (Wasko 2001). The indirect mediatization is highly visible through licensing, i.e., the ever more intensive use of the media's symbolic content (heroes, narratives, etc.) in toys. Through licensing, toys offer a re-enactment or modified rehearsal of the media stories with which the child is already familiar.

As a consequence of direct and indirect mediatization, both play and toys have undergone several alterations. In the following analysis we will consider these changes using the concepts of imaginarization, narrativization, and virtualization. To illustrate the process of mediatization, we will provide a historical case study of the toy manufacturer LEGO that will focus on how toys have changed due to both new market conditions and a changing children's culture, which both stimulate media influence. Before exploring the historical developments, we will take a look at some broader social and cultural developments that will provide a backdrop for our understanding of the contemporary mediatization of play: the changing notion of childhood, the commercial convergence between media, toys, and advertising, and the development of computer gaming as a dominant play activity among children and adolescents.

The transformation of childhood

Not only have toys and play been altered, but a change in the very notion of childhood and adolescence has taken place. In his pioneering work on the history of childhood, Philippe Ariès (1962) demonstrates that, at any given time, the concept of childhood and the view of the child are influenced in important ways by specific cultures. In a theoretical overview of paradigms informing research on childhood, Allison *et al.* (1998) point to a general development in the understanding of children and childhood. Earlier research focused on the concept of the child as "becoming" a human being, by considering the different developmental stages from infant to adult, while newer research to a far greater degree considers the child as a "being," i.e., an already existing social and cultural character. Previously, researchers would see the child as an unfinished human being, whereas contemporary research to a greater degree perceives the child as a well-founded individual, whose competences and culture should not be reduced to a developmental stage on the way to mature adulthood. This shift from "becoming" to "being" does not imply that the child is considered to be passive. On the contrary, instead of focusing on the child's need to learn and accommodate to the demands of the adult world, newer strands of research consider the child to be an active and self-reliant individual who interacts with his or her social environment in various ways, without necessarily being guided by an overall developmental path toward adulthood.

It is, of course, not only within research that the concept of childhood and youth has changed. To some extent, we find parallel changes in ideas about childhood and youth in society in general. Childhood and youth have increasingly emerged as separate realms of experience and culture that not only exist separately from the adult world, but also in various aspects exhibit distinct qualities that are at odds with the culture of adults. The children's world is ascribed a series of positive values such as play, fantasy, and creativity, in contrast to the adult world's heavy burden of work, routine, and duties. Youth is very often understood as a time of opportunity, between the innocence of childhood and the duties of adulthood. Youth denotes a sphere of personal development, sexual exploration, and new social relationships. Thus, in high modernity, youth is the realm of individual self-realization *par excellence*; but precisely because of this potential, young people are expected to demonstrate a high degree of reflexivity, in order to create their own lives and identities in a society where the norms and experience of the older generations no longer provide sound guidelines (Ziehe 1989).

The differentiation of childhood and youth as separate cultural domains, ruled by values other than those of adult society, is related to certain general and long-term transformations in modern society that became very prominent in the period after World War II. Industrialization and urbanization separated the family's home from the workplace and gradually made children unimportant to the labor force. The family gradually lost several social functions and duties, and through this process it was now possible to put more emphasis on the emotional and personal aspects of the relationships among family members. At the same time, the extension of compulsory education meant that children and young people would spend the first 10–20 years of their lives outside the institutions of adult society. In this way, children and young people were no longer expected to become part of, or to contribute to, the adult world. In actual fact, they came to spend many years in another social world of school, family, and leisure time, in which life as a child, adolescent, and young person would be regulated by other norms than those of the adult world. The rapidly expanding consumer market in the post-war period also increased opportunities for, and the importance of, leisure activities in the growing children and youth cultures.

These developments in the notion of childhood and youth are also reflected in the media supplied to these segments of the population, including the media's choice of topics and modes of address toward children and young people. In her historical analysis of Danish television for children and young people, Christensen (2006) demonstrates how children's television of the 1950s was dominated by programs in which children demonstrated their skills in a variety of ways (physically, artistically, cognitively, etc.) in order to prove that they were almost as good as adults. Similarly, television programs aimed at younger people did not deal with a specific youth culture, but were driven by an adult ethos of lending the younger generation a helping hand by providing advice and good ideas on their way to adulthood. From the 1960s and onward, television for children and young people increasingly sought to give children and young people their own voice and to portray society from the perspective of the children and young people themselves. In the 1960s and 1970s, this shift in perspective often made way for a new social realism with a political tone and a critique of the social and cultural conditions faced by children and young people in both Denmark and other countries, especially in the Third World. In the 1980s, children's television became more and more inward-looking, with focus on the children's own world, and cultivated an interest in fantasy, magic, and creative play. Children were hereby portrayed as "free and resourceful individuals in contrast to the reality fixated and unimaginative adults" (Christensen 2006: 87; my translation). Starting in the 1990s, both children's and young people's television became more integrated into a consumer culture, and children and young people were portrayed and addressed as competent individuals who created their own identities through consumption, not least the consumption of media products.

Kids getting older younger

Together with other social factors, the media have redrawn the boundaries between the cultures of children, young people, and adults. As the example of Danish television demonstrates, the media have raised the value of children and youth cultures, but at the same time they have given children and young people access to the experience of topics that hitherto were reserved for adults (Meyrowitz 1986). Of special interest to the analysis of toys and media is the changing relationship between childhood and youth. During the last several decades, a general change in children's media and consumer habits is discernable, and among market analysts this development is labeled K.G.O.Y., i.e., Kids Getting Older Younger. Put simply, at an earlier age children begin to develop behavior, including consumer behavior, that is more teenage-like, and as a consequence children between the ages of roughly 8 and 12 are labeled "tweens" or "tweenagers," i.e., a contraction of "in between" and "teenagers." This new age group reflects a development by which children at an early age become more conscious of their physical appearance (choice of clothes, makeup, hairstyle, etc.) and start to dress like teenagers, while their leisure activities become more "mature," including the consumption of a wide range of media products, such as music, television, movies, computer games, mobile phones, the Internet, etc. There is also a biological aspect to the children's earlier maturity, in that girls are beginning to reach puberty at an earlier age.

The changing consumer habits among children are partly a consequence of the intensification of marketing aimed at younger age groups, with the differentiation of this target group into age segments. Cook and Kaiser (2004) trace the history of the "tween" category back to the 1940s in the United States. At that time, the teenager was gradually developed as a marketing segment by the clothing industry, and as a result the "preteen" arose as a precursor to the "tween" category. Kay Hymowitz (2000) considers Mattel's promotion of the Barbie doll in 1959 as the key toy marking the beginning of "the media's teening of childhood" (Hymowitz 2000: 110; quoted from Cook and Kaiser 2004: 212).

With Mattel's Barbie series, girls' play with dolls was no longer focused on caretaking and nurturing, but was brought into a teenage and adult universe of romance, lifestyle, and consumption. This has, not least, resulted in the increased sexualization of girls, giving rise to occasional public debates concerning, for example, the sale of g-string underwear to young girls. The more recent expansion of the marketing of clothes, cosmetics, and other lifestyle products for younger boys will undoubtedly also increase the sexualization of "tween" boys. For the toy industry in general, however, the early maturing of children poses a serious problem, because it reduces the number of years that children actually play with toys. The earlier children are introduced to a tween or teenage culture, the faster they will put the toys on the back shelf and distance themselves from toys as something childish. In order to compensate for this development, the toy industry seeks to develop toys with a more mature lifestyle component and to achieve further product differentiation according to age group, allowing for a gradual reduction of the level of "childishness" for each age group.

The cultural concept of adult identity has also changed. In a traditional or early modern society, old age would usually be considered an index of maturity and experience, thereby requiring younger people to respect their elders. In the era of high modernity, age has become a problem, not least due to society's incessant demands for flexibility and innovation of the workforce. For instance, the call for lifelong learning and further education in most sectors of society reflects that completing an education and getting a job are no longer a culminating point in a person's life. As an adult, you can no longer expect to live on already achieved knowledge or skills, but must – like younger people – be prepared to continually learn, abandon well-known skills and procedures, and learn new methods in order to keep pace with society's demands. Concurrently, becoming older also poses a cultural problem, as youth has become the ideal for adults. In their physical appearance and social activities, adults and, in particular adult females, must look younger and display youthful behavior. Parallel to the K.G.O.Y. phenomenon, the older generations are subject to the A.S.Y.L. trend, i.e., Adults Staying Younger Longer. The paradox is that the processes that are responsible for childhood and youth acquiring the status of independent cultures, with separate norms and behaviors compared to the adult world, also cause the adult identity to feed on the normative ideals of the self-same childhood and youth. Play and creativity are no longer juxtaposed with the work-life of adults, but to some extent have become an important productive force in high modernity. Richard Florida's (2004) celebration of the "creative class" is one of many examples of how play and creativity are assigned key roles in the so-called knowledge economy.

The fact that the media bring children and young people into closer contact with adult themes such as sex, violence, and alcohol, and promote adult-like beauty ideals and consumer habits, has been subject to severe cultural criticism from both academics and the broader public. Examples of such criticism from academic circles include David Elkind's *The Hurried Child: Growing Up Too Soon, Too Fast* (1981) and Neil Postman's *The Disappearance of Childhood* (1982). Although their academic approaches are not the same, they are both concerned that children are not allowed to stay children for as long as they apparently did before, but instead become premature grown-ups who are exposed to problems they are neither emotionally nor socially mature enough to handle.

David Buckingham (2000) convincingly examines how this cultural criticism is often based on a conservative sentimentalism about childhood as the threatened or lost kingdom, while also promoting a cultural political agenda aimed at reconstructing a period in which parental authority, together with a society based on the values of a print culture, may reassert adult control over children's access to knowledge and experience. Such an agenda is often based on middle-class values and fails to see that, in the past, not all children lived a protected life behind the walls of a well-functioning family. As Stephanie Coontz (2000) also documents, contemporary ideas and values about family, gender, and childhood are saturated with nostalgia about the healthy, safe, and well-functioning family life of the past.

Buckingham (2000) also points to quite another kind of sentimentalism in both media research and the general public regarding children and their media use. It is the widespread notion of the "competent child" that endows the child – precisely because of his or her childish nature (spontaneity, curiosity, etc.) – with a set of innate talents to master the media for creative purposes. According to this view, children's early and massive use of computers, the Internet, and mobile phones is seen as empirical evidence of such innate competence. The general focus of reception studies on the audience's own use of the media has similarly underpinned the notion of the competent child, and downplayed the possible influence of the media system on the user's choice and reception of media products (see also Chapter 1). The first kind of sentimentalism often finds its supporters among cultural critics in the public sphere, while the second kind is often advocated by spokesmen for the media industry. As Buckingham (2000: 105) suggests, the discussion of children and the media is "often reduced to a simple choice between these two positions: if one is false, then the other must necessarily be true." Either the media are dangerous and children must be protected against them, or children are competent users of media that will enrich their childhoods. Both standpoints rest on an essentialist view of children and their media use in which the individual child's abilities and actions are considered in isolation. In contrast, Buckingham (ibid.: 105–6, emphasis in original) wants to argue "for a more fully *social* account of the relationship between children and the media, which situates our analysis of the audience within a broader understanding of social, institutional and historical change." It is precisely such an approach we will follow in the subsequent analysis of the mediatization of play.

The interplay between the toy and media industries

The relationship between the toy and media industries began to develop in the post-war years in the United States, where a fully commercial broadcasting industry was developing, in contrast to the European continent, which was dominated by publicly regulated radio and television services. In fundamental terms, the interplay between the toy and media industries began with the introduction of children's television, consisting of cartoons and other forms of entertainment programs, in the 1950s. An important step was taken in 1955 with the success of *Disney's Mickey Mouse Club*, a mixed program for children and youngsters. Until then, advertisers had shown little interest in children's television, but now toy advertising became an important part of the commercial breaks during the hours that quickly became institutionalized as the permanent time slots for children's television: weekday afternoons and Saturday mornings (Kline 1993). Disney was also behind another important event in 1955: the film premiere of *Davy Crockett, King of the Wild Frontier*, based on the Davy Crockett television series, and this film was followed by a major merchandise marketing effort consisting of clothing, toys, games, playing cards, etc. (Wasko 2008).

Starting in the 1960s, children's programming became an established and growing ingredient of American television, and subsequently the marketing of goods targeted at the children segment expanded (Engelhardt 1986; Kline 1993). Bringing advertising, television programs and toys into a common circuit provided a new economic synergy. The American toy manufacturer Mattel's television advertising strategy is considered to be crucial to this development:

> Mattel's decision to advertise toys to children on national television fifty-two weeks a year so revolutionized the industry that it is not an exaggeration to divide the history of the American toy business into two eras, before and after television.
>
> *(Stern and Schoenhaus 1990: 55)*

The fictional universes of children's television were opened up to licensing and merchandising, and toys were increasingly advertised on television, not only in commercials, but also via fictional television series that to some extent were transformed into half-hour advertisements for toy products. At the end of the 1960s, the consequences of this cooperation between the media, toy, and advertising industries had become so visible that it spurred counter-reactions. The American Public Broadcasting Service (PBS) developed *Sesame Street* as an educational and quality alternative to the commercial competitors; but *Sesame Street* itself was criticized for its narrative style (Hendershot 1999), which was not that different from commercial children's television. Moreover, *Sesame Street* also had considerable income from the merchandising of characters, etc. The controversy surrounding the major American toy manufacturer Mattel's "Hot Wheels" model car series illustrates the general development and conflict (Engelhardt 1986). In addition to selling the "Hot Wheels" toys, the American network ABC broadcast a cartoon of the same name, featuring the cars as the most prominent ingredient. A competitor filed a complaint to the American Federal Communications Commission (FCC), arguing that the cartoon should in effect be considered a commercial for "Hot Wheels." The FCC sustained the claim that this type of cooperation was contrary to the public nature of the television medium, and ABC cancelled the cartoon series. The FCC's ruling on this case stated that:

> [T]here can be no doubt that in this program, Mattell receives commercial promotion for its product beyond the time [allowed] for commercial advertising. ... We find this pattern disturbing ... for [it] subordinates programming in the interest of the public to programming in the interest of salability.
>
> *(quoted from Engelhardt 1986: 75)*

During the 1970s, different citizens' groups attempted, through lobbying, etc., to counter the most striking consequences of the new commercial synergy between television and toys. The Reaganism of the 1980s, however, provided a political context favorable to increased commercial interaction between the media and toy industries. The deregulation of American television during the Reagan administration allowed the further commercialization of children's television, which developed into the toy industry's most important channel of communication with its customers, the children. Currently, with the deregulation of television in Europe and elsewhere since the 1980s, the cooperation between television and toy manufacturers has also become visible in many other countries.

The commercial partnership between the television, advertising, and toy industries affected the character of both toys and play. As Cross (1997) suggests in his detailed study of the American toy industry, play became divorced from the constraints of parents and their realities. The new toys were not just modern versions of old toys:

> [T]he fantasy playthings of the 1980s and 1990s represent something more. Toys have become part of a vast interconnected industry that creates novel fantasies for profit. This industry encompasses movies, TV shows, videos, and other media. It embraces licensed images that appear from everything from caps and lunch boxes to toys. Those fantasies designed for the youth market celebrate a world free from real adults.
>
> *(Cross 1997: 188)*

Television commercials and cartoons are particularly suitable for the promotion of toys that include, or simply consist of, fictional characters. Television's narrative and visual depictions of fictional characters could present the toys in attractive ways, and as a result an endless series of fictional characters, each with his or her own specific character traits and accessories (weapons, clothes, etc.), was introduced in the toy market: Barbie and Ken, G. I. Joe, He-Man, My Little Pony, Spider-Man, Ninja Turtles, Pokémon, Bratz, etc. The synergy among the different industries revolving around television advertising for children has undoubtedly affected children's consumer choices, including their choice of toys. A comprehensive review of 25 years of research on the consumer socialization of children concludes that "the evidence to date provides strong support for the influence of television advertising on children's product preferences and choices" (John 1999: 207). For example, a Canadian study compared children's wish lists for Santa Claus and found that children exposed to cable television advertising for character toys twice as often put such toys on their lists, compared to children who did not have this television access (Kline 1993: 322).

Although television was the crucial medium for initiating the interplay between media, advertising, and the toy industry, other media have increasingly played a role in this circuit: cartoons, films, music, etc. The integration of computer, Internet, and mobile media in particular has changed the relationship between toys and the media, making online gaming a dominant and commoditized form of play. What began as a commercial interaction between different commodities and cultural phenomena has developed into a field where the borders between toys and media are less clear and in many cases are disappearing. Toys are increasingly becoming computer-based and connected to the online world, first and foremost in the form of computer games, but other types of toys are also equipped with microchips and software and have become intelligent, interactive, or accompanied by a virtual world on the Internet. At www.barbie.com, Mattel incorporates playing with Barbie dolls into a virtual world of games, videos, and tips about fashion. Children's play with plush animals is similarly integrated into a virtual and commoditized environment. In 2005, the company Ganz became highly successful with its series of plush toys called Webkinz. By activating a digital code on the plush animal, the child can play with it in the virtual Webkinz world (Wasko 2010).

Since the late 1990s, media companies like Nintendo, Sony, and Microsoft have emerged as major players in the toy business, and traditional toy manufacturers have lost market shares, or have been forced to develop toys with a media component. The media are no longer secondary aspects of toys; nor do they primarily function as advertisers of the "real" toy product. The media have been integrated into toys and play itself, and the physical toys may just as well promote the media as vice-versa. Yet the growing synergy between the media and toy industries is not only a result of new marketing opportunities. The aforementioned changing consumer habits of children and young people have also brought the toy industry closer to the media. As children become more and more infatuated with the media in their daily lives, toy manufacturers are forced to follow suit and accommodate to this new reality. The media–advertising–toy circuit began as a way to increase toy sales, but the media have gradually developed from a commercial partner to a cultural environment and socio-economic reality to which toy manufacturers are obliged to adjust.

Apart from opening a new toy market, the media also provide new incentives for the renewal of existing products and for much more elaborate communication and modes of contact with consumers. When a consumer purchases an item of media hardware, he or she will be inclined to demand a continuous supply of new software, in order to sustain the attractiveness of playing with the hardware, e.g., new computer games, new movies, new songs, etc. Soccer as a form of play, for instance, has been transformed into a major media business via computer games that invite the players to renew their existing software on a yearly basis when new versions and expansion packages of the same software are released. Furthermore, digital technologies, in combination with the Internet, provide an opportunity for marketing, distribution, and direct sales to the customers. Additionally, the Internet is used to create virtual communities in order to promote children's contact with and attachment to toy products and brands, for instance, by playing games and talking to other children via the company's community site. As stated by the head of K Zero, a British company specializing in the commercial potentials of virtual communities, concerning the incentive of virtual play: "The motivation for these companies to create virtual playgrounds is simple: It's an extension of the real world toy play and keeps the children in a 'branded' frame of mind" (De Mesa 2008: 1).

Children controlling media usage

The growing importance of media in the lives of children and young people in a very simple, yet important, way is reflected in the number of media they have access to, and the amount of time they spend using them. Radio, television, and various media for listening to music have been accessible to children and young people for several decades, and interactive media like the Internet and mobile telephones have spread rapidly during the last two decades. In addition to the growing number of media that children and young people have access to, and the increasing number of hours spent on media consumption, there is a qualitative shift in the growing influence that children and young people have gained over their own media consumption. This is because the media have become more interactive, allowing children and young people to participate in mediated communication of various kinds, and children and young people have gained greater control of the situations in which the media are consumed, not least because children and young people today own many more media devices and have direct access to them from their own bedrooms.

According to the *EU Kids Online* survey of media use among children and young people aged 9–16 in 25 European countries in 2010, the absolute majority of children and young people use the Internet. Particularly in northern Europe, almost everyone in this age group has some form of access to the online world: Finland (98 percent), Norway (98 percent), United Kingdom (98 percent), Poland (97 percent), and Germany (86 percent). In southern Europe, the access is still somewhat more limited, but most children and young people have access: Spain (80 percent), Turkey (65 percent) and Greece (59 percent) (Livingstone *et al.* 2011: 163). On average, 93 percent of European children using the Internet go online at least weekly, and 60 percent go online every day or almost every day. The home is the most common location for Internet use (87 percent of users) followed by the school (63 percent). Forty-nine percent have access to the Internet from their bedrooms, and 33 percent via mobile or other handheld devices (Livingstone *et al.* 2011: 5). The older the children get, the more time they spend on the Internet: 9–10 year-old users spend roughly an hour a day, while 15–16 year-old users spend double that amount of time. Gender seems to play a minor role regarding the time spent on the Internet (Livingstone *et al.* 2011: 26). See Table 5.1 for details.

As noted, approximately half of the users have online access from their own bedrooms, and here we find the same pattern of young people having more access from their own bedrooms compared to younger children (see Table 5.2). There

TABLE 5.1 Internet use in minutes by European children and young people on an average day in 2010

All children and young people	88
Girls	85
Boys	91
9–10 years	58
11–12 years	74
13–14 years	97
15–16 years	118

The basis is children and young people aged 9–16 using the Internet.
Source: EU Kids Online survey (Livingstone *et al.* 2011: 25)

TABLE 5.2 Location of Internet use by European children and young people in 2010

	Own bedroom at home	At home, but not in own bedroom
All children and young people	49	38
Girls	47	39
Boys	50	37
9–10 years	30	55
11–12 years	42	43
13–14 years	52	34
15–16 years	67	23

The basis is children and young people aged 9–16 using the Internet.
Source: EU Kids Online survey (Livingstone *et al.* 2011: 20)

are, however, considerable national variations as regards children and young people's control of Internet resources. For instance, in Denmark, 74 percent of users have access from their own bedrooms, and in the United Kingdom 52 percent of users have this kind of access, while only 37 percent of Hungarian children and young people use the Internet from their own bedrooms.

In the case of children's use of mobile phones, we find similar patterns. The Eurobarometer survey in 2008 reports that 64 percent of children (6–17 years of age) in Europe use a mobile phone of their own. Children in Spain (48 percent) and France (50 percent) are the least likely to have a mobile phone of their own, whereas children in Lithuania (88 percent) and Finland (87 percent) are the most frequent owners of mobile phones. Again we find important age differences, indicating that the older the child is, the more likely he or she is to have a mobile phone of his or her own. At the age of 6 years, 11 percent of European children use a mobile phone of their own. At the age of 11, 64 percent will have a mobile phone, and at the age of 17, almost everyone (95 percent) will use a mobile phone of their own (Eurobarometer 2008: 19–20).

Bovill and Livingstone (2001) were among the first to discuss the emergence of media-rich bedrooms for children in Europe. Concurrently with modernization and growing affluence in the second half of the twentieth century, children in the western world increasingly have their own bedroom, and they spend a considerable amount of their leisure time in their bedrooms, either alone or together with friends or siblings. There are naturally many national and social differences, but compared to earlier times, more lower-income families have acquired sufficient domestic space to allow children to have their own bedrooms too. With the growing number of media available in the household in general, and in the children's bedrooms in particular, the domestic space of the family and children is further individualized and privatized, allowing each of the family members to disengage him- or herself from the communal family space and pursue individual interests involving media consumption. The privatization of the emerging bedroom culture also implies that children have acquired a new and independent presence in the household. Earlier, they would to a greater extent play outside with other children, but now they have the opportunity to be present in the family household without necessarily being subject to a high degree of parental control. In general, the entry of the media into children's bedrooms increases the level of media consumption, at the same time as parents' influence on the content of their children's media usage diminishes. Parents have not lost control of their children's media behavior completely, but increasingly parents have to negotiate the norms of appropriate media behavior with their children in a new context "which pits a discourse of new opportunities and consumer choice against one of the parental duties to manage appropriately the social development of their children" (Bovill and Livingstone 2001: 14).

The children's media-rich bedrooms not only individualize and privatize media consumption, but also connect the children to society at large, surpassing the authority of their parents. Access to various mass media exposes them to a multiplicity of experiences and social spheres in the adult world (Meyrowitz 1986), and the spread of interactive media (mobile phones, computer games, the Internet, etc.) allows them to connect to dispersed social networks of other children and young people. At the time of the cross-national study by Bovill and Livingstone (2001), the introduction of interactive media to children's bedrooms was still restricted, due to high prices and low-speed networks, but since then such media have become the standard inventory in children's bedrooms in many countries, including the USA and northern Europe. Recent figures from Denmark may serve to illustrate the diversity of media in children's bedrooms, even among young children. In 2011, 34.4 percent of Danish children aged 5–7 years had their own television sets, among the 13–18-year-olds, the figure was 75.7 percent. DVD players and recorders are also very frequent: among the 8–12 age group, 26.6 percent had a DVD player in their bedrooms, while 46.2 percent of the 13–18 age group had one (see Table 5.3). Few in the 5–7 age group had a computer in their own bedrooms, but more than one-third of the tweens did. Among the 13–18 age group, almost everyone will have either a laptop or a stationary computer. Internet access from the bedroom follows a similar pattern, so that many tweens and young people may access various websites and virtual communities on their own. A PlayStation 2 was found in the rooms of 21.7 percent of the 8–12-year-old children, in particular among the boys, and to this figure we must add the presence of several other types of games consoles: for example, the Xbox, PlayStation 3, etc. For instance, the Nintendo WII was found in 15.4 percent of teenagers' room. Various types of mobile music players (MP3, iPod, etc.) become popular around the ages of 8–12, and here the girls are a little more likely to possess them. Owning a mobile phone is a reality for most 8–12-year-olds, and among 13–18-year-olds ownership of a mobile phone is almost universal. Via access to the media from their own bedrooms, children and young people have acquired greater independence in their use of the media, but it is also worth noting that they may increasingly access the media in a multitude of social settings such as kindergartens, schools, libraries, youth clubs, cafés, etc.

TABLE 5.3 Various types of media that children and young people have in their own rooms in Denmark in 2011

	5–7-year-olds			8–12-year-olds			13–18-year-olds		
	Total	*Boys*	*Girls*	*Total*	*Boys*	*Girls*	*Total*	*Boys*	*Girls*
Television – CRT or flat-screen	34.4	36.9	31.8	59.1	60.6	57.5	75.7	77.2	74.1
DVD player/ recorder	20	18.7	21.4	26.6	22.9	30.5	46.2	40.3	52.4
PC/computer	9	9.5	8.4	18.3	22.9	13.5	21.6	33.7	8.9
Laptop PC/ computer	10	5.7	14.4	32.6	26.5	39	75.2	67.9	82.9
Internet access	18.7	14.7	22.9	42.8	44.4	41.2	74.2	75.7	72.6
PlayStation 2	8.5	10.9	6.0	21.7	32.2	10.6	25.4	33	17.3
Nintendo WII	3.7	3.8	3.6	12.8	15.2	10.2	13	15.4	10.5
MP3 player	11.2	8.3	14.2	23.8	19.1	28.8	37.4	36.9	38
iPod	8.1	4.5	11.8	21.2	15.6	27.1	52.9	47.4	58.6
Own mobile phone	5.4	3.6	7.2	77.1	74.6	79.8	94.6	93.7	95.5

By percentage of the age group. Sample size for each of the age groups: 5–7-year-olds, N=404; 8–12-year-olds, N=709; and 13–18-year-olds, N=911.

Source: Gallup's *Children and Youth Index* (Autumn 2011)

As households become more and more saturated with media, the play activities of all ages are gradually mediatized. As mentioned earlier, computer games represent a direct mediatization of play and it is increasingly being recognized that computer games signify an important change in the leisure and play activities in society. For example, a political resolution adopted by the European Parliament stressed "that video games are one of the favourite recreational activities of citizens of all ages and social origins" and called for various political measures to regulate the market for computer games, in order to both stimulate the educational use of computer games and counter the potential dangers of "incorrect use of video games by minors" (European Parliament 2009: 4).

The amount of time children and young people spend on computer and video games may be seen as one indicator of the importance of this form of mediatized play. Computer games can be played on a variety of media platforms and today many children and young people have access to these media in their homes, but also elsewhere in kindergartens, schools, youth clubs, etc. Tables 5.4 and 5.5 give an overview of the time children and young people "on an average weekday" in 2011 spent on PC computer games and online games, respectively. A majority of all age groups spent at least some time playing PC games, but the amount of time varied considerably across age groups and gender. Among the 5–7-year-olds, there is not much difference between the two genders, but the older they get, the more PC games become a male activity. This is particularly the case with the 13–18-year-old boys, among whom we find a larger number of heavy users. Within this age group, 23.1 percent of the boys spent three hours or more on PC

TABLE 5.4 Time spent playing computer games on PCs by children and young people in Denmark in 2011. Answers to the question: "How much time do you spend playing PC computer games on an average weekday?"

	5–7-year-olds			8–12-year-olds			13–18-year-olds		
	Total	Boys	Girls	Total	Boys	Girls	Total	Boys	Girls
Do not spend time on	45.7	43.1	48.3	33.2	25.4	41.4	47.0	22.1	73.1
Less than 30 min.	37.9	36.9	39	24.1	25	23.2	13.8	15.2	12.3
30 min. to 1 hour	8.6	10.6	6.5	20.1	21.8	18.2	11.1	17.2	4.7
1–2 hours	2.8	3.6	2	12.0	14.7	9.1	10.4	16.9	3.5
3–4 hours	0.2	0.4	0	3.7	5.7	1.6	9.2	15.8	2.3
5–6 hours	0	0	0	0.5	0.8	0.2	2.9	5.2	0.4
More than 7 hours	0	0	0	0.5	0.9	0	1.4	2.1	0.8
No answer	4.4	3.6	5.3	6.0	5.7	6.2	4.2	5.6	2.7

By percentage of the age group. Sample size for each of the age groups: 5–7-year-olds, N=404; 8–12-year-olds, N=709; and 13–18-year-olds, N=911. The time ranges are simplified in order to make it easier for children to respond.

Source: Gallup's *Children and Youth Index* (Autumn 2011)

TABLE 5.5 Time spent playing online computer games by children and young people in Denmark in 2011. Answers to the question: "How much time do you spend playing online computer games on an average weekday?"

	5–7-year-olds			8–12-year-olds			13–18-year-olds		
	Total	Boys	Girls	Total	Boys	Girls	Total	Boys	Girls
Do not spend time on	50.6	47.9	53.3	26.7	22.8	30.9	41.3	29.1	54.1
Less than 30 min.	31	32.4	29.6	26.2	22.3	30.2	22.6	20.4	24.9
30 min. to 1 hour	10.1	11.3	8.9	22.7	24.9	20.4	10.3	11.8	8.7
1–2 hours	3.6	4.3	2.9	13.1	14.8	11.4	8.8	12.1	5.4
3–4 hours	0.2	0.4	0	5.3	7.9	2.6	8.7	15.4	1.6
5–6 hours	0	0	0	0.3	0.7	0	2.2	3.8	0.4
More than 7 hours	0	0	0	0.7	1.1	0.2	1.3	1.9	0.7
No answer	4.4	3.6	5.3	5	5.6	4.3	4.9	5.5	4.2

By percentage of the age group. Sample size for each of the age groups: 5–7-year-olds, N=404; 8–12-year-olds, N=709; and 13–18-year-olds, N=911. The time ranges are simplified in order to make it easier for children to respond.

Source: Gallup's *Children and Youth Index* (Autumn 2011).

games on an average weekday. At the same time, we see that three out of four of the 13–18-year-old girls did not spend any time playing PC games on weekdays. We find similar patterns for the use of online computer games, although the girls played online games more often than PC games.

Computer games have not only become widely popular among children and young people, but are also becoming a prominent adult leisure activity. A national survey conducted by the American Entertainment Software Association (ESA) reported in 2012 that the average American game player was 30 years old; 32 percent of all players were under 18 years old; 31 percent were between 18–35 years old; and 37 percent were 36 years or older (ESA 2012: 2). The data from the ESA study also showed that computer gaming is not limited to a brief period or phase of a person's life. On average, the adult American game player has been playing for 14 years, the average man for 16 years, and the average woman for 12 years (ESA 2012: 5). The mediatization of play may historically have started in childhood and youth, but it has successively spread to the adult population.

However, these quantitative indicators of the mediatization of children and young people's play and social life in general do not provide insight into how the media have changed the cultural experiences and practices of children and young people. In order to complement the quantitative approach with a qualitative understanding of the mediatization of play, the following case study of LEGO will discuss how the old construction toy, the LEGO brick, has gradually been integrated into the cultural and economic circuit of the media; and how, through this process, both the idea of play and the cultural values embedded in the play with LEGO toys have been transformed. In addition to already existing LEGO research, the case study is based on written sources from the LEGO company (e.g., LEGO 1982), including the LEGO catalogs and advertising, publicly available industry information (e.g., the website www.lego.com), and internal documents provided by the LEGO company.

LEGO's way to the media industry

The key LEGO product, the LEGO brick, was introduced in 1955 under the heading "LEGO System in Play." Starting in the 1930s, LEGO's founder Ole Kirk Christiansen had created toys using wood and other materials, but from the beginning of the 1950s the company began to develop the LEGO bricks, and in 1958 the coupling system that enabled the bricks to stick together with a "click" was invented. When a fire in 1960 destroyed the company's warehouse containing wooden toys, it was decided to concentrate all efforts on one single product: the LEGO brick. Since then, LEGO has become one of Denmark's industrial success stories, reflecting how a small, local carpenter's workshop was transformed into a global toy company that – unlike many of its competitors – has maintained a positive reputation among industrialists, parents, children, and educational professionals alike. LEGO has managed to project the image of a socially responsible company with a product that is not only fun to play with, but also has educational qualities. LEGO bricks are not associated with violence, sex, political viewpoints, or controversial topics of any other kind, and the company has deliberately sought to develop an image of the LEGO brick as something with which both parents and children can feel perfectly safe. These values have generally been an advantage for the company, since both parents and educators recommend children's play with LEGO bricks. Nevertheless, during the last decades this safe image of LEGO has also come to present a problem, because children increasingly engage in more teenage-like leisure activities, influenced by adult topics circulating in the media. For the growing generation of "tween"-agers, the safe image could easily be synonymous with childish.

Compared with many other international toy companies, LEGO was a late starter in adjusting to the increased competition from media companies and engaging itself in media activities. This was partly a consequence of the company's own culture. In spite of its early international orientation, it was a family-owned company that throughout the post-war period had expanded on the basis of its own ideas and earnings (Poulsen 1993). The company and its management were characterized by a Christian, Jutlandic culture (Byskov 1997) that was also reflected in the values of social responsibility embodied in the LEGO toy and play. The management strategies were generally conservative, and control of the business empire was firmly located in the main office in the small provincial town of Billund in Denmark (Cortzen 1996; Hansen 1997).

LEGO's late reaction to the changing toy market was also due to the fact that the LEGO company had not seen itself as an all-round producer of toys, let alone a provider of children's entertainment. Instead, it considered itself to be a producer of a particular type of toy: construction toys. According to this view, LEGO was not in outright competition with other international toy companies like Mattel or Hasbro. Within its own niche, construction toys, it had pursued a stable and robust growth strategy and had successfully become the leader within this confined market area. It was not until the 1990s that LEGO began to change its strategy and perception of the company. The crucial element of this change was a conceptual shift whereby LEGO would no longer be identified by its physical product: the bricks. Instead, the inherent values of LEGO, understood as quality in play, were to be the future bearer of the company's identity and activities. This conceptual change was in principle already anticipated in the late 1970s by Kjeld Kirk Kristiansen, the CEO of LEGO at that time, when he began to talk about LEGO as a concept, rather than a product. In a speech in March 1978 he said:

> Today, it is primarily a product identity (LEGO = construction toy), but in the future the name LEGO – in the eyes of the consumer – should aspire to become "*LEGO* = *a company that produces and markets creative and stimulating quality toys for all ages*".
>
> (Kristiansen 1978: 10–11; his emphasis)

In reality, however, this declaration of intent did not have major consequences before the mid-1990s, when the toy market had already changed and LEGO began to experience financial difficulties. In the 1980s and first part of the 1990s, LEGO was still focused on construction toys, and innovations were concentrated on product differentiation by developing new thematic product universes for different age groups. In her analysis of the brand development in LEGO, Pernille Gjøls-Andersen (2001) shows how the management of LEGO gradually came to recognize that LEGO did not have the same status and attraction for children as before. LEGO had gradually become a toy that parents and grandparents would celebrate, but the children themselves were no longer finding the building bricks very exciting. As a project manager from the Product Development Division in LEGO phrased it:

> The fact that our product is outdated is terrible, but it is not news to us. We saw it coming years ago. When I came to LEGO there was already research showing that it is only boys who sing in choir who like LEGO. Boys today talk about RAM and hard disks, but they don't talk about the newest LEGO model. So when LEGO is purchased it is because of the tears in the eyes of their grandparents.
>
> *(Quoted from Gjøls-Andersen 2001: 166)*

Another problem was the increased emphasis on construction work when children built the ever more complex and detailed LEGO models. In the LEGO company's Annual Report for 1998, it was pointed out that the company should move "away from many difficult building instructions for beautiful but perhaps overly pre-determined results (i.e., models) and back to our products' core values – to the joy of creating something, giving space to imagination and a wealth of possibilities" (The LEGO Group Annual Report 1998). In other words, LEGO's heavy emphasis on the construction aspect had turned children's play into work. In contrast to this, the expanding media culture seemed far more entertaining and attractive, and for LEGO the development of media activities was one way to get the playfulness back into the toys.

With stagnating earnings in the mid-1990s and a huge deficit in 1998, the road was paved for a change in the company's strategy. As a result, a much larger array of toys, lifestyle products, and entertainment products for children was launched, and in addition to the construction toys, three new commercial areas were formed: LEGOLAND amusement parks, LEGO Lifestyle products, and LEGO Media products. According to the new strategy, LEGO was to become a global and brand-driven enterprise that no longer focused on one particular product. Instead, the various activities were to be held together by the values of the LEGO brand. Accordingly, the declared ambition of the LEGO company was to become the strongest brand among families with children in 2005. LEGO was not necessarily to become the biggest or the most profitable company, but its brand was to be known and loved by families with children.

In order to achieve this goal, an aggressive growth strategy was developed, including the development of new products, expansion of sales in new markets, and the opening of LEGO brand stores and new amusement parks in the United States and Germany. Among the LEGO Lifestyle products, children's clothes became a prominent product line. The ambition was that "LEGO Kids Wear should be among the world's strongest brands among children's clothes in year 2005" (LEGO press release: "Big Global Venture with LEGO Kids Wear" 1999). In the area of the media, the expansion was headed by the new LEGO Media division, which in particular was to intensify the development of computer games, but also stimulate cooperation with other media companies and develop LEGO movies, television series, cartoons, magazines, etc. Through these new activities,

LEGO was now in a different competitive situation. Earlier, the company had to defend its leading position in the construction toy niche against pirate products and newcomers to the construction toy market. Now, LEGO was in fierce competition with major toy companies and some media companies, of which several were much bigger than LEGO, and it had to compete in new lines of commerce such as children's clothes, where it had little or no experience.

The expansive global growth strategy that LEGO adopted in the late 1990s resulted in a mediatization of its toy products, but mediatization was neither part of the company's deliberate strategy, nor was this concept applied by the management or employees. The mediatization was an un-intentional side-effect of the company's expansion into a global market of lifestyle, entertainment, media, and information technologies for children and young people. At various stages, several sub-divisions of LEGO were involved in the development of media-related products, and occasionally there was internal disagreement, with developments in several directions without any overall coordination (Karmark 2002). For the purpose of this overview, we will distinguish analytically between the different stages in the mediatization of LEGO products. Initially, the media were primarily conceived as *channels of information*. Apart from advertising, which LEGO had used from an early stage, the media gained a foothold as an alternative way of communicating building instructions and distributing the product catalog. Instead of providing building instructions on paper, the LEGO submarine in 1997 was accompanied by a CD-ROM with various building suggestions, while an interactive CD-ROM catalog on LEGO Technic was also released in 1997. Then followed a phase in which the media were considered to be a *supplementary and supporting* activity. Media products were developed, but they had a limited and subordinate role in the overall product assortment: for example, an early computer game like LEGO Chess did not have a clear relationship with the other product lines. The next step was to consider the media as an *integrated* element of all major product lines. In around 2000, media products were treated on a par with physical products (e.g., computer games related to the various thematic universes), and intelligent bricks were developed that allowed the user to control the final structure, e.g., robots in the CyberMaster and MindStorms series.

Media- and, not least, information technology-based products acquired an important *image* function. Although the media products were still in the minority in quantitative terms, they became highly visible in the marketing of the LEGO brand and products, and they furthermore played an important role in the communication of the company's transformed image. LEGO was now considered a provider of both high-quality and high-technology products that were playful, improved learning, and were reaching out to users through web communities, etc. At this stage, the role of the more traditional brick products was downplayed. As an illustration of this tendency, the LEGO catalog in 2000 displayed the title "The Toy of the Future," and computer games, intelligent bricks, the website www.lego.com, etc. were used as symbols of LEGO's new image. By associating itself with digital media, LEGO would no longer be the toy of the parents' generation, but the toy of present and future generations.

After severe losses in 1998, LEGO's business improved in 1999, but 2000 ended with a new deficit. Nevertheless, sales were increasing steadily, and in 2001–2 the company achieved a profit that created confidence in the new strategy. This positive development, however, was completely disrupted by catastrophic deficits in 2003 and 2004, forcing the company to reconsider its entire strategy. With the prospect of yet another billion-dollar deficit, the ambition of becoming the strongest brand among families with children was abandoned. The expansive growth strategy had moved the company into business areas where it had no, or very limited, expertise, and in order to solve the financial difficulties some of these business areas were either discarded (like LEGO Kids Wear) or outsourced to companies with greater expertise or better financial capacity. The LEGOLAND amusement parks were thus sold to external partners, but continued to use the LEGO brand. A renewed focus on the brick products was announced, but this did not lead LEGO to give up on its media activities. Instead, it reflected how the strategy in general was over-ambitious and that the exclusive focus on the brand, and not on the products, was insufficiently thought out. Therefore, LEGO today continues its development of computer games, just as the company is proceeding with media license products like Star Wars, Batman, Bob the Builder, Indiana Jones, Harry Potter, and Lord of the Rings. In 2009, LEGO's executive vice-president Mads Nipper estimated that licensed products generated approximately 25–30 percent of LEGO's total retail sales globally (Berman *et al.* 2009; see also Annicelli and Peterson 2008). More and more computer games and media-related products are being developed, but instead of trying to produce these media products itself, LEGO leaves the production of computer games, films, etc. to dedicated media companies.

In the case of LEGO, from an analytical perspective mediatization seems to involve three different, but mutually dependent aspects: imaginarization, narrativization, and virtualization. Imaginarization is a process by which the symbolic content of the toy comes to refer to an imagined world, rather than to an existing reality (present or historical). The physical brick is still at the center of the play, but it is used to create non-realist fantasy universes. Narrativization is understood as a process through which the bricks, due to their physical design, marketing, or an accompanying text, motivate play with narrative qualities. A narrative is a sequence of events (e.g., a fight, pursuit, etc.) organized within the unity of an action that is endowed with human interest and takes the shape of a human project (Bremond 1973). Important to this aspect has been the development of LEGO figures with human characteristics. Virtualization is understood as a process by which the bricks lose their physical and tactile sensory form and become represented in virtual universes. Transferring the physical bricks to a pictorial representation on a screen reduces the tactile experience of manipulating physical objects, but at the same time the visual specificities of the bricks can be highlighted via the possibility of visual manipulation (enlargements, color changes, etc.).

It must be stressed that play as a social and psychological activity always involves elements of more or less imagined character and narrative formats, while the play itself may constitute a kind of virtual space of interaction. Therefore, the process of mediatization does not imply an absolute shift from a realistic, non-narrative play in the physical world to an imaginary and narrative play in a virtual environment. Earlier forms of play would also draw on fantastic stories, just as the contemporary mediated forms of play may involve imitations of the real world and lack narrative forms. However, the massive presence of the media in children's lives in general, and the increased interaction between the media and toy industries in particular, have intensified the imaginary, narrative, and virtual aspects of children's play. By virtue of their institutional resources, technological possibilities, and wide repertoire of narratives, the media enable these aspects to become more prominent in children's play than they were before.

Imaginarization

At the beginning, the LEGO brick was literally a brick for building a house. In line with this, for many years LEGO bricks were first and foremost elements with which to construct models of the physical inventory of the modern world: houses, roads, cars, trains, etc. As the picture from a LEGO brochure in 1960 illustrates (Figure 5.1), play was understood as construction, and the purpose of play was to build lifelike representations of the urban environment that at that time was being built in Denmark, Germany, and other European markets for the LEGO company. The toy bricks were gradually differentiated with more specialized bricks that

FIGURE 5.1 Picture from LEGO brochure, 1960.

allowed for more detailed representations of real-world objects. The bricks were also differentiated according to age, with the big DUPLO bricks for younger children (from 1967), while Technic LEGO was introduced for older children (from 1977, but with gear kits already in 1970), allowing for greater technical refinements. Gradually the models also became divided according to thematic universes, such as towns, railroads, outer space, etc.

The different types of LEGO bricks and models reflected a common perception of the child as the small engineer who, with the help of technical instruction manuals, would combine systematic planning with a talent for construction. Play focused on the production of an object and was informed by an ambition to imitate the external physical world. The age differentiation was not motivated by consideration of children's different interests at various ages, or differences between children and youth cultures. Instead, the age classifications of the LEGO models reflected a developmental conception of how the child gradually matures into an adult. As the child grows older, he/she gradually acquires more advanced engineering skills and therefore becomes capable of handling ever more complex and demanding construction tasks.

Like other toy products, the LEGO bricks were gradually transformed from the 1970s and onward. The thematic universes of the brick models gained a more and more imaginary and fictional character. The brick models replicated the real world to a decreasing degree, and instead came to represent the inventory of fantasy worlds: space (from 1979), knights (from 1984), pirates (from 1989), Islanders (from 1994), the Wild West (from 1996), and others. These fantasy worlds in part made use of existing genres already circulating in popular media culture, and in part reworked these into specific LEGO versions of the genres in question. The development of the space series is emblematic of the process of imaginarization. In the first part of the 1970s, LEGO presented models of rocket launchers and lunar landing vehicles from the American space program. With the Space series from 1979, the space exploration theme was gradually transformed into a purely fictional subject matter, building upon the science fiction genre's mythological descriptions of high-tech civilizations, cosmic warfare, and man's conflict with robots and aliens. The Slizer, Rock Raiders, and *Star Wars* series from 1999 marked a provisional culmination of this development.

By entering these imaginary worlds, LEGO had moved a long way from the replication of the existing modern world, while at the same time the level of potential dramatic conflict had increased. While the old LEGO town presented a positive and conflict-free social world, the new imaginary space world portrayed a more dangerous landscape. In 1988, the LEGO catalog invited the child to play with suggestions such as "What about becoming the mayor of the city?" In comparison, the suggestion on LEGO's website in 2000 concerning the Slizer battle robots sounded somewhat more aggressive:

> In a faraway galaxy, a new and strange life form has been found. Eight powerful characters control their separate worlds. They fight nature,

monsters. ... and each other! Continue through the galaxy to see the battle zones where the fights and games will take place.

(www.lego.com 2000)

The imaginary worlds have expanded, but they have not replaced the reality-depicting LEGO models. Instead, we see a change in how the real world is portrayed in various thematic universes. Basically, the real world is increasingly dramatized and influenced by imagery from genres of media fiction. The changes in LEGO's depiction of the modern urban environment provide an interesting illustration of this development. The LEGO catalogs' presentations of a truck in respectively 1984 and 1996 are reproduced in Figures 5.2 and 5.3. In 1984, the truck passes by a garage in a small provincial town. There are a lot of police officers around, but everybody in this harmonious universe seems friendly, cooperative, and happy. In the 1996 catalog, the presentation of the truck has been transformed into spectacular scenery from a major American city. The truck has become a "runaway truck" that, according to the accompanying cartoon, will "crash everything," so everyone has to "run for your lives." The police station seems to be located in a Californian bay with palm trees, and the truck is depicted as flying through the air twice: as a close-up at the front, in order to demonstrate speed and velocity, and in the distance, flying across a damaged highway bridge with a Manhattan cityscape as a backdrop. The provincial idyll has been replaced by an American action universe that no longer focuses on the usefulness of the vehicle, but instead is fascinated by the speed and destructive force of the runaway machine. The scene of the runaway truck flying over a damaged bridge resembles well-known scenes from American action movies such as *Runaway Train* (1985), *Terminator II* (1991), and *Speed* (1994). The imaginarization of LEGO not only moves the urban depictions from the Danish provinces to the American metropolis, but also informs them with the imagery of popular American culture. More recently, in 2012, the computer game *LEGO City Undercover* with a gameplay not unlike *Grand Theft Auto* has transformed the LEGO City brick environment into a world of crime in which the detective Chase McCain chases villains.

As a supplement to the boyish fantasy worlds, LEGO also introduced bricks aimed particularly at girls. In the beginning we find very simple dolls' houses (from 1971) that invite play of a realistic nature that is focused on family life, nurture, and childcare. Later there are more imaginary worlds like Fabuland (from 1979), Paradisa (from 1992), Belville (from 1994), and Scala (from 1997), with less emphasis on construction work and reality depiction, and more focus on emotional relationships in fantasy worlds. Fabuland introduces a world full of fabled animals for younger girls, and Paradisa, Belville, and Scala invite play for both younger and older girls, focusing on a luxurious leisure lifestyle (skiing, horseback riding, surfing, fashion, etc.) à la Barbie, *Baywatch*, or fairy-tale worlds of castles, fairies, and witches.

As the imaginarization gradually advanced, the sets of LEGO became organized according to the same genres and sub-genres as are known from media fiction, and

FIGURE 5.2 LEGO catalog from 1984: presentation of a truck in a provincial town.

FIGURE 5.3 LEGO catalog from 1996: presentation of a truck in an American metropolis.

in particular the genres that are preferred by LEGO's primary target group of boys aged five to 16 years: the adventure genre (about knights, pirates, Red Indians, and explorers) and the action genre (about racing, the police, the fire brigade, space, etc.). At the end of the 1980s, popular media genres had established themselves as important thematic categories for LEGO bricks, and the development in the 1990s was characterized by further evolution in this direction (variation and differentiation of genre elements) and an approximation to specific fantasy worlds that circulated in the media. Some of LEGO's thematic universes from the 1990s were similar to well-known fictional films. The LEGO adventurer Johnny Thunder, who in the inter-war period explores pyramids, flies in balloons, etc., had allusions to the Indiana Jones movies by Steven Spielberg. Similarly, the "Little Forest Friends" DUPLO brick series for younger children had similarities with the fictional universe of the Smurfs. This tendency was perhaps most evident in a particular Johnny Thunder series that featured dinosaur hunting on a tropical island: the similarity to the *Jurassic Park* narratives was rather obvious. Although these universes were not licensed, and also displayed differences in terms of names and details, they may be considered to be forerunners of the subsequent licensing of a variety of media stories and characters.

LEGO's expansive global strategy from the late 1990s led LEGO to buy media characters. In 1998, LEGO reached an agreement with Disney that allowed LEGO to use characters from the Mickey Mouse and Winnie the Pooh universes. In the same year, an agreement was signed with Lucas Entertainment for the *Star Wars* series. This was related to the *Star Wars* revival introduced with the premiere of the new "first" *Star Wars* movie. In 2000, LEGO introduced a soccer series in connection with the Euro2000 games, using the French soccer player Zidane as a licensed character. That same year, LEGO also made a deal with Warner Brothers concerning the *Harry Potter* movies, allowing LEGO to develop *Harry Potter* brick universes. For the younger children, a DUPLO series with *Bob the Builder* was made possible via an agreement with HIT Entertainment PLC, also in 2000. The use of popular media stories and characters has continued up to the present day with, for example, *LEGO Spider-Man* in 2003, *LEGO Batman* in 2006, *LEGO Indiana Jones* in 2008, *LEGO Prince of Persia* in 2010, and *LEGO DC Super Heroes* and *LEGO Lord of the Rings* in 2012.

As a result, the LEGO brick packages are not only organized thematically according to the different fictional genres and imaginary universes, but they are increasingly *representations of specific fictional universes* that are already promoted – and owned – by other media industries. The licensing agreements are, from one viewpoint, a traditional example of cross-branding, in which two brands (e.g., *Star Wars* and LEGO) join forces in order to reach a wider audience than each of them could achieve alone. However, as should be obvious from the aforementioned, this kind of licensing agreement has a stronger impact on the product than the latter's association with yet another brand. The media brands become an important component of the toys, transforming both the imagery of the bricks and the character of the play.

Narrativization

Although the LEGO sets were organized according to thematic universes during the 1970s and 1980s, they did not have many narrative elements. In terms of narrative, the thematic worlds were very open and it was left to the children themselves to create their own stories in relation to their play with the bricks. The construction work, on the other hand, was organized in carefully outlined sequences, as suggested in the accompanying building instructions. Accordingly, there was a considerable difference between the highly scripted construction work and the ensuing free play with the brick models. The building instructions gave detailed advice on how and when to use every single brick, but afterwards there was practically no advice or suggestions concerning the play.

From the mid-1980s onwards, a rudimentary narrativization of the different thematic universes began to take place, for example, with the introduction of different clans in the knights and space universes (Lion and Black Knights from 1985; Blacktron from 1987; Space Police from 1989; and M-tron from 1990). The brick universes hereby suggest simple narratives, typically fights or wars between different clans, etc. Due to LEGO's adherence to positive social values, violent behavior and warfare have typically either been absent or very downplayed in both bricks and advertising, and in any case moved to a distant past (the knights) or remote future (space), making the violence less realistic. In the case of bricks referring to a recognizable contemporary world, the rudimentary action was focused on scientific discoveries, instead of individual aggression or war. In the 1990s, LEGO sets suggested narratives about the exploration of space (Iceplanet from 1993), the deep sea (Aquazone from 1995, and Divers from 1997), and polar regions (Arctic from 2000). These narratives were about human survival in hostile environments, and not so much about fights with other humans. Similar non-violent narratives were suggested with Time Cruisers from 1996, about traveling in time, and Res-Q from 1998, about risky rescue operations.

At the end of the 1990s, LEGO in practice gave up its strict non-violence policies. Several brick series that quite openly suggested aggression and battle were released, for instance, the Competition series from 1998, with LEGO models shooting at each other, the Ninja series from 1999, inspired by Hong Kong martial arts, and the Slizer series from 1999, about fighting robots. Race car series like Speed Slammers and Robo-Riders focused on confrontation and destruction, such as when the Battle Cars in the Speed Slammers series were announced with the slogan "Build 'em and bash 'em!" Yet the narratives were still quite rudimentary in nature.

One of the great obstacles to introducing narratives in LEGO toys was the lack of character traits in the LEGO figures. LEGO introduced some family figures in 1974, and from 1978 they were equipped with movable arms and legs, but for many years they were not thought of as possible narrative agents. The figures were very small and displayed no character traits, and mostly served a decorative function by making the brick structures look livelier. In order to create a narrative, you need specified roles (the good, the evil, the helper, etc.) and a set of personal character traits (strength, wisdom, nerve, etc.) that suggest possible chains of events and solutions to conflicts (Greimas 1974). In other words, the roles and character traits of narrative agents demarcate a set of likely action schemata that children can draw on in their construction of fictional narratives in play. The modest size of the LEGO figures, however, only allows for a limited degree of character drawing and individualization, and consequently they were not very suitable for narrative play.

In order to overcome this obstacle, LEGO has sought to differentiate the figures in various ways, for instance, by introducing named figures to serve as protagonists in specified thematic universes. Accompanying media have helped to narrativize the bricks: since the 1990s, sales catalogs, advertising, magazines, films, computer games, television, and theme parks have increasingly been used to develop character drawing and to sketch out main storylines. For instance, in the LEGO catalogs, short cartoons are used to portray named figures in key narrative sequences. In 1998, LEGO began to develop the *LEGO Adventures* magazine for children together with Egmont's media division in Great Britain. It was first published in Great Britain in 1999, and subsequently in Poland, the Czech Republic, and Spain. The magazine format allowed for longer cartoon stories about the different thematic universes, and a stronger development of character traits. Today, the website, www.lego.com, has become the central platform for the company's communication with its customers, and this is not least used to present video stories and online games featuring key characters in relation to virtually all brick products.

License agreements with various media companies have given LEGO access to many fictional protagonists, like Harry Potter, Batman, and many others. This has greatly improved the differentiation of fictional LEGO characters and the level of individual characterization. The media fictions not only provide a narrative context for the play, but also offer highly developed roles and characters to be enacted in the play. In the *LEGO Batman* series, for instance, the LEGO figures become Batman, Catwoman, the Joker, the Penguin, and many others, and their character traits are further developed on LEGO's website, in animated LEGO movies, cartoons, posters, etc. The license agreements are not restricted to fictional characters. In LEGO's sports series, real people have been transformed into LEGO figures; e.g., LEGO's NBA collector's series that portrays each named NBA player as a LEGO figure. LEGO's computer games have also promoted the narrativization of the bricks by displaying the figures in various action sequences that the child can then re-enact in the play with the physical bricks. The computer games have furthermore stimulated the development of the figures toward fuller and more realistic characters by giving them smoother movements, realistic skin colors, various facial expressions, etc.

Apart from developing the small decorative figures into narrative characters, LEGO has also sought to create new figures that are more suitable for story-based play. The LEGO Bionicle in particular has been a major successful attempt to develop a new product as a combination of action figures and construction toys. The Bionicle series was launched in 2001 and consists of a set of figures that are much larger than the usual LEGO figures. Although the figures must be built before they can be used, the construction work is very limited and there is far more emphasis on the mythological storyline concerning the Bionicle universe in general and the narrative sequences that characterize the individual Bionicle action figures in particular. To support the narrative development of the Bionicle figures, a wide range of media products has been produced, including computer games and feature films. In 2001, the Bionicle film *The Mask of Light* was released; in 2004, *Legends of Metru Nui*; in 2005, *Web of Shadows*; and in 2009 *The Legend Reborn*, all with a duration of one and a quarter hours. In addition to the Bionicle part of the regular LEGO website, there is a special website for the Bionicle series dedicated to the narrative itself: www.bioniclestory.com (Figure 5.4). As action figures, LEGO Bionicles differ from the other brick toys, and Bionicle's relationship with LEGO is somewhat downplayed. Bionicle does not share the same web address as LEGO and the product brand is generally just as important, if not more important than the company brand. Furthermore, the Bionicle story also features more elements that may be attractive to an emerging teenage identity. From the Bionicle website you can download special Bionicle music, and the Bionicle story itself is generally much darker, more violent, and dystopian than usually found in LEGO narratives. After a decade's success with Bionicle the concept has been transformed into a rather similar product series called *Hero Factory*, from 2010. Concurrently with the launch of this new series of action figures, new storylines were introduced, supported by an animated television series later sold on DVD.

FIGURE 5.4 The website www.bioniclestory.com contributes to the narrativization of the action figures from the LEGO Bionicle series.

Virtualization

By virtue of imaginarization, the LEGO bricks are increasingly used to build fantasy worlds inspired by the fictional genres of the media, and through narrativization, play becomes a storytelling activity that draws on, re-circulates, and develops existing media narratives. Mediatization further entails a virtualization in which the bricks and the construction work lose some of their physical traits in favor of a symbolic representation and interaction. This is most obvious in the case of LEGO computer games, in which the physical bricks are replaced by a visual representation, and the play is performed through the manipulation of a joystick, mouse, and keyboard.

The relationship between the virtual worlds of the computer games and the brick worlds has not been without ambiguity. On the one hand, there is a clear iconographic resemblance betweens games and bricks, because the game worlds are made of bricks and the actors in the games are LEGO figures. There is also a thematic connection between some of the games and the brick worlds, since most of the games are presented as belonging to a particular thematic brick universe, like the computer game *LEGO Rock Raiders*. On the other hand, many of the different LEGO games make use of existing game genres and game play, etc., so that some games seem more like a LEGO version of existing adventure or chess games, rather than a virtual adaptation of a specific thematic brick universe. The brick iconography is common to both games and physical bricks, but not least in newer games the play and representations are less bound by the physical features of the bricks. In an early game like *Panic on the LEGO Island*, the figures moved with the same rigid movements known from the physical figures. Yet in later games, such as *Action Team*, the body movements had become softer and more natural. At first, LEGO was not very successful with its computer games, but the *LEGO Star Wars 2* game from 2006 turned out to be a tremendous hit and was followed by the *LEGO Indiana Jones* and *LEGO Batman* games in 2008. In 2007, LEGO initiated the development of its own Massive Multiplayer Online Game (MMOG), named the LEGO Universe, in cooperation with the company NetDevil, but this did not attract sufficient numbers of users and closed in 2012. Instead of this major online play universe, LEGO has continued its development of online games related to the individual product lines like LEGO City and LEGO Dino.

Virtualization entails not only that bricks are moved into the media, but also that the media become built into the bricks. An interest in intelligent control of brick models was developed very early in the LEGO company, and this became formalized in 1989 via cooperation with the Massachusetts Institute of Technology (MIT), where Seymour Papert was promoted as the first "LEGO professor of learning research." Seymour Papert contributed to the creation of the programming language Logo that was later used as the command and control language, LEGO TC Logo, for the LEGO bricks used in education. With the introduction of LEGO Mindstorms in 1998, LEGO created an educational robot system that appealed to a larger consumer market. In the same year, another robot system called Cybermaster was put on the market. Cybermaster primarily involved the remote steering of robots and suggested action rather than learning. From the two competing series, LEGO decided to give priority to the Mindstorms product. This was subsequently developed to make the programming part more intuitive and to expand the possible range of stimuli (such as pressure, temperature, light, etc.) that robots could respond to. The Mindstorms series constitutes an intelligent type of toy in which play focuses on the control of various physical interactions through logical interaction sequences programmed on a computer and downloaded into robots. It is not the bricks that become virtual, since the play is very much about the interaction between the brick-made robots and the physical environment. Instead, the physical action itself is virtualized, whereby interaction sequences are subject to formal and abstract programming procedures. Instead of moving the robot model around with your hand, action and interaction with the environment are pre-programmed as abstract logical sequences. As a consequence, the play is de-narrativized in favor of an experimental play with more abstract cause-and-effect relationships.

Virtualization is also visible in products that have the explicit aim of producing media representations. The best example of this kind of virtualization is the LEGO Studios Steven Spielberg MovieMaker Set from 2000 that contains a small web camera and video editing software. With this, children could make their own LEGO movies, and due to the agreement with Steven Spielberg, the set was put on the market with various suggestions of imitations and partial parodies of the *Jurassic Park* movie. In addition to the camera and video editing software, several LEGO sets with film scenes were introduced on the market, allowing the children to direct and record various key scenes from Steven Spielberg's movies. Another example of toys aimed at media production is the computer game LEGO Friends from 1999. It was targeted particularly at girls, and the purpose of the game was to produce a music hit with a girl band. Through these initiatives, LEGO has not only created products that re-enact fictional media worlds, but the toys themselves serve as a means to produce entertaining media productions.

The Internet has furthermore made it possible for the LEGO company and its fans to establish virtual worlds for communication and interaction. As stated earlier, the Internet has become more and more important for LEGO's own communication with its customers and the wider public; but apart from such marketing and public relations, the Internet also serves to create greater mutual contact between the company and users. Brincker (2003) shows how the developers of Bionicle wished to create a "deep story," and the Internet provided a forum via which users could gradually involve themselves in the story as it developed. Such Internet activities now follow all major LEGO products, so it is not only possible for the users to get inspiration from the LEGO company, but also from other users. An online club for LEGO enthusiasts, My LEGO Network, has been created, and a "Brickipedia," resembling Wikipedia, as well as unofficial websites for LEGO enthusiasts, have continued to develop. Like other companies, LEGO also seeks to involve users in product development, and the Internet plays an important role for this purpose (Lauwaert 2007).

As a final aspect of the virtualization process, we will mention the increased role of the LEGO brand itself in the development of the company. When LEGO's founder Ole Kirk Christiansen began to manufacture toys back in the 1930s, advertising and marketing were only weakly developed, and it is reported that Ole Kirk Christiansen was almost an opponent of advertising. In his portrait of the LEGO company, Jan Cortzen cites Ole Kirk Christiansen as saying that "advertising is not something we will emphasize. [...] We will put our efforts into quality and only that – then the rest will follow. Just make the products better, then people will ask for them" (Cortzen 1996: 135; my translation). According to this philosophy, it is the product and its inherent qualities that determine the success of a company. In comparison, quite another company philosophy was published by LEGO in 2004, in the document "about us – corporate information from LEGO":

> It is not possible to separate our company from our brand – the two share a foundation and values. In the pursuit of our mission we will focus on building our brand. Our brand goes beyond our logos and trademarks and extends to the relationship a person has with our company through products and services.
>
> *(www.lego.com 2004)*

As Gjøls-Andersen (2001) and others have documented, LEGO's global ambitions from the 1990s and onward were guided by a brand-led strategy via which the core values of the company were no longer to be identified by the product, but by a set of values articulated via the brand. In other words, the LEGO company itself became virtualized, since its activities were no longer to have their primary focus on the physical product, but on a set of ideas related to play and learning. As mentioned earlier, LEGO had to revise its expansive growth strategy due to severe losses in 2003 and 2004, and to some extent the company gave up the exclusive focus on the brand and reintroduced a focus on the products. Yet the LEGO brand continues to play an important role, and the company is not likely to return to the founder Ole Kirk Christiansen's market philosophy from the age of industrialization. In the 2010s, there is still a market for construction toys, especially if you understand how to combine the construction aspect with new components and ideas from the world of the media. According to a representative from one of LEGO's competitors, the toy firm Geomag, the innovative challenge for the future construction toy is to marry the old and new category values: "taking the basic building blocks, the concepts of construction, and bringing in something new in an environment where children are so tech savvy, and being able to fill that desire at the same time" (Bohen 2006: 17).

The transformation of play

In this case study I have examined the history of LEGO's construction toy and the development of this particular company. In the first decades, the inherent values of play were taken from the world of engineering. The hero of the early LEGO bricks was the engineer who constructed the buildings and machines of the modern world. Through play with the LEGO bricks, the child him/herself could become a young engineer who created replicas of the material wonders of the industrial society. As mediatization progressed, heroes and values stemming from the media industry's repertoire of adventurous heroes gradually replaced the engineer. LEGO's new heroes are not to the same extent occupied with the slow, laborious work of construction, but are far more devoted to action in exotic places and fantasy worlds, and to some extent also engaged in different kinds of violent – yet morally legitimate – destruction.

The growing influence from fictional media worlds, at the expense of the engineering paradigm, in many ways resembles the changes Leo Lowenthal reported in his study of biographies of famous people in magazines in the first part of the twentieth century (Lowenthal 1961). In the early years of the twentieth century, magazines portrayed prominent people in industry, political leaders, and famous scientists, and the biographies were preoccupied with their achievements in the social sphere of work. Half a century later, these "idols of production," as Lowenthal labels them, have been supplanted by a new class of heroes: the "idols of consumption." The new idols have not earned their fame through hard work, intelligence, or political leadership, but have become famous through exposure in the media. What interests the media is not the Hollywood star's education, knowledge, or working life, but his/her adventurous lifestyle and leisure activities. They are heroes due to their experiences in the sphere of consumption. This change can also serve as a general conceptual distinction between different historical phases in the cultural values of toys.

As this case study demonstrates, the LEGO bricks have become subject to imaginarization, narrativization, and virtualization. It should be noted, however, that we cannot infer a change in children's play directly from the changes in their toys. Children may use toys in various ways that are not anticipated by toy manufacturers, and the change in children's play must be considered within the broader context of "social, institutional and historical change" (Buckingham 2000: 105–6). But when we consider that LEGO's history is parallel to a general development in the toy business and embedded within a general change in the leisure and play activities of children and young people, we can draw the conclusion that the story of this particular construction toy can serve to illustrate the general mediatization of play. Furthermore, the theory of mediatization suggested in this book may be considered to be a contribution to the broader framework that Buckingham (2000) is calling for, in order to understand the changing relationship between children and the media.

Even though children may use toys according to their own ideas and purposes, there is nevertheless reason to believe that the properties of the toy affect how children play. Kline (1999), for instance, has demonstrated that the ways in which a toy is characterized and presented in marketing and advertisements do make a difference with regard to the subsequent play with the toy. Using Gibson's (1979) concept of *affordances*, we argued in Chapter 2 that a given medium influences the ways in which it is used for communication and interaction, due to its technolo-gical, aesthetic, and institutional features. In a similar vein, a toy will possess a set of affordances that encourages certain types of play, but limits others, and in general has a structuring impact on the children's mode of interaction with the toy. Such affordances may be material or technological (e.g., the microchips and software in the interactive doll), symbolic (e.g., discourses and narratives in advertising and other media), or institutional (e.g., prices and policies regarding advertising targeted at children). How the more specific interplay between toy, media, and play is spelled out is first and foremost an empirical question that cannot be answered within the limits of this chapter.

Finally, we will address two important consequences of the mediatization of play: how children's play became integrated with a global consumer culture, and how toy manufacturers became dependent on the fluctuations of the media industry. Researchers of play and toys like Sutton-Smith (1986) and Kline (1993) have pointed to how children's excessive use of toys for play is a historically recent phenomenon. As Sutton-Smith expresses it, "the history of play is largely a history without toys for children" (Sutton-Smith 1986: 26). In premodern societies, chil-dren's play often took place in groups without the use of any toys. The use of artifacts designed for play and games was rather to be found in the adult world. Toys for children emerged in the upper classes and the higher middle classes during the eighteenth and nineteenth centuries and gradually spread to other social classes, concurrently with the general improvements in living conditions during the twentieth century. Play gradually became a more individual activity that took place either at home or close to the household, and the significance of play became somewhat narrower, meaning children's activities with toys. To some extent, the toy came to isolate the individual child and to bring his/her activities under the supervision of the parents, while toys became important as presents to signify the emotional ties between parents and children in the nuclear family.

Compared to this early modern development, the process of mediatization points in another direction: through the media, children are connected to the larger world beyond the walls of the home. This gives them access to the global media culture's reservoir of fantasy worlds, narratives, and virtual interaction spaces. This implies that children's play is detached from the parents' world, so that it becomes more difficult for adults to control the play of children. Children's play becomes influenced by the logic of a popular media culture dominated by new themes, patterns of communicative behavior, and normative values. Through the mediatization of play, children are brought into close contact with a predominantly market-driven and global consumer culture that is not least subject to the demands of fashion, i.e., the demands for continuous updates and incessant consumption (Christensen 1986).

The mediatization of play also affects the toy industry. From an economic viewpoint, Michael Wolf (1999) has pointed out that the entertainment industry of the media plays an increasingly larger role in society. The entertainment industry itself has expanded, at the same time as entertainment components are added to other kinds of goods and services. Products that until a few years ago would have been considered the antithesis of entertainment are being dressed up with a touch of entertainment. Flight and train travel, telephony, clothing, food, etc. are either adding a slice of entertainment (in-flight entertainment consoles, happy ring tones, etc.) or are symbolically associated with the world of media entertainment. Media stars and brands become tools to provide ordinary consumer goods with an extra level of satisfaction and attention. As a result, entertainment media and other businesses become intertwined:

> Brands and stars have become the same thing. Stars attract us to entertainment products. Brands attract us to other kinds of products. In the emerging world economy, where entertainment and the laws of the entertainment business infuse more and more of the rest of the world of commerce and culture, successful businesses need star brands to bring consumers through the door.
>
> *(Wolf 1999: 28)*

The media industry as a dominant element of the entertainment business may be used as a short cut by other companies to expand into new markets. By associating an already known media brand and its stars (*Harry Potter*, *Batman*, etc.) with its own products, a toy company like LEGO can extend the reach and improve the reputation of its own brand. Compared to the costs of building the company's brand using its own resources, the licensing of media stars – despite extremely high license costs – may prove to be a cheaper and faster solution.

Such a strategy, however, is not without costs. Once a company has established ties to the media industries, it is not easy to drop them again. The company will usually be obliged to update the media component on a continuous basis by releasing products relating to the newest episodes and characters of the media product in question. Once the toy is associated with the media narrative, the customer will see the toy as an artifact belonging to the media narrative. As a consequence, more industries, including toy industries, are becoming dependent on the successful promotion of media products and the general ups and downs of the media industry. As the then executive vice-president of LEGO, Poul Plougmann explained when the year 2003 began to look very bleak for the LEGO company: "We were aware from the outset that this year would be a difficult one – partly because there were no movie premieres to tie in with major series such as LEGO Harry Potter and LEGO Star Wars" (LEGO press release, 29 August 2003). Play and toys have become intertwined with the media. This has not only brought children and toy manufacturers closer to the stars of the media brands, but also made both of them more dependent on the technological, symbolic, and economic logic of the media.

6

THE MEDIATIZATION OF HABITUS

The social character of a new individualism

Introduction

In the preceding chapters we have argued that mediatization is one of the transformative processes of high modernity, on a par with – as well as intertwined with – other major processes of (high) modernity such as globalization, secularization, and individualization. Hopefully, the interconnections between mediatization and other major transformative processes have been demonstrated through the various individual studies of politics, religion, and play, yet the primary focus so far has been on the role of the media, whereas other processes of modernity have served primarily as a context or secondary factor in the analyses. In this chapter, the relationship between mediatization and other major processes of modernity, in this case *individualization*, becomes the focal point of our discussion.

The aim is more precisely to discuss how mediatization processes affect the relationship between the individual and society, with particular emphasis on how the media enable, structure, and change how individuals acquire normative orientation and enter into social relations with each other. Although mediatization may change specific social institutions such as politics, education, and research in various ways (Strömbäck 2008; Friesen and Hug 2009; Rödder and Schäfer 2010), it may also have a more general influence, across different social institutions, on how social cohesion is reproduced in society at large. At this general level, it will be argued that mediatization stimulates the development of a *soft individualism* that depends on *weak social ties*. The social character proliferating in mediatized and highly modernized societies is neither characterized by a strong, self-dependent individualism nor by strong collectivism in the shape of obedience to powerful organizations, or a close-knit family unit. Instead, a paradoxical combination of individualism and sensibility toward the outside world has gained ground, while strong social ties toward family, school, and workplace are subject to increased competition from weaker social ties enabled via media networks. These developments are at least partly a reflection of how the formation of the individual's social character – its habitus – has become influenced by extended and interactive media networks.

The relationship between the individual and society is integral to one of the most classic sociological questions concerning how society is possible, i.e., how the "big" entities of society like institutions or nations connect with the "small" units of society: individuals in situated interaction. From a bottom-up perspective, the question is how individuals' actions and relations with each other are constitutive of the larger social units of society; and from a top-down perspective, the question is how the big institutions of society like politics, family, education, and industry (re)produce specific relations between humans, and either motivate or force them to act and interpret the world in specific ways that synchronize the individual with society at large. Key sociological contributions to this discussion provide the basis for our examination of the question. Max Weber's (1904) study of the protestant ethic and its importance to the development of the industrious and self-controlled individual of early capitalism provides a classic example of how psychological character traits may be partly constitutive of broader social transformations. His ideas have, for instance, been further developed by Colin Campbell (1987) in his study of the development of a romantic sensibility and its influence on consumer culture. Norbert Elias' (1939) study of the civilizing process and the refinement of manners within European courts is another important contribution to our understanding of how social norms concerning eating, sex, violence, and social class have historically become internalized as a kind of second nature, i.e., a socially acquired, yet strong psychological disposition to follow acceptable rules of social behavior. Pierre Bourdieu (1998a, 1998c) uses the concept of habitus to transcend the contradiction between the demands of the external and objective social world and the inner and subjective dispositions that guide the actions and interpretations of the social actor. Similarly, Anthony Giddens' (1984) structuration theory seeks to surpass the traditional dichotomy between macro- and micro-sociology and explain how social institutions are both reproduced and changed through individual social agents' reflexive use of institutional resources.

Habitus and social character

By using the notion of social character and its further development with the concept of habitus, the aim is furthermore to give the all-pervading discussion of cultural identity a stronger sociological twist. Following newer strands of cultural theory of high or postmodernity, the demise of tradition and the rise of self-reflexive subjectivity impel the individual to construct his or her own identity (Beck, 1992; Giddens, 1991). Under conditions of vast and rapid changes due to globalization, urbanization, flexible modes of production, etc., the construction of cultural identity becomes a lifelong process in which the individual may acquire multiple, and to some extent contradictory, identities. There is little doubt that, from the perspective of the individual, the construction of one's own cultural and social identity has become a far more pertinent issue and problem, since identity is to a much lesser extent passed on through traditions. However, discussions of cultural identity tend to take the individual's subjective experience at face value, and correspondingly underestimate the presence of common characteristics of lifestyles within specific social segments of the population, and the ways in which the cultural and social self-perception of the individual are informed by the cultural and social contexts in which the individual lives. Rethinking the concepts of social character and habitus may provide us with an opportunity to consider the influence of the media on cultural and social identity in a way that avoids the pitfalls of both determinism and voluntarism. As such, social character or habitus do not equal social or cultural identity, but denote the general dispositions by which an individual relates to and interacts with his or her surroundings. Social character and habitus provide a conceptualization of the interface between identity formation and the social and cultural context. Social character and habitus are thus not intended to replace identity, but are concepts that allow us to specify how identity is mediated through social and cultural circumstances, including the media.

The concept of social character has almost disappeared from the vocabulary of modern sociology, yet at an earlier stage it played an important role in both social theory and empirical analysis. For the social psychologist Erich Fromm (1941), who came from the Frankfurt School of critical theory, social character was a key concept and he defined it as "*the essential nucleus of the character structure of most members of a group which has developed as the result of the basic experiences and mode of life common to that group*" (1941: 305, italics in original). Fromm combined a psycho-analytical understanding of the subject, as influenced by unconscious and biological drives, with a partly Marxist sociology of society's influence on consciousness and behavior. Already in Sigmund Freud's psychoanalysis, we find a theory of how, through suppression and internalization of the norms of parental authority, sexual drives are channeled into socially acceptable dispositions and actions. While Freud's theory primarily dealt with the psychological aspects of consciousness and subconsciousness, Fromm developed a social psychology in which societal aspects played a more prominent role. Others worked along the same lines, among them Wilhelm Reich (1933), whose study of the mass psychology of fascism also combined psychoanalysis with critical social theory.

Later studies have sought to identify the traits of a national social character. For example, Bellah *et al.* (1985) have sought to identify the American character and mentality, and Sennett (1998) has provided a critical analysis of how newer forms of flexible labor may be detrimental to the healthy development of personal character. In contrast to many of his predecessors and contemporaries, David Riesman (1950), whose study of the changing American social character we shall return to later, was not dominated by a psychoanalytical approach. We can describe his work as a combination of social and cultural analysis, since he examined the importance of structural and material developments (population growth, class composition, etc.) by studying how these were experienced by individuals and groups. It was the acknowledgment of changing social experiences in the home, the workplace, the city, and the mass media that led him to develop the theory of the other-directed character.

There are several reasons for the disappearance of social character from the agenda of sociology. The "cultural turn" in sociology during the last decades, and the rise of social constructivism, has put cultural identity on the agenda to the extent that this concept has almost monopolized current thinking of the role of the individual in modern society, including the field of media studies. The relationship between the media, culture, and the individual social agent has thus become almost synonymous with the interplay between media, culture, and identity. Social character as a concept has, however, not only disappeared due to a recent intellectual trend in sociology or other strands of research, but also because of its internal weaknesses. The notion of social character has had a touch of essentialism, by which social character was seen as the innate core of the nation, the authoritarian state, or a primitive society. In this way the concept lost track of the relational and dynamic aspects between individual and society that it potentially should be able to grasp, and in addition variations and differences were downplayed in the analysis. The early influence from psychoanalysis also contributed to this essentialism, because a few psychoanalytical concepts of sexual and mental dispositions (Oedipus complex, subconscious desires, etc.) came to dominate the perception of how biology, society, and character formation were interconnected. Concurrently with the decline of psychoanalytical theory, the concept of social character lost some of its theoretical underpinnings.

As Meisenhelder (2006) has argued, we may consider Pierre Bourdieu's concept of habitus as the sociological successor to the concept of social character. Through habitus, Bourdieu also wishes to grasp the fundamental social character of the individual agents' actions and interpretations of their positions in society. Via habitus, the individual develops a particular lifestyle and set of practices and value orientations that justify the hierarchical position of the individual and make it meaningful. At the same time, habitus informs the individual to think and act appropriately across different social fields. As Bourdieu puts it, "habitus is this generative and unifying principle which retranslates the intrinsic and relational characteristics of a position into a unitary lifestyle, that is, a unitary set of choices of persons, goods, practices" (Bourdieu 1998c: 8). Lifestyle is built upon a set of classificatory schemata by which the individual makes distinctions within different social fields such as politics, food, leisure activities, etc. (Bourdieu 1998a). Habitus does not provide full-fledged interpretations or directions for action in any particular situation, but consists of a practical, cognitive, and affective, as well as bodily, disposition that guides interpretation and action.

There is little doubt that Bourdieu's concept of habitus is better equipped to describe the couplings between the individual and society than the earlier notion of social character. Habitus allows us to consider how the schemata of interpretation and action are intertwined with the structural position of an individual, a particular group, or social class across a range of social fields. Habitus thus combines an understanding of social power and class with the specific historical trajectory of a given individual, group, or social class. What is missing in Bourdieu's theoretical framework is a psychological dimension that allows us to understand the interplay between societal development and individual psychology, including emotional and cognitive processes. Furthermore, Bourdieu provides little help concerning the role of the modern media in society, including the media's influence on habitus and lifestyle formation. His writings on media (Bourdieu 1998b) are unfortunately among his least informed analyses.

Although Bourdieu's theoretical framework in many ways is more advanced than the concept of social character, I will take my point of departure in Riesman's analysis of the changing social character in the mid-twentieth century United States. Riesman's general diagnosis of the other-directed social character contains some fruitful insights regarding the role of the media in the construction of habitus. Furthermore, he has a remarkable sensitivity to the psychological and social contradictions of the search for individual autonomy, and the collective underpinnings of this independence:

> The presence of the guiding and approving "others" is a vital element in his whole system of conformity and self-justification. Depriving him of the sociability his character has come to crave will not make him autonomous, but only anomic […] if the other-directed man is seeking autonomy, he cannot achieve it alone. He needs friends.
>
> *(Riesman 1950: 327)*

As we shall see, social character in Riesman's analysis points to structural changes at a far more general level than the habitus of specific social classes and groups addresses. In *The Lonely Crowd* Riesman addresses the experiences of the expanding middle class in great detail within a particular historical period. His main argument nevertheless concerns the large-scale, indeed epochal, change in character traits in different phases of modernity. Due to the increased mediatization of society, these character traits have proliferated way beyond the specific class and historical period within which they emerged. Subsequently, I shall return to the connection between these character traits, habitus, and the media.

From gyroscope to radar

Riesman's notion of social character is somewhat similar to Erich Fromm's concept, as he considers social character to be the mechanism via which society gets its members to *want* to act in the ways they *have* to act as members of society. In continuation of this, he considers social character to be a "mode of conformity," i.e., the psychological and social dispositions that make an individual or group act in accordance with the demands of a given society and culture. Although this may sound rather deterministic, the argument is not that everybody automatically conforms to the demands of society. As Riesman points out, many people will develop a character that to a lesser degree conforms to societal pressures, yet the less the character fits the social context, the greater the psychological and social costs for the individual. Due to this pressure, social character will gradually accommodate the demands of society, but since character is formed not least through childhood and adolescence, the social character of many people will often lag behind the challenges of modern society. Furthermore, Riesman (1969: 6) stresses that conformity is not all there is to social character: "'mode of creativity' is as much a part of it."

Riesman stipulates a typology of three ideal social characters: the traditional, the inner-directed, and the other-directed. The traditional character is governed by shame, exercised by the extended family and community in agrarian, traditional society, whereas the inner-directed character is regulated by the feeling of guilt, internalized by the individual through his or her upbringing in industrial, modern society. The other-directed character is not so much regulated by guilt as by a diffuse anxiety for not being recognized and loved by his or her contemporaries. Riesman's argument about the transition from the traditional to the inner-directed character follows along the lines of Max Weber's account of how the spread of protestant ethics fostered the self-controlled character and work ethos suitable for early capitalism. Riesman's original contribution lies in his vivid and detailed analysis of the emergence of the other-directed character.

The rapid growth of the consumer society in the mid-twentieth-century United States changed the demands that society made of the individual. Expanding consumer opportunities and leisure time created the conditions for a psychology of affluence: the importance of being a hardworking individual was gradually challenged by the lure of the market to become a good consumer. While the upbringing of the inner-directed character had stressed the need for modesty and good manners, the other-directed character had to enjoy spending money and be able to give grounds for consumer choices. Earlier, work had defined most of existence, but now life outside the factory and office gained importance: sociability, dining, sports, and sex not only acquired more time and space, but also became topics for discussion and evaluation. In this new cultural environment, the norms of the inner-directed character were of little use, and increasingly the individual had to search for normative orientation in the contemporary world. As Riesman puts it, the tool used by the inner-directed character for social navigation, the *gyroscope*, was gradually replaced by the *radar* of the other-directed character, guiding his or her constant search through the external world for both recognition and normative orientation. This change may also be considered a shift from "conscience" to "consciousness" (Wouters 2011): the other-directed individual is not governed by the "super-ego" of the Victorian gentleman, but by the "ego" of the twentieth century modern man. He is less inclined to be "bowing to the rules of a rigorous conscience – and [has] greater awareness of others and of the pressures they exercise" (Wouters 2011: 157). The other-directed character is not characterized by a particular lifestyle or norm as such, since these will change over time. The hallmark of the other-directed character is the very disposition to monitor the surroundings through peer groups and media:

What is common to all other-directeds is that their contemporaries are the source of direction for the individual – either those known to him or those with whom he is indirectly acquainted, through friends and through mass media. This source is of course "internalized" in the sense that dependence on it for guidance in life is implanted early. The goals towards which the other-directed person strives shift with that guidance: it is only the process of striving itself and the process of paying close attention to the signals from others that remain unaltered throughout life.

(Riesman 1950: 22, italics in original)

The inner-directed character lived in a class-divided society and often had to uphold his status vis-à-vis persons from other classes (servants, workers, etc.), but the other-directed character increasingly comes to live surrounded by people of more or less the same social class: the expanding middle class. Concurrently, people are no longer defined solely by class, but also by lifestyle. This does not necessarily imply that social divisions become less important, but the competence to read social divisions becomes more sophisticated. As one of many examples, Riesman (1950: 74) suggests that Europeans coming to the United States are likely to think "that salesgirls, society ladies and movie actresses all dress alike, as compared with the clear status differences of Europe." This is, however, only a superficial similarity, and in order to decode the subtle status differences, the American "must look for small qualitative differences that signify style and status" (ibid.).

In the new urban reality, with millions of people, big offices, and large public institutions, the modern American also has to interact with many more people. Knowledge of fashion, taste, and norms in general becomes important in this new environment where the boundary between the known and the unknown is no longer as evident as before. Social and organizational skills become imperative if you want to make a career in modern commerce, and in some sectors work acquires an element of sociability. Quoting Paul Lazarsfeld, Riesman points to a shift in attention from the bank account to the expense account: in a modern organization you should not only work, but also live, feel a sense of community, and be a consumer at meetings, business dinners, and during travel, etc. Work relations become infused with personal relations, as the other-directed character puts "into work all the resources of personalization, of glad handling, of which his character is capable, and just because he puts so much energy and effort into work, he reaps the benefit of thinking it important" (Riesman 1950: 310–11).

Today, many of Riesman's observations are commonplace and they have, for instance, been supported by Joshua Meyrowitz's study (1986) of the rise of a so-called "middle-region" behavioral norm, i.e., a performative model, mixing personal and public behavior, that is not least promoted by the media. Inglehart's (1990) study of the spread of post-materialist values in postmodern societies also shares similarities with Riesman's argument. When Riesman wrote it, however, he was ahead of his time, to such an extent that he was misunderstood. As Riesman mentions himself, in many quarters his book was received as a story of decline, in which the inner-directed hero lost ground to the weak other-directed character, who was far too dependent on the approval and norms of his peer group and the mass media. Such an interpretation does not do justice to Riesman's argument, and the title of the book *The Lonely Crowd* (which was not Riesman's suggestion) bears some of the responsibility for this reception. In general, Riesman is more optimistic than pessimistic about the new social character, just as he is generally positive toward the growth of "new" media like radio, television, recorded music, etc., because these foster an increased sociability for the other-directed character, in contrast to books and newspapers that drew the inner-directed character away from the group.

Riesman's analysis has its strength in the sweeping overview of cultural change in American society and the cross-disciplinary approach that allows it to discern parallel developments in very different sectors of society. Its strength also points to a weakness. In general, Riesman seeks to attribute too many different cultural and social developments to the change in social character. As a consequence, it becomes somewhat unclear how detailed we may be able to specify the new social character. On the one hand, Riesman tends to say that it is basically the urge to monitor the surroundings, in order to achieve recognition and normative orienta-tion, that makes up the other-directed character (cf. the preceding citation). On the other hand, his numerous examples and insightful sense of detail suggest a far more elaborate and specified social character. In order to make use of Riesman's character study for our discussion of mediatization, we will choose the narrow definition of the other-directed character. Consequently, the core characteristic of the other-directed character is his or her highly developed sensibility toward an extended network of both persons and media. In other words, we will consider the other-directed disposition as the instrument of character formation, rather than the outcome or full-fledged profile of the social character itself.

Riesman's approach has been criticized for not being able to connect the multiplicity of cultural changes reflected by the new social character to more fundamental, macro-social phenomena (Meisenhelder 2006). This is correct to the extent that Riesman himself only provides indirect links between social character and macro-social expla-nations such as the division of labor, urbanization, etc. But this apparent weakness may rightly also be considered the very strength of the argument. Riesman seeks to depict how the emerging modern world *is experienced* in new ways and expands the possibi-lities for social interaction, and how the inner-directed character fails precisely due to the changing modern experience and new modes of interaction. In order to under-stand the connection between macro- and micro-social phenomena, i.e., the inner ties between institutions and social actors, we have to consider the structure of both human experience and the interactional realms constituted by institutions (including media), since they are the connecting node between macro and micro phenomena.

Weak ties and sociability

Besides the transformation of social character, Riesman also noticed a change in social relations and forms of interaction. Formerly, functional and formal relationships became gradually more personal, and sociability spread to many social spheres as an important mode of interaction. In order to understand these changes in forms of relations and interaction, we shall consider Mark Granovetter's study of weak social ties and Georg Simmel's notion of sociability. In sociology, the distinction between strong and weak social ties is not well-defined. In general, the frequency, reciprocity, importance, and duration of interactions between people are considered as indicators of whether the ties between them are strong or weak. Thus, a married couple would usually be an example of people with mutual strong ties, whereas two people standing in a line at a supermarket counter would have very weak or non-existing social ties with each other. Usually, strong social ties are considered important for the general cohesion of society, but Granovetter (1973) argues that weak social ties are, in some respects, superior to strong social ties, and consequently we can talk about the "strength of weak ties."

Granovetter's original analysis concerned the relationships and flow of information among people looking for a new job. Where you might think that people you are more strongly attached to would provide the best starting point when looking for information, it turned out that weak social ties provided a better flow of information. People with strong social ties with each other may have strong reciprocal commitments but, when it comes to information flow, such relationships tend to circulate already known information. Weak social ties involve less responsibility, but they usually provide individuals with more and newer information about the world outside – in Granovetter's case, information about available jobs. As regards the spread of information in social networks, Granovetter (1973: 1366) concludes: "whatever is to be diffused can reach a larger number of people, and traverse greater social distance (i.e., path length), when passed through weak ties than strong."

Granovetter also suggested that social cohesion could benefit from weak social ties. Strong ties within a small group of people may ensure unity (e.g., in the family, or among friends), but weak social ties across such groups are important to keep the larger social unit together. If strong social ties come to dominate, there is a danger of social separation, as the information circulating within these groups primarily tends to confirm already existing knowledge and opinions about the external world. This is the problem of the ghetto and the small village community: as strong as they may be internally, they face a gradual decline unless they develop ties with the surrounding society. Social structures only consisting of weak social ties do, of course, also have inherent problems, since both society and the individual need long-lasting and binding commitments. Thus, the question of social cohesion is not a simple choice between strong or weak social ties, but about the overall composition and balance between social relations of different strength and type.

It is exactly this composition and balance between different social relations that the process of mediatization affects. As Schulz (2004) has pointed out, mediatization involves an extension, substitution, amalgamation, and accommodation of face-to-face encounters with mediated encounters and, through these processes, both weak and strong social ties come to be influenced by the affordances of the media. Generally, both the mass and the interactive media expand the individual's opportunities to monitor the external world and regulate his or her interaction with other persons, real or virtual. Thus, as each individual needs less effort to acquire information about both close and distant surroundings, he or she may not only be able to multiply and intensify distant – and formerly weak – relationships, but the information flow within stronger social ties will also intensify and bring these close-knit relationships into far more direct and continuous contact with the external world. Individual media may direct the attention of the individual toward the social environment in different ways. Generally, mass media and Internet-based media may extend the individual's encounters beyond the realm of strong ties, but mobile phones tend primarily to strengthen social ties between family and friends (Ling 2008).

In order to master the growing number of weak social ties, the media support forms of interaction that are suitable for such more casual and less binding relationships. In his historical analysis of broadcasting, Scannell (1996) considers *sociability* to be one of the key modes of interaction that radio and television promote. In order to address a mass audience situated at home, radio, and subsequently television had to develop forms of communication that were appropriate for this particular situation, and sociability proved to be a successful mode of address. Sociability may not, however, be a particular characteristic of broadcast media, but a far more general feature of communicative forms promoted by the media (Hjarvard 2005). To a great extent, social networking media, such as Messenger, Facebook, and LinkedIn, also thrive on sociability as the preferred mode of interaction.

Georg Simmel (1971) accentuates the playful character of sociability, i.e., sociability is interaction without any other purpose than the interaction itself. As such, it may be considered a social time-out in which more binding social roles are temporarily suspended. From a utilitarian point of view, it is purposeless, but it nevertheless serves the purpose of making the social company of others enjoyable. We may object to Simmel's interpretation in which he exaggerates the playfulness of sociability. Like other modes of interaction, sociability adheres to social norms and expectations that may vary according to culture and social class, and within these respective circles sociability also serves a disciplining function: if you do not behave according to the specific etiquette of sociability, you may lose the recognition of your fellow peers. Accordingly, there is a world of difference between the sociability of a business dinner, a birthday party in a low-income community, and the rector's annual reception at a university. Joshua Meyrowitz's (1986) diagnosis of the spread of a "middle-region" behavioral norm by the electronic media in general, and television in particular, shares many of the same characteristics as Scannell's notion of sociability. Middle-region behavior is, like sociability, a balancing act between the private and the public, and between front stage and backstage. With the spread of sociability that balances between the private and the public, and at least partially suspends the binding social roles of strong ties, the media both encourage and make possible a continuous monitoring of the wider social environment through weak social ties.

The mediatization of habitus

Three of Riesman's observations concerning the other-directed character seem of special relevance to the construction of habitus in a mediatized society. First, the formation of habitus is to a greater extent shaped through interaction with *contemporary* society. Second, habitus is reproduced through an *intensified monitoring* of an *extended* social environment, and third, *recognition* becomes an important regulatory mechanism for the development of self-esteem and behavior. Since Riesman wrote about the rise of the other-directed character, the process of mediatization has made both mass and interactive media far more widespread tools for human interaction in almost all parts of society. Consequently, the media intervene in all three of the aforementioned aspects of habitus formation.

The media produce a continuous representation of our contemporary society that is accessible for everybody in almost all social institutions. Today's political realities, the consumer offers of tomorrow, and the contemporary problems of personal life, are all continuously updated and available to the modern individual. The media may also be a source of historical knowledge about the norms and behavior of yesterday, but this will usually be interpreted within a contemporary framework. In a certain sense, humans have, of course, always lived in their con-temporary world, but earlier this world was less connected to the wider society. Thus, the possibility of local worlds being out of sync with the development in other parts of society was generally more prevalent in older and less media-saturated societies. Concurrently with the proliferation of both the mass and interactive media, the individual will increasingly come to live in closer and more immediate contact with the wider society, and as a consequence, the metabolism between society and individual habitus formation also increases.

The intensified monitoring of an extended social environment is not only stimulated by a concern for general orientation, but is also motivated by the increased problematization of all social spheres, from politics to sex, in high modernity. The growing number of choices and risks makes it imperative for the individual to make decisions, and in order to motivate and justify such decisions, knowledge about current norms and trends becomes important. As Martin Eide and Graham Knight (1999: 526) observe, the media increasingly both problematize and offer solutions to the dispositions of everyday life:

> Far from erasing the troubles and difficulties of everyday life, the growth of knowledge, expertise and channels of communicating information and help has expanded the scope of problematization, and with it the kind of restless orientation to the life-world that modernity ferments. A profusion, and con-fusion, of new forms and media of help, advice, guidance and information about the management of self and everyday life continues to develop.

Modern journalism is responding to this new social function and has developed new themes and genres to deliver advice to the modern individual about not only politics, but also consumer choices, health, children's upbringing, etc. As such, the press is not only the fourth estate, the vigilant watch-dog of political power, but also the "fourth service estate": the helpful provider of service for the modern individual (Eide 1992). In addition to journalistic media a variety of commercial and civil services use digital media (Internet and mobile apps) to offer everything from medical advice to parenting assistance. Through such information and guidance the media provide input to the individual's rationalization of his or her norms and practices, i.e., the lifestyle of the individual.

It is not only the individual that seeks the media, but the media also seek the individual. In an ever more commercial media environment, audience maximization has become an important logic of the media, and consequently the media make efforts to comply with the audience's demand for orientation in formats that correspond to the lifestyle of the particular audience in question. The growth of audience and consumer research has greatly increased the knowledge about audiences and their composition in terms of gender, age, income, education, lifestyle, consumer choices, etc. Accordingly, the media will strive to produce content that is in accordance with the lifestyle of attractive segments of the population. Earlier, the media were either in service to other institutions, addressing a socially defined group according to, e.g., political interest (the partisan press), or the media were cultural institutions addressing a generalized public by promoting a common national culture. Today, the media are less steered by such social interests or common cultural values, and are more likely to produce and circulate content in ways that will meet the lifestyle preferences of different segments of the population. Lifestyle magazines, format radio, and cable television are examples of mass media that allow more individualized, lifestyle-based consumption patterns to emerge, but the spread of digital and interactive media has multiplied the ability of the media and users to converge around shared lifestyles, i.e., practices and representations with a shared value orientation that are positioned vis-à-vis the other media consumption patterns of other groups.

Through the segmentation of media products, the media have become more sensitive to differences in audience lifestyles than before, but there are also limits to the extent that the media will reflect already existing lifestyles. Whether or not a given segment of the population will be served by the media – and have its lifestyle represented in magazines, websites, or television programs – depends on the economic attractiveness of the particular segment, as well as other factors such as the size of a particular media market, competitive pressures, generic conventions and trends, etc. Typically, the media will seek to accommodate several audience segments in one product by putting several lifestyle components into the same product. For instance, the use of focus group research in media organizations often serves to ensure that a new product strikes the right balance between the key target groups of the media in question.

The media are also governed by fashion, i.e., a demand for continuous innovation of taste. In order to be read, heard, or seen, not only today but also tomorrow, a media product will have to renew both its form and content on a continuous basis, and consequently it will often be ahead of its audience in terms of lifestyle preferences. The role of guide and advisor for modern individuals also ensures that the media content will emphasize the discussion of new developments and trends, rather than recycling existing knowledge, but the intensity and direction of such renewal will, of course, vary according to the particular lifestyle segments that are addressed. Both as a result of market considerations and the requirements of fashion, the media not only reflect, but also construct, lifestyles. As a result, they come to modify the norms and practices that different segments of society are offered as guidance for modern life.

On the whole, we may say that the media *socialize taste*, because media products are not only (like all cultural artifacts) positioned within a hierarchical structure of cultural distinctions and cultural capital, but are also deliberately developed and tested in order to cultivate specific lifestyle preferences among audiences and may, as such, contribute to a reconfiguration of lifestyle patterns. Media usage patterns will, of course, reflect existing lifestyle differences, but media consumption as a social practice will also inform the renewal of lifestyles and their cultural value vis-à-vis other lifestyles, as the media bundle people together in new configurations around cultural objects and practices. For example, during the last decade, lifestyle television focusing on interior decoration has usually been dominated by lower-middle-class values, and via these programs such values are spread to larger elements of the population (Christensen 2008). Contrary to postmodern hypotheses about the disappearing importance of traditional demographic categories (e.g., Maffesoli 1996) such as class, age, gender, and education in terms of social behavior, consumer choice, and media usage, there is still ample evidence of the relevance of such categories. Media usage also varies systematically according to such parameters as age, gender, social class, education, and ethnicity (Bennett *et al.* 2006; Hjarvard 2002b; Roux *et al.* 2007). However, as Bourdieu also points out, categorical distinctions such as class or age may not influence habitus directly, but are mediated via the lifestyle of the particular individual and group in question. In a highly modernized society in which organized interests (parties, unions, churches, etc.) have a less significant position, lifestyle comes to play a more important role as mediator of both cultural and social hierarchies. With the media actively linking various networks of audiences around media-influenced lifestyles, they become part of the reproduction and renewal of cultural and social distinctions in the population.

Recognition via the media

The media constitute an arena in which the individual may perform, communicate, and act, and subsequently acquire recognition. Riesman (1950) did not unfold his notion of recognition, but his basic argument was that the search for recognition plays a more important role for the other-directed character's social integration, compared to earlier types of social character. Social theorist Axel Honneth (1996) has developed a distinction between three forms of recognition in modern society that is useful for our discussion. The first type of recognition, *love*, concerns close emotional bonds, such as between parents and children, husband and wife, and in close friendships. From this primary recognition, the individual achieves a funda-mental *self-confidence*. The second type of recognition, *respect*, regards the wider society's acknowledgment of the individual's moral accountability, from which follows a set of universal rights as a responsible, legal subject in society. This type of recognition is based on reason and provides the individual with the right to vote, protection against violation by others, etc. From this type of recognition, the individual acquires *self-respect* as an equal person among other fellow citizens. The third type of recognition, *esteem*, is partly emotional, partly rational; yet in contrast to the first two, it is not unconditional. It stems from the recognition by others of individuals' achievements as part of a social group, e.g., their ability to solve pro-blems in the workplace, be good neighbors, etc. Through such recognition as a valuable element of cooperative effort and community, the individual achieves *self-esteem*. The three types of recognition each belong primarily to a specific sphere of society: recognition through love takes place in the private and intimate sphere; recognition through respect takes place in the public sphere; and recognition through esteem is exercised in the social sphere. Although the first type of recog-nition may be considered primary, since it is a precondition for humans to develop the ability to enter into mutual relationships with each other, the three types of recognition are not an order of priority. Achieving self-confidence, self-respect, and self-esteem are all important to the exercising of individual autonomy. More negatively, Honneth also identifies three types of violations of recognition: violation of the body, the rights, and the ways of life.

Honneth himself does not consider the role of the media in relation to the processes of recognition. But in view of the mediatization process, the media have come to create a series of new interactional spaces and forms through which recognition may be exercised, and the boundaries between the three types may also become less clear. In a mediatized society, the very representation and visibility of an individual or group may be a valuable recognition, both as a private, public, and social person. Many social networking media such as Facebook, LinkedIn, MySpace, etc. are not only forums for communication and contact, but also media for the recognition of various private, social, and public achievements. As Kaare and Lundby (2008) point out, with the emergence of digital media, new formats for self-representation have become more widespread, and through these self-representations, the individual may authenticate his or her own biographical story and achieve collective recognition of personal identity. Similarly, both fictional and factual mass media products allow audiences to study the recognition of various individuals, social groups, and public figures, and newer forms of reality television series are constructed to dramatize the inclusion and expulsion of individuals from a group. Entertainment programs like *Survivor* and *X Factor* are intense studies of the social play between recognition and violation of the self, both as a private individual, a public figure, and a person belonging to a social group.

As the media project sociability as a dominant mode of interaction in many institutional contexts, the media come to influence how recognition is exercised as love, respect, and esteem. Due to the partly private, partly public nature of sociability, recognition through the media will often assume both an emotional and rational form. When private individuals or families present profiles on the Internet and make friends with others, this private and emotional recognition will also be submitted to a generalized and public notion of what should be recognized as positive and important personal qualities. When a politician wants to recognize (or violate) a given group's political or social issue (e.g., homeowners' mortgage problems, homosexuals' access to child adoption, etc.) this takes place not only via rational deliberation and appropriate legislation, but is also usually accompanied by a media performance in which the politician seeks to show sympathy and an ability to interact with the types of persons in question (or the very opposite). Thus, rational arguments need emotional performance in order to prove the authenticity of the public recognition. As regards the third type of recognition, social esteem, we may say that the media have generally expanded the opportunities to achieve such recognition. With increased access to engage in both weaker and stronger social relationships through the media, it not only becomes possible to achieve such recognition through the media, but more effort is also required to sustain it.

Soft individualism

The provocative insight from Riesman was to turn the relationship between individual autonomy and social belonging upside down. The inner-directed character gained his autonomy through a withdrawal from, or distance to, his contemporary world, since he predominantly relied on himself, or rather on the normative framework installed in him by parents and other authorities at an early stage in life. For the other-directed character, such autonomy is no longer possible, not because he is weaker, but for the reason that it becomes less helpful to rely on such old normative frameworks. If he sought to do this, he would not become autonomous, but merely decoupled from society. Instead, the other-directed character achieves autonomy through the ability to connect to the larger and contemporary social networks. Riesman clearly recognized the media as an important factor in this process, but the mediatization of society has undoubtedly accelerated since Riesman took stock of the mid-twentieth-century United States. As a result, the logic of the media in terms of technology, organization, and aesthetics – in short the affordances of the media – has come to mold the way people communicate, act, and sustain relationships with each other.

The other-directed character of the present mediatized society is marked by a soft individualism. Modern individuals are increasingly left to produce their own biographies in a society that celebrates everyone's right to be as individual as possible. Yet this is a soft form of individualism, since it deviates from earlier forms of individualism in its deep reliance on and sensibility toward the external world. It represents a more reflexive and flexible form of self-governance, compared to the inner-directed character (Wouters 2011). However, the softness does not imply that the individual is less integrated in society than before. Beck (1992) talks about the institutionalization of the individual biography in order to describe the new forms of dependency between the individual and society when older types of institution such as class, Church, or family become less important to the individual. Accordingly, we may say that the media increasingly provide an important framework in all spheres of society for such institutionalization of the individual biography. As the media become resources for the development of lifestyle and moral orientation, and for sustaining social relationships, they serve to reproduce and renew the habitus of the individual. Whether or not we consider this institutionalization of individual biography as negative or positive, as a "mode of conformity" or a "mode of creativity," is quite another matter: the argument here only points to the integrative function of the media. As Riesman noted, the other-directed character needs friends in order to achieve autonomy. Increasingly, we may add, he also needs the media.

7

EPILOG

Consequences and policies of mediatization

Diverse consequences

In this book we have studied mediatization processes at several levels, theoretically as well as empirically. In the theoretical Chapters 1–2 we have characterized mediatization as a major transformative process of high modernity on a par with urbanization, globalization, and individualization. Mediatization is defined as the process whereby culture and society to an increasing degree become dependent on the media and their logic and this process is furthermore characterized by a duality in that the media have acquired the status of a semi-independent institution in society at the same time as they become integrated into the very fabric of social life in other social institutions and cultural spheres. In Chapters 3–5 we explored the influences of media within particular institutional contexts and in Chapter 6 we have gone beyond any single institutional context in order to consider the development of individualism in high modernity. Precisely because the media have become integrated into society, their influence is also dependent on the particular contexts in which they are used. As the preceding chapters have demonstrated, mediatization may have considerable influence, but also very different consequences, depending on the specific social institution or phenomenon – politics, religion, play, or habitus – in question. Table 7.1 presents an overview of the key consequences of mediatization regarding the various institutions and phenomena.

In this book we have adopted an institutional perspective on mediatization in order to analyze social and cultural transformation at the meso level. The aim has been to understand long-term transformations in culture and society and at the same recognize the complexities of development within different spheres of society. By considering mediatization theory as a middle-range theory, we have sought to avoid the pitfalls of both the grand claims typical of macro-level theorizing and the celebration of heterogeneity typical of certain micro-level analysis.

TABLE 7.1 Key characteristics and outcomes of mediatization as regards various social and cultural institutions and phenomena

Mediatization of politics	The media as an industry of opinion and arbitrator of public consent to political viewpoints and actions
	Media influence political agenda-setting process
	Extended networks of political communication
	Conversationalization and personalization of politics
	A new class of media-based political commentators
Mediatization of religion	The media become a dominant source of information and experience concerning religion
	Three forms of mediatized religion emerge:
	• religious media
	• journalism on religion
	• banal religion
	The media serve integrative social functions hitherto performed by the Church, such as community, rituals, moral advice, etc.
Mediatization of play	Increased dependency between the media industry, the toy industry, and the advertising industry
	Imaginarization of play
	Narrativization of play
	Virtualization of play
Mediatization of habitus	Habitus is reproduced through an intensified and extended monitoring of the contemporary world
	Recognition of the individual through media networks serves social integration
	Soft individualism and the growing importance of weak social ties

An institutional perspective at the meso level has allowed us to make generalizations across the situational contexts of micro-social encounters, but prevented us from making totalizing accounts of how the media influence culture and society in general irrespective of time, space, and context. The question of the right level of generalization is, in the final analysis, not to be solved theoretically, but is an empirical question, since any general tendencies claimed are required to be substantiated empirically. What we may denote theoretically as "meso-level" developments can, in practice, turn out to be located at different points on the scale between micro, meso, and macro, depending on the particular issue and institution we are examining. Nonetheless, a theoretically based meso-level approach serves a heuristic function, since it is driven by the ambition to discern systematic patterns of change across time and space within a particular institutional framework. At the same time, such an approach is skeptical of over-generalizations that lose sight of social and cultural differences and the interplay between media and other social factors.

In continuation of this, mediatization theory is *not* to be understood as the theory of a "media society" that is created or conditioned by the media alone. Instead, mediatization theory presents a sociological framework within which to consider how the media, within a particular historical phase of high modernity, have developed into a semi-independent institution in society, while also becoming integrated into a variety of social and cultural institutions; and how the media come to influence society in a variety of ways via this process of differentiation, integration, and interaction with other social and cultural institutions. Because mediatization is linked to a particular period of history, and conditioned by the interplay with other social and cultural developments, there is nothing "natural" or inevitable about the development. We may also imagine the possibility of a *de*-mediatization of particular social institutions, making them less influenced by the media and more dominated by other types of steering logic. For instance, the "global war on terror" has in some cases curtailed the independence of the journalistic media and made political, religious, and military prerogatives more dominant in the public representation of terrorism, war, and conflict.

Media politics: big and small

The media have acquired greater independence in society and today are far more likely to be driven by professional and commercial factors than steered by the interests of other social and cultural institutions. Since the media help to constitute a common world of experience in society as a whole, and increasingly facilitate communication and interaction between institutions, groups, and individuals, they are, however, not to be regarded as yet another commercial activity, on a par with clothing or shoe manufacturing. The media serve important social and cultural functions because they enable society to understand itself and act as a collective entity, both at the level of big politics and at the small-group level of family and friendships. Processes of mediatization have made culture and society more dependent on the media, at the same time as the media have become more independent and commercial. How the media system is structured, and how the various media operate, become more important for other institutions' ability to serve their social and cultural purposes. Questions of media policy, such as which media companies dominate a particular media sector, what resources are available for content production and distribution within various genres and media, and who has access to these resources, etc., become important not only for the media themselves, but increasingly for other institutions in society too. As Curran *et al.* (2009) have demonstrated in comparative studies the political-economic structures of news media (i.e., commercial, public service, or combinations hereof) do make a difference in terms of the kind and amount of information that is offered to the public. Traditionally, media policies have focused on two major issues: the facilitation of informed political deliberation; and the protection of "vulnerable" segments of the population, in particular children and young people. In the present mediatized environment of converging media, media policies must expand their scope and take account of how national and global media structures and resources may facilitate – or counteract – vital collective functions within a variety of social and cultural institutions.

Concurrently with the process via which the media become part of the inner workings of other social institutions such as family and education, the traditional types of media policy are no longer sufficient. As a supplement to the "big" media policy of society as such, e.g., the governance of media markets, public service institutions, etc., there is growing need for a "smaller" media policy for civil society. A media policy for civil society concerns the use of the media within the smaller social unit, such as the school, workplace, family, etc. Due to the presence of the media in all social and cultural settings, in many everyday contexts it is increasingly important to consider which media should be available and kept open, and at what times and for which purposes. These are not abstract questions, but reflect problems that cut right to the heart of contemporary social arrangements. For instance, how many media is it beneficial to take with you on vacation to ensure that the family has a good time together? To what extent should employees be allowed to use private media during working hours, and should the management be able to screen employees' email or Facebook accounts?

The media represent a tremendous resource for social interaction, but they also – as considered in Chapter 2 – make the individual social units vulnerable, in view of the ease with which both insiders and outsiders can enter and leave the conversation and interaction within, for instance, the family, the workplace, and the school. Following the virtualization of interaction, participation in a social activity is to a lesser extent prompted by physical presence, and becomes more of an optional choice between several available options. In order to function as a collective unit, family members, co-workers, or teachers and pupils, need to agree on a common understanding of the situation at hand. In order to do this, they increasingly need to consider how they make use of the media in particular settings. Such a media policy of the civil society is already in the making, since families, schools, and workplaces are seeking to apply various rules to the use of the media, for instance, by banning mobile phones in the classroom, or restricting Facebook use in the office. However, such types of media policy are often developed on an *ad hoc* basis and frequently entail a negative and restrictive focus on what not to do with the media. A media policy of the civil society would need to consider the enabling, delimiting, and structuring influences of the media, and how to balance the demands of the collective needs with the individual's requirements. Such a media policy for the "smaller" aspects of life is not only about making explicit rules, but also about creating a responsible and open dialog between members on how to make the best use of the media in a civil, i.e., socially constructive, manner. This clearly involves normative and political questions, and the individual social unit, such as the school or workplace, would certainly need to consider its own media policies in relation to the rules, norms, and practices in other spheres of society. Through mediatization, the *modus operandi* of the media has come to influence a larger part of society, but the media are not ungovernable. Through a combination of a wider set of media policies for the big society, and media policies for the smaller units of civil society, it is possible to make the media serve culture and society, and not the other way around.

BIBLIOGRAPHY

Agger, G. (2005) *Dansk tv-drama* (*Danish Television Drama*), Frederiksberg: Samfundslitteratur.

Alexander, J. C. (1981) "The Mass News Media in Systemic, Historical, and Comparative Perspective," in Katz, E. and Szecskö, T. (eds) *Mass Media and Social Change*, Sage Studies in International Sociology, 22, London: Sage, pp. 17–51.

Allern, S. (2007) "From Party Press to Independent Observers? An Analysis of Election Campaign Coverage Prior to the General Elections of 1981 and 2005 in Two Norwegian Newspapers," *Nordicom Review* 29(2): 63–79.

Allern, S. and Ørsten, M. (2011) "The News Media as a Political Institution," *Journalism Studies* 12(1): 92–105.

Allern, S. and Pollack, E. (eds) (2012) *Scandalous! The Mediated Construction of Political Scandals in Four Nordic Countries*, Gothenburg: Nordicom.

Allison, J., Jenks, C., and Prout, A. (1998) *Theorizing Childhood*, Cambridge: Polity Press.

Altheide, D. L. and Snow, R. P. (1979) *Media Logic*, Beverly Hills, CA: Sage.

——(1988) "Toward a Theory of Mediation," in Anderson, J. A. (ed.) *Communication Yearbook*, 11: 194–223.

Anderson, B. (1991) *Imagined Communities: Reflections on the Origin and Spread of Nationalism*, London: Verso.

Annicelli, C. and Peterson, K. M. (2008) "Properties, Properly. A Decade Later, LEGO's Licensed Lines Still Growing," *Playthings* 4(12): 11.

Ariès, P. (1962) *Centuries of Childhood, A Social History of Family Life*, New York: Vintage Books.

Asp, K. (1986) *Mäktiga massmedier: Studier i politisk opinionsbildning* (*Powerful Mass Media: Studies in Political Opinion Formation*), Stockholm: Akademilitteratur.

——(1990) "Medialization, Media Logic and Mediarchy," *Nordicom Review* 11(2): 47–50.

Asp, K. and Esaiasson, P. (1996) "The Modernization of Swedish Campaigns: Individualization, Professionalization, and Medialization," in Swanson, D. L. and Mancini, P. (eds) *Politics, Media, and Modern Democracy: An International Study of Innovations in Electoral Campaigning and Their Consequences*, Westport: Praeger, pp. 73–90.

Aubert, V. (1975) *Sosiologi* (*Sociology*), Oslo: Universitetsforlaget.

Auslander, P. (1999) *Liveness: Performance in a Mediatized Culture*, London: Routledge.

Austin, J. L. (1962) *How to Do Things with Words*, Oxford: Clarendon.

Barrett, J. L. (2004) *Why Would Anyone Believe in God?* Walnut Creek: AltaMira.

Bastiansen, M. and Dahl, M.- F. (2008) *Norsk mediehistorie* (*The History of Norwegian Media*), 2nd edition, Oslo: Universitetsforlaget.

Baudrillard, J. (1981) *For a Critique of the Political Economy of the Sign*, St. Louis, MO: Telos Press.
——(1994) *Simulacra and Simulations*, Ann Arbor: University of Michigan Press.
——(1995) *The Gulf War Did Not Take Place*, Bloomington: Indiana University Press.
Beck, U. (1992) *Risk Society: Towards a New Modernity*, London: Sage.
Bellah, R. N., Madsen, R., Sullivan, W. M., Swidler, A., and Tipton, S. M. (1985) *Habits of the Heart: Individualism and Commitment in American Life*, Berkeley: University of California Press.
Bennett, T., Savage, M., Silva, E., Warde, A., Gayo-Cal, M., and Wright, D. (2006) *Media Culture: The Social Organisation of Media Practices in Contemporary Britain*, British Film Institute. Online. Available at www.bfi.org.uk/about/pdf/social-org-media-practices.pdf (accessed 26 May 2012).
Berger, P., Sacks, J., Martin, D., Weiming, T., Weigel, G., Davie, G., and An-Naim, A. (eds) (1999) *The Desecularization of the World: Resurgent Religion and World Politics*, Washington DC: Ethics and Public Policy Center.
Bergmann, J. R. (1993) *Discreet Indiscretions: The Social Organization of Gossip*, New York: Aldine de Gruyter.
Berman, S. Fitzgeorge-Parker, L., and Boston, W. (2009) "The Real Toy Story," *CNBC Business*, November 2009: 46–48. Available at: www.cnbcmagazine.com/story/the-real-toy-story/1061/1.
Billig, M. (1995) *Banal Nationalism*, London: Sage.
——(2005) *Laughter and Ridicule*, London: Sage.
Blumer, H. (1954) "What is Wrong with Social Theory?" *American Sociological Review* 19(1): 3–10.
Blumler, J. G. and Gurevitch, M. (1981) "Politicians and the Press: An Essay on Role Relationships," in Nimmo, D. D. and Sanders, K. R. (eds) *Handbook of Political Communication*, Beverly Hills, CA: Sage, pp. 467–97.
Blumler, J. G. and Katz, E. (eds) (1974) *The Uses of Mass Communications, Current Perspectives on Gratifications Research*, Beverly Hills, CA: Sage.
Blumler, J. G. and Kavanagh, D. (1999) "The Third Age of Political Communication: Influences and Features," *Political Communication* 16(3): 209–30.
Bogason, P. (2001) *Fragmenteret forvaltning: demokrati og netværksstyring i decentraliseret lokalstyre* (*Fragmented Government: Democracy and Network Governance in Decentralized Local Government*), Aarhus: Systime.
Bohen, C. (2006) "Building Blocks. Construction Toys Hold Their Own in Today's Tech-crazy Toy Market," *Playthings* 5(12): 16–17.
Bomholt, J. (1964) *Stil Ind: DR Årbogen 1963–64* (*Tune in: Denmark's Radio's Yearbook 1963–64*), Copenhagen: DR.
Bondebjerg, I. (2007) "Power and Personality: Politicians on the World Wide Web," *Northern Lights* 5(1): 119–40.
Boudon, R. (1991) "Review: What Middle-Range Theories Are," *Contemporary Sociology* 20(4): 519–22.
Bourdieu, P. (1993) *The Field of Cultural Production: Essays on Art and Literature*, Cambridge: Polity Press.
——(1998a) *Distinction: A Social Critique of the Judgement of Taste*, London: Routledge.
——(1998b) *On Television*, London: Pluto Press.
——(1998c) *Practical Reason: On the Theory of Action*, Cambridge: Polity.
——(2005) "The Political Field, the Social Science Field, and Journalistic Field," in Benson, R. and Neveu, E. (eds) *Bourdieu and the Journalistic Field*, Cambridge: Polity Press, pp. 29–47.
Bovill, M. and Livingstone, S. (2001) "Bedroom Culture and the Privatization of Media Use," in Livingstone, S. and Bovill, M. (eds) *Children and their Changing Media Environment: A European Comparative Study*, Mahwah, NJ: Lawrence Erlbaum Associates, pp. 179–200.
Boyer, P. (2001) *Religion Explained: The Human Instincts that Fashion Gods, Spirits and Ancestors*, London: William Heinemann.
Bremond, C. (1973) *Logique du récit* (*Logic of the Narrative*), Paris: Éditions du Seuil.

Brincker, B. (2003) "Clash of Communities: A Study of the LEGO Product Bionicle," paper presented at the conference "New Media, Technology and Everyday Life in Europe," London, April 2003.

Brown, S. (2003) *Crime and Law in Media Culture*, Buckingham: Open University Press.

Bruce, S. (2002) *God is Dead: Secularization in the West*, Oxford: Blackwell.

Bruns, A. (2005) *Gatewatching: Collaborative Online News Production*, New York: Peter Lang.

——(2008) "The Active Audience: Transforming Journalism," in Paterson, C. and Domingo, D. (eds) *Making Online News: The Ethnography of New Media Production*, New York: Peter Lang, pp. 171–84.

Buckingham, D. (2000) *After the Death of Childhood: Growing Up in the Age of Electronic Media*, Cambridge: Polity Press.

Byskov, S. (1997) *Tro, håb og legetøj: landsbyfolk og industrieventyr i Billund 1920–1980 (Faith, Hope, and Toys: Village People and Industrial Adventure in Billund 1920–1980)*, Grindsted: Overgaard Bøger.

Campbell, C. (1987) *The Romantic Ethic and the Spirit of Modern Consumerism*, Oxford: Basil Blackwell.

Campbell, H. A. (2010) *When Religion Meets New Media*, New York: Routledge.

Carey, J. (1989) *Communication as Culture: Essays on Media and Society*, Winchester, MA: Unwin Hyman.

Castells, M. (1996) *The Information Age: Economy, Society and Culture*, vol. 1–3, Oxford: Blackwell.

——(2001) *The Internet Galaxy, Reflections on Internet, Business, and Society*, Oxford: Oxford University Press.

——(2009) *Communication Power*, New York: Oxford University Press.

Christensen, C. L. (1986) "Krop og form – et spørgsmål om stil" ("Body and Form – A Question of Style"), in Christensen, C. L. (ed.) *Slidser. En bog om mode (Slits – A Book about Fashion)*, Aarhus: Modtryk, pp. 55–72.

——(2006) "Børne-og ungdoms-tv" ("Television for Children and Youth"), in Hjarvard, S. (ed.) *Dansk tv's historie (The History of Danish Television)*, Frederiksberg: Samfundslitteratur, pp. 65–104.

——(2008) "Livsstil som tv-underholdning" ("Lifestyle as TV Entertainment"), *MedieKultur* 24(45): 23–36.

Christensen, H. R. (2010) "Religion and Authority in the Public Sphere, Representations of Religion in Scandinavian Parliaments and Media," Ph.D. dissertation, Aarhus: Department of Theology.

——(2012) "Mediatization, Deprivatization, and Vicarious Religion: Coverage of Religion and Homosexuality in the Scandinavian Mainstream Press," in Hjarvard, S. and Lövheim, M. (eds) *Mediatization and Religion: Nordic Perspectives*, Gothenburg: Nordicom, pp. 63–78.

Clark, L. S. (2005) *From Angels to Aliens: Teenagers, the Media, and the Supernatural*, Oxford: Oxford University Press.

Cohen, B. C. (1963) *The Press and Foreign Policy*, Princeton: Princeton University Press.

Cohen, J., Tsfati, Y., and Sheafer, T. (2008) "The Influence of Presumed Media Influence in Politics: Do Politicians' Perception of Media Power Matter?" *Public Opinion Quarterly* 72(2): 331–44.

Cook, D. T. and Kaiser, S. B. (2004) "Betwixt and Be Tween: Age Ambiguity and the Sexualization of the Female Consuming Subject," *Journal of Consumer Culture* 4(2): 203–27.

Cook, T. C. (1998) *Governing with the News: The News Media as a Political Institution*, Chicago: University of Chicago Press.

Coontz, S. (2000) *The Way We Never Were: American Families and the Nostalgia Trap*, New York: Basic Books.

Corner, J. (2003) "Mediated Persona and Political Culture," in Corner, J. and Pels, D. (eds) *Media and the Restyling of Politics*, London: Sage, pp. 67–84.

Cortzen, J. (1996) *LEGO manden – historien om Godtfred Kirk Christiansen* (*The LEGO Man – The History of Godtfred Kirk Christiansen*), Copenhagen: Børsen.

Cottle, S. (1999) "From BBC Newsroom to BBC News Centre: On Changing Technology and Journalist Practices," *Convergence: Journal of New Information and Communication Technologies* 5(3): 22–43.

——(2006a) *Mediatized Conflict*, Maidenhead: Open University Press.

——(2006b) "Mediatized Rituals: Beyond Manufacturing Consent," *Media, Culture & Society* 28(3): 411–32.

Couldry, N. (2003a) "Media Meta-Capital: Extending the Range of Bourdieu's Field Theory," *Theory and Society* 32(5/6): 653–77.

——(2003b) *Media Rituals: A Critical Approach*, London: Routledge.

——(2008) "Mediatization or Mediation? Alternative Understandings of the Emergent Space of Digital Storytelling," *New Media & Society* 10(3): 439–57.

——(2012) *Media, Society, World. Social Theory and Digital Media Practice*, Cambridge: Polity.

Cross, G. (1997) *Kids' Stuff: Toys and the Changing World of American Childhood*, Cambridge, MA: Harvard University Press.

Crystal, D. (2011) *Internet Linguistics, a Student Guide*, London: Routledge.

Curran, J., Lyengar, S., Lund, A. B., and Salovaara-Moring, I. (2009) "Media System, Public Knowledge and Democracy: A Comparative Study," *European Journal of Communication* 24(1): 5–26.

Dahlgren, P. (2006) "Doing Citizenship: The Cultural Origins of Civic Agency in the Public Sphere," *Cultural Studies* 9(3): 267–86.

Dansk Folkeparti (2001) *Valgkampsvideo* (*Danish People's Party: Election Campaign Video*).

Dayan, D. and Katz, E. (1992) *Media Events: The Live Broadcasting of History*, Cambridge: Harvard University Press.

Demerath N. J. III (2003) "Secularization Extended: From Religious 'Myth' to Cultural Commonplace," in Fenn, R. K. (ed.) *Sociology of Religion*, Oxford: Blackwell, pp. 211–28.

De Mesa, A. (2008) "Toy Brands Don't Play Around in Virtual Worlds." Online. Available at www.brandchannel.com/features_effect.asp?pf_id=430 (accessed 18 June 2012).

Deuze, M. (2007) *Media Work*, Cambridge: Polity Press.

Dewey, J. (1927) *The Public and its Problems*, New York: Henry Holt.

Djerf-Pierre, M. and Weibull, L. (2001) *Spegla, granska, tolka* (*Mirroring, Investigating, Interpreting*), Stockholm: Prisma.

Dobbelaere, K. (2002) *Secularization: An Analysis at Three Levels*, Brussels: P.I.E.-Peter Lang.

Eide, M. (1992) *Den fjerde servicemakt* (*The Fourth Service Estate*), Bergen: Institutt for massekommunikasjon, University of Bergen.

Eide, M. and Knight, G. (1999) "Public/Private Service: Service Journalism and the Problems of Everyday Life," *European Journal of Communication* 14(4): 525–47.

Eisenstein, E. L. (1979) *The Printing Press as an Agent of Change*, Cambridge, MA: Cambridge University Press.

Elias, N. (1939; 1978) *The Civilizing Process*, vol. 1–2, Oxford: Blackwell.

Elkind, D. (1981; 2007) *The Hurried Child: Growing Up Too Fast, Too Soon*, Cambridge, MA: Da Capo Press.

Engelhardt, T. (1986) "The Shortcake Strategy," in Gitlin, T. (ed.) *Watching Television*, New York: Pantheon, pp. 68–110.

Entman, R. M. (1993) "Framing: Toward Clarification of a Fractured Paradigm," *Journal of Communication* 43(4): 51–58.

ESA (2012) *Essential Facts About the Computer and Video Game Industry*. Report published by the Entertainment Software Association (ESA). Online. Available at http://esa.create-send2.com/t/y-i-jrxmk-l-i/ (accessed 12 May 2012).

Eurobarometer (2008) *Towards a Safer Use of the Internet for Children in the EU – A Parents' Perspective*. Analytical report, Flash Eurobarometer 248. Brussels: EU Commission. Online. Available at http://ec.europa.eu/information_society/activities/sip/docs/eurobarometer/analy ticalreport_2008.pdf (accessed 16 October 2012).

European Parliament (2009) *Report on the Protection of Consumers, in Particular Minors, in Respect of the Use of Video Games*, Report no. 2008/2173(INI), Brussels: Committee on the Internal Market and Consumer Protection.

Fairclough, N. (1995) *Media Discourse*, London: Arnold.

Fenton, N. (2010) *New Media, Old News, Journalism and Democracy in the Digital Age*, London: Sage.

Fischer, C. S. (1992) *America Calling: A Social History of the Telephone to 1940*, Berkeley: University of California Press.

Florida, R. (2004) *The Rise of the Creative Class: And How it's Transforming Work, Leisure, Community and Everyday Life*, New York: Basic Books.

Fornäs, J. (1995) *Cultural Theory and Late Modernity*, London: Sage.

Friesen, N. and Hug, T. (2009) "The Mediatic Turn: Exploring Concepts for Media Pedagogy," in Lundby, K. (ed.) *Mediatization, Concept, Changes, Consequences*, New York: Peter Lang, pp. 63–83.

Fromm, E. (1941; 1965) *Escape From Freedom*, New York: Avon Books.

Galal, E. (2002) "Al-Jazeera – Borgerlig offentlighed i den arabiske medieverden" ("Al-Jazeera: Public Sphere in the Arab Media World"), in Qvortrup, L. (ed.) *Mediernes 11 September* (*The Media's 9/11*), Copenhagen: Gyldendal, pp. 101–15.

——(2008) "Magic Spells and Recitation Contests: The Quran as Entertainment on Arab Satellite Television," *Northern Lights: Film and Media Studies Yearbook* 6(1): 181–96.

Galal, E. and Spielhaus, R. (2012) "Covering the Arab Spring: Middle East in the Media – the Media in the Middle East," *Global Media Journal*, German Edition 2(1): 1–6.

Ghanem, S. (1997) "Filling in the Tapestry: The Second Level of Agenda-Setting," in McCombs, M., Shaw, D. L., and Weaver, D. (eds) *Communication and Democracy*, Mahwah, NJ: Lawrence Erlbaum, pp. 3–15.

Gibson, J. J. (1979) *The Ecological Approach to Visual Perception*, Boston: Houghton Mifflin.

Giddens, A. (1984) *The Constitution of Society*, Cambridge: Polity.

——(1990) *The Consequences of Modernity*, Cambridge: Polity.

——(1991) *Modernity and Self-identity*, Cambridge: Polity Press.

——(1992) *The Transformation of Intimacy: Sexuality, Love, and Eroticism in Modern Societies*, Palo Alto: Stanford University Press.

Gilhus, I. S. and Mikaelsson, L. (1998) *Kulturens refortrylling: Nyreligiøsitet i moderne samfunn* (*The Re-enchantment of Culture: New Religions in Modern Societies*), Oslo: Universitetsforlaget.

Gjøls-Andersen, P. (2001) "A Case Study of the Change of Brand Strategy in Lego from a Focus on the Famous Building Brick to Introducing a Broad Variety of Lego Products in the Children's Universe," Ph.D. series no. 18. 2001, Copenhagen: Copenhagen Business School.

Goffman, E. (1956) *The Presentation of Self in Everyday Life*, Edinburgh: University of Edinburgh.

Granovetter, M. (1973) "The Strength of Weak Ties," *American Journal of Sociology* 78(6): 1360–80.

Greimas, A. J. (1974) *Struktural Semantik* (*Structural Semantics*), Copenhagen: Borgen.

Gripsrud, J. and Weibull, L. (eds) (2010) *Media, Markets and Public Spheres*, Bristol: Intellect.

Gulati, G. J., Just, M. R., and Crigler, A. (2004) "News Coverage of Political Campaigns," in Kaid, L. L. (ed.) *Handbook of Political Communication Research*, Mahwah, NJ: Lawrence Erlbaum Associates, pp. 237–56.

Gunther, A. C. and Storey, J. D. (2003) "The Influence of Presumed Influence," *Journal of Communication* 35(2): 199–215.

Habermas, J. (1962; 1989) *The Structural Transformation of the Public Sphere*, Cambridge: Polity Press.

——(1990) "Vorwort" ("Introduction"), in Habermas, J. *Strukturwandel der Öffentlichkeit* (*The Structural Transformation of the Public Sphere*), Frankfurt: Suhrkamp, pp. 11–50.

Hallin, D. and Mancini, P. (2004) *Comparing Media Systems*, Cambridge: Cambridge University Press.

Hansen, O. S. (1997) *LEGO og Godtfred Kirk Christiansen (LEGO and Godtfred Kirk Christiansen)*, Frederiksberg: Bogfabrikken.

Hart, P. and Fairness & Accuracy in Reporting (FAIR) (2003) *The "Oh really?" Factor, Unspinning Fox News Channel's Bill O'Reilly*, New York: Seven Stories Press.

Hartley, J. (2009) "Journalism and Popular Culture," in Wahl-Jørgensen, K. and Hanitzsch, T. (eds) *The Handbook of Journalism Studies*, London: Routledge, pp. 310–24.

Hemmingsen, M. and Sigtenbjerggaard, M. (2008) "Tre i en: Rollen som politisk kommentator" ("Three in One: The Role as Political Commentator"), *Politik* 11(4): 72–83.

Hendershot, H. (1999) "Sesame Street: Cognition and Communications Imperialism," in Kinder, M. (ed.) *Kids' Media Culture*, Durham: Duke University Press, pp. 139–77.

Hepp, A. (2012) "Mediatization and the 'Moulding Force' of the Media," *Communications* 37(1): 1–28.

Hernes, G. (1978) "Det mediavridde samfunn" ("The Media-Twisted Society"), *Samtiden* 86(1): 1–14.

Hills, M. (2002) *Fan Cultures*, London: Routledge.

Hjarvard, S. (1999) *Tv-nyheder i konkurrence (Television News in Competition)*, Frederiksberg: Samfundslitteratur.

——(2001) "News Media and the Globalization of the Public Sphere," in Hjarvard, S. (ed.) *News in a Globalized Society*, Göteborg: Nordicom, pp. 17–39.

——(2002a) "Simulated Conversations: The Simulation of Interpersonal Communication in Electronic Media," in Jerslev, A. (ed.). *Realism and "Reality" in Film and Media*: Northern Lights 2002, Copenhagen: Museum Tusculanum Press, pp. 227–52.

——(2002b) "Seernes reality" ("The Audience's Reality"), *MedieKultur* 18(34): 92–109.

——(2003) "A Mediated World: The Globalization of Society and the Role of Media," in Hjarvard, S. (ed.) *Media in a Globalized Society*, Copenhagen: Museum Tusculanum Press, pp. 15–53.

——(2004a) "The Globalization of Language. How the Media Contribute to the Spread of English and the Emergence of Medialects," *Nordicom Review* 25(1–2): 75–97.

——(2004b) "From Bricks to Bytes. The Mediatization of a Global Toy Industry," in Bondebjerg, I. and Golding, P. (eds) *European Culture and the Media*, Bristol: Intellect, pp. 43–63.

——(2005) *Det selskabelige samfund (A Culture of Sociability)*, Frederiksberg: Samfundslitteratur.

——(2008a) "The Mediatization of Society, A Theory of the Media as Agents of Social and Cultural Change," *Nordicom Review* 29(2): 105–34.

——(2008b) "The Mediatization of Religion, A Theory of the Media as Agents of Religious Change," *Northern Lights 2008*, Bristol: Intellect.

——(2010a) "Die Mediendynamik der Mohammed-Karikaturen-Krisen" ("The Media Dynamics of the Mohammed Cartoon Crisis"), in Hepp, A., Höhn, M., and Wimmer, J. (eds) *Medienkultur im Wandel (Changing Media Culture)*, Konstanz: UVK Verlagsgesellschaft, pp. 169–80.

——(2010b) "The Views of the News: The Role of Political Newspapers in a Changing Media Landscape," *Northern Lights* 8(1): 25–48.

——(2011) "The Mediatization of Religion: Theorising Religion, Media and Social Change," *Culture and Religion* 12(2): 119–35.

——(2012a) "Three Forms of Mediatized Religion: Changing the Public Face of Religion," in Hjarvard, S. and Lövheim, M. (eds) *Mediatization and Religion: Nordic Perspectives*, Gothenburg: Nordicom, pp. 21–44.

——(2012b) "Media and Communication Studies in a Mediatized World," *Nordicom Review* 33(1): Supplement: 27–34.

Hjarvard, S. and Lövheim, M. (eds) (2012) *Mediatization and Religion: Nordic Perspectives*, Gothenburg: Nordicom.

Hobsbawm, J. and Lloyd, J. (2008) *The Power of the Commentariat*, London: Editorial Intelligence, Ltd.

Højsgaard, M. T. (2005) "Cyber-religion: On the Cutting Edge Between the Virtual and the Real," in Højsgaard, M. T. and Warburg, M. (eds) *Religion and Cyberspace*, London: Routledge, pp. 50–63.

Højsgaard, M. T. and Warburg, M. (eds) (2005) *Religion and Cyberspace*, London: Routledge.

Honneth, A. (1996) *The Struggle for Recognition: The Moral Grammar of Social Conflicts*, Cambridge: Polity Press.

Hoover, S., Clark, L. S., and Rainie, L. (2004) *Faith Online*, Washington, DC: Pew Internet and American Life Project. Online. Available at www.pewinternet.org/~/media/Files/Reports/2004/PIP_Faith_Online_2004.pdf.pdf (accessed 16 October 2012).

Hoover, S. M. (2006) *Religion in the Media Age*, London: Routledge.

Horkheimer, M. and Adorno, T. W. (1944; 1989) *Dialectic of Enlightenment*, London: Verso.

Horsfield, P. (forthcoming) "The Ecology of Writing and the Shaping of Early Christianity," in Lundby, K. (ed.) *Religion Across Media: From Early Antiquity to Late Modernity*, New York: Peter Lang.

Horten, G. (2011) "The Mediatization of War: A Comparison of the American and German Media Coverage of the Vietnam and Iraq Wars," *American Journalism* 28(4): 29–53.

Horton, D. and Wohl, R. (1956) "Mass Communication and Para-Social Interaction: Observation on Intimacy at a Distance," *Psychiatry* 19, pp. 215–29.

Høybye, A., Buchhace, B., Lund, M., and Wagner, S. (eds) (2007) *Politisk spin (Political Spin)*, Copenhagen: Akademisk.

Hughes, T. P. (1994) "Technological Momentum", in Smith, M. R. and L. Marx (eds) *Does Technology Drive History? The Dilemma of Technological Determinism*, Cambridge, MA: MIT Press, pp. 101–13.

Hutchby, I. (2001) "Technologies, Texts and Affordances," *Sociology* 35(2): 441–56.

——(2003) "Affordances and the Analysis of Technologically Mediated Interaction: A Response to Brian Rappert," *Sociology* 37(3): 581–89.

Hymowitz, K. (2000) *Ready or Not: Why Treating Children as Small Adults Endangers Their Future – and Ours*, San Francisco: Encounter Books.

Inglehart, R. (1990) *Culture Shift in Advanced Industrial Society*, Princeton, NJ: Princeton University Press.

Inglehart, R. and Welzel, C. (2005) *Modernization, Cultural Change, and Democracy – The Human Development Sequence*, Cambridge: Cambridge University Press.

Innis, H. A. (1951) *The Bias of Communication*, Toronto: University of Toronto Press.

James, J. D. (2010) *McDonaldisation, Masala McGospel, and Om Economics – Televangelism in Contemporary India*, New Delhi: Sage.

Jamieson, C. H. (1988) *Eloquence in an Electronic Age: The Transformation of Political Speechmaking*, Oxford: Oxford University Press.

Jenkins, H. (1992a) *Textual Poachers: Television Fans and Participatory Culture*, New York: Routledge.

——(1992b) "'Strangers No More, We Sing': Filking and the Social Construction of the Science Fiction Fan Community," in Lewis, L. (ed.) *The Adoring Audience: Fan Culture and Popular Media*, London: Routledge, pp. 208–37.

Jenkins, H. and Thorburn, D. (eds) (2003) *Democracy and New Media*, Cambridge, MA: MIT Press.

Jensen, K. B. (ed.) (2003) *Dansk mediehistorie (The History of Danish Media)*, vol. I–IV, Frederiksberg: Samfundslitteratur.

Jensen, K. B. (forthcoming) "Definitive and Sensitizing Conceptualizations of Mediatization," *Communication Theory*.

Jenssen, A. T. (2007) "Den medialiserte politikken" ("Mediatized Politics"), in Jenssen, A. T. and Aalberg, T. (eds) *Den medialiserte politikken (Mediatized Politics)*, Oslo: Universitetsforlaget, pp. 9–24.

Jenssen, A. T. and Aalberg, T. (eds) (2007) *Den medialiserte politikken (Mediatized Politics)*, Oslo: Universitetsforlaget.

John, D. R. (1999) "Consumer Socialization of Children: A Retrospective Look at Twenty-Five Years of Research," *Journal of Consumer Research* 26: 183–213.

Kaare, B. H. and Lundby, K. (2008) "Mediatized Lives. Autobiography and Assumed Authenticity in Digital Storytelling," in Lundby, K. (ed.) *Digital Storytelling, Mediatized Stories*, New York: Peter Lang, pp. 105–22.

Kahn, K. F. and Kenny, P. J. (2002) "The Slant of the News: How Editorial Endorsements Influence Campaign Coverage and Citizens' Views of Candidates," *American Political Science Review* 6(2): 381–94.

Karmark, E. (2002) "Organizational Identity in a Dualistic Subculture – A Case Study of Organizational Identity Formation in Lego Media International," Ph.D. series 22.2002. Copenhagen: Copenhagen Business School.

Kaun, A. (2011) "Mediatization versus Mediation: Contemporary Concepts under Scrutiny. Research Overview from Riksbankens Jubileumsfond," in Fornäs, J. and Kaun, A. (eds) *Medialisering av kultur, politik, vardag och forskning: Slutrapport från Riksbankens Jubileumsfonds forskarsymposium i Stockholm 18–19 augusti 2011 (Mediatization of Culture, Politics, Everyday Life and Research: Final Report from Riksbankens Jubileumsfond's Research Symposium in Stockholm, 18–19 August 2011)*, Södertörn: Medierstudier vid Södertörn, pp. 16–38. Online. Available at http://urn.kb.se/resolve?urn=urn:nbn:se:sh:diva-12829 (accessed 28 June 2012).

Kitch, C. (2003) "Mourning in America: Ritual, Redemption, and Recovery in News Narrative after September 11," *Journalism Studies* 4(2): 213–24.

Kline, S. (1993) *Out of the Garden. Toys, TV, and Children's Culture in the Age of Marketing*, London: Verso.

——(1995a) "The Play of the Market: On the Internationalization of Children's Culture," *Theory, Culture & Society* 12(2): 103–29.

——(1995b) "The Promotion and Marketing of Toys: Time to Rethink the Paradox?" in Pellegrini, A. D. (ed.) *The Future of Play Theory*, Albany: State University of New York Press, pp. 165–87.

——(1999) "Toys as Media: The Role of Toy Design, Promotional TV and Mother's Reinforcement in the Young Males (3–6) Acquisition of Pro-social Play Scripts for *Rescue Hero* Action Toys," paper presented to the ITRA Conference in Halmstadt, Sweden.

Koch, H. (1945) *Hvad er demokrati? (What is Democracy?)*, Copenhagen: Samvirke serien.

Kristensen, N. N. (2000) "Journalistik som profession: Om journalistens rolleplacering i et professionssociologisk perspektiv" ("Journalism as a Profession: On the Role of the Journalist Seen from the Sociology of Profession"), in *Sekvens 2000: Årbog for Film-& Medievidenskab*, Copenhagen: University of Copenhagen, pp. 159–84.

——(2006) "Spin in the Media – the Media in a (Self-) Spin?" *Tidsskriftet Politik* 9(2): 54–63.

Kristiansen, K. K. (1978) "Indlæg til Marts-konferencen" ("Contribution at March Conference"). March 7, 1978. Billund: LEGO.

Krotz, F. (2007a) *Mediatisierung: Fallstudien zum Wandel von Kommunikation (Mediatization: Case Studies of Communicative Change)*, Wiesbaden: VS Verlag für Socialwissenschaften.

——(2007b) "The Meta-Process of Mediatization as a Conceptual Frame," *Global Media and Communication* 3(3): 256–60.

——(2009) "Mediatization: A Concept with Which to Grasp Media and Societal Change," in Lundby, K. (ed.) *Mediatization: Concept, Changes, Consequences*, New York: Peter Lang, pp. 21–40.

Kunelius, R., Eide, E., Hahn, O., and Schrøder, R. (eds) (2007) *Reading the Mohammed Cartoons Controversy*, Bochum/Freiburg: Projekt Verlag.

Langer, A. I. (2007) "A Historical Exploration of the Personalisation of Politics in the Print Media: The British Prime Ministers (1945–99)," *Parliamentary Affairs* 60(3): 371–87.

——(2010) "The Politicization of Private Persona: Exceptional Leaders or the New Rule? The Case of United Kingdom and the Blair Effect," *International Journal of Press/Politics* 15(1): 60–76.

Lauwaert, M. (2007) "The Place of Play: On Toys, Technological Innovations and Geographies of Play", Ph.D. dissertation, Maastricht: Maastricht University.

Lazarsfeld, P. F., Berelson, B., and Gaudet, H. (1944) *The People's Choice: How the Voter Makes Up His Mind in a Presidential Campaign*, New York: Columbia University Press.

LEGO (1982) *50 år i leg (Fifty Years in Play)*, Billund: LEGO.

Lewis, J. (ed.) (2003) *The Encyclopaedic Sourcebook of UFO Religion*, New York: Prometheus Books.

Liebes, T. and Katz, E. (1990) *The Export of Meaning, Cross-Cultural Readings of Dallas*, New York: Oxford University Press.

Lindhardt, J. (2004) "Overtro er det glade vrøvl" ("Superstition is Sheer Nonsense"), *Dagbladet Politiken*, 3 January.

Ling, R. (2008) *New Tech, New Ties, How Mobile Communication is Reshaping Social Cohesion*, Cambridge, MA: The MIT Press.

Lippmann, W. (1922; 1992) *Public Opinion*, New York: Free Press.

——(1925; 1993) *The Phantom Public*, Brunswick, NJ: Transaction Publishers.

Livingstone, S. (2009) "On the Mediation of Everything: ICA Presidential Address 2008," *Journal of Communication* 59(1): 1–18.

Livingstone, S., Haddon, L., Görzig, A., and Ólafsson, K. (2011) *Risks and Safety on the Internet: The Perspective of European Children. Full Findings*, London: LSE, EU Kids Online Network. Available at www2.lse.ac.uk/media@lse/research/EUKidsOnline/EU%20Kids%20Online%20reports.aspx (accessed 13 June 2012).

Lövheim, M. (2005) "A Space Set Apart? Young People Exploring the Sacred on the Internet," in Sumiala-Seppänen, J., Lundby, K., and Salokangas, R. (eds) *Implications of the Sacred in (Post)Modern Media*, Gothenburg: Nordicom, pp. 255–72.

——(2008) "Rethinking Cyberreligion? Teens, Religion, and the Internet in Sweden," *Nordicom Review* 29(2): 205–17.

——(2012) "A Voice of Their Own: Young Muslim Women, Blogs and Religion," in Hjarvard, S. and Lövheim, M. (eds) *Mediatization and Religion: Nordic Perspectives*, Gothenburg: Nordicom, pp. 129–45.

Lövheim, M. and Axner, M. (2011) "Halal-TV: Negotiating the Place of Religion in Swedish Public Discourse," *Nordic Journal of Religion and Society* 24(1): 57–74.

Lövheim, M. and Lynch, G. (2011) "The Mediatisation of Religion Debate: An Introduction," *Culture and Religion* 12(2): 111–17.

Lowenthal, L. (1961) *Literature, Popular Culture, and Society*, Englewood Cliffs: Prentice-Hall.

Lull, J. (1990) *Inside Family Viewing, Ethnographic Research on Television's Audiences*, London: Routledge.

Lund, A. B. (2004) "Niche Nursing Political Networks: Priming and Framing before Spinning," *Modinet Working Paper* no. 9, University of Copenhagen. Online. Available at www.modinet.dk/pdf/WorkingPapers/No9_Niche_Nursing_Political_Networks.pdf (accessed 4 April 2012).

Lundby, K. (2009a) "Introduction: 'Mediatization' as Key," in Lundby, K. (ed.) *Mediatization: Concept, Changes, Consequences*, New York: Peter Lang, pp. 1–18.

——(2009b) "Media Logic: Looking for Social Interaction," in Lundby, K. (ed.) *Mediatization: Concept, Changes, Consequences*, New York: Peter Lang, pp. 101–19.

Lundby, K. and Lövheim, M. (eds) (forthcoming) Special issue on religion and media of *Nordic Journal of Religion and Society*, 26(1), 2013.

Lyengar, L. and Hahn, K. S. (2009) "Red Media, Blue Media: Evidence of Ideological Selectivity in Media Use," *Journal of Communication* 59(1): 19–39.

Lynch, G. (2011) "What Can We Learn from the Mediatization of Religion Debate?" *Culture and Religion* 12(2): 203–10.

Maarek, P. J. (2011) *Campaign Communication and Political Marketing*, Oxford: Wiley-Blackwell.

McCombs, M. (2004) *Setting the Agenda: The Mass Media and Public Opinion*, Cambridge: Polity.

McLuhan, M. (1964) *Understanding Media: The Extensions of Man*, London: Routledge and Kegan Paul.

McManus, J. (1994) *Market-driven Journalism: Let the Citizens Beware?* Thousand Oaks, CA: Sage.

McNair, B. (2000) *Journalism and Democracy: An Evaluation of the Political Public Sphere*, London: Routledge.

Maffesoli, M. (1996) *The Time of the Tribes*, London: Sage.

March, J. G. and Olsen, J. P. (1989) *Rediscovering Institutions: The Organizational Basis of Politics*, New York: The Free Press.

Martin-Barbero, J. (1997) "Mass Media as a Site of Resacralization of Contemporary Culture," in Hoover, S. and Lundby, K. (eds) *Rethinking Media, Religion and Culture*, Thousand Oaks, CA: Sage, pp. 102–16.

Marwick, A. E. and Danah, B. (2010) "I Tweet Honestly, I Tweet Passionately: Twitter Users, Context Collapse, and the Imagined Audience," *New Media & Society* 13(1): 114–33.

Mazzoleni, G. and Schulz, W. (1999) "'Mediatization' of Politics: A Challenge for Democracy?" *Political Communication* 16(3): 247–61.

Meisenhelder, T. (2006). "From Character to Habitus in Sociology," *The Social Science Journal* 43(1): 55–66.

Merton, R. K. (1946; 1971) *Mass Persuasion: The Social Psychology of a War Bond Drive*, Westport, CT: Greenwood Press.

——(1957) *Social Theory and Social Structure*, Glencoe, IL: Free Press.

Meyer, B., and Moors, A. (2006) "Introduction," in Meyer, B. and Moors, A. (eds) *Religion, Media, and the Public Sphere*, Bloomington: Indiana University Press, pp. 1–25.

Meyrowitz, J. (1986) *No Sense of Place: The Impact of Electronic Media on Social Behavior*, New York: Oxford University Press.

——(1993) "Images of Media: Hidden Ferment – and Harmony – in the Field," *Journal of Communication* 43(3): 55–66.

Middleton, R. (1990) *Studying Popular Music*, Milton Keynes: Open University Press.

Møller, T. and Kiellberg, J. (2011) "Kommentatorer fylder mere og mere" ("Commentators Are Used Ever More Frequently"), InfoMedia analysis reproduced in *Politiken*, 14 October.

Morley, D. (2000) *Home Territories, Media, Mobility and Identity*, London: Routledge.

Murdock, G. (1997) "The Re-Enchantment of the World: Religion and the Transformations of Modernity," in Hoover, S. M. and Lundby, K. (eds) *Rethinking Media, Religion and Culture*, London: Sage, pp. 85–101.

——(2008) "Re-Enchantment and the Popular Imagination: Fate, Magic and Purity," *Northern Lights. Film and Media Studies Yearbook* 6: 27–44.

Mutz, D. C. (1989) "The Influence of Perceptions of Media Influence: Third Person Effects and the Public Expression of Opinions," *International Journal of Public Opinion Research* 1(1): 3–23.

Negrine, R. (2008) *The Transformation of Political Communication: Continuities and Changes in Media and Politics*, Basingstoke: Palgrave.

Nimmo, D. and Combs, J. E. (1992) *The Political Pundits*, New York: Praeger.

Norman, D. (1990) *The Design of Everyday Things*, New York: Doubleday.

Norris, P. (2000) *A Virtuous Circle: Political Communications in Postindustrial Societies*, Cambridge: Cambridge University Press.

Norris, P. and Inglehart, R. (2004) *Sacred and Secular: Religion and Politics Worldwide*, Cambridge: Cambridge University Press.

Ong, W. J. (1982) *Orality and Literacy: The Technologizing of the Word*, London: Methuen.

Örnebring, M. (2009) "The Two Professionalisms of Journalism: Journalism and the Changing Context of Work," Working Paper, Reuters Institute for the Study of Journalism, University of Oxford. Online. Available at: http://reutersinstitute.politics.ox.ac.uk/Fileadmin/documents/publications/The_Two_Proffessionalisms_of_Journalism_Working_Paper.pdf. (accessed 30 November 2012).

Ørsten, M. (2005) "Nyhedsinstitutionen: Et ny-institutionelt perspektiv på den medierede politiske kommunikation" ("The News Institution: A Neo-Institutional Perspective on Mediated Political Communication"), *Økonomi & Politik* 78(3): 13–28.

Orton, J. D. and Weick, K. E. (1990) "Loosely Coupled Systems: A Reconceptualization," *Academy of Management Review* 15(2): 203–23.

Palmer, J. (2000) *Spinning into Control*, London: Leicester University Press.

Partridge, C. (2008) "The Occultural Significance of 'The Da Vinci Code'", *Northern Lights. Film and Media Studies Yearbook 2008* 6(1): 107–26.

Peck, J. (1993) *The Gods of Televangelism: The Crisis of Meaning and the Appeal of Religious Television*, Cresskill, NJ: Hampton Press.

Pedersen, P. T. (ed.) (1964) *TV – tør vi? (Television – Do We Dare?)*, Copenhagen: Høst og Søns Forlag.

Petersen, L. N. (2010) "American Television Fiction Transforming Danish Teenagers' Religious Imaginations," *Communications* 35(3): 229–47.

——(2012) "Danish 'Twilight' Fandom: Transformative Processes of Religion," in Hjarvard, S. and Lövheim, M. (eds) *Mediatization and Religion: Nordic Perspectives*, Gothenburg: Nordicom, pp. 163–82.

Pew Research Center (2010) "New Media, Old Media. How Blogs and Social Media Agendas Relate and Differ from Traditional Press," Report from the Pew Research Center's Project for Excellence in Journalism, May 23. Online. Available at http://pewresearch.org/pubs/1602/new-media-review-differences-from-traditional-press (accessed 3 May 2012).

Plummer, K. (2003) *Intimate Citizenship: Private Decisions and Public Dialogues*, Seattle: University of Washington Press.

Postman, N. (1982) *The Disappearance of Childhood*, New York: Delacorte Press.

Poulsen, P. T. (1993) *LEGO – en virksomhed og dens sjæl (LEGO – A Company and its Soul)*, Copenhagen: Schultz.

Preiss, R. W., Gayle, B. M., Burrell, N., Allen, M., and Bryant, J. (2007) *Mass Media Effects Research – Advances Through Meta-Analysis*, Mahwah, NJ: Lawrence Erlbaum.

Preston, P. (2009) *Making the News: Journalism and News Cultures in Europe*, London: Routledge.

Pyssiäinen, I. and Anttonen, V. (eds) (2002) *Current Approaches in the Cognitive Science of Religion*, London: Continuum.

Reich, W. (1933; 1978) *The Mass Psychology of Fascism*, London: Penguin.

Richards, J., Wilson, S., and Woodhead, L. (eds) (1999) *Diana: The Making of a Media Saint*, London: I. B. Tauris Publishers.

Riesman, D. (1950) *The Lonely Crowd: A Study of the Changing American Character*, New Haven: Yale University Press.

——(1969) *The Lonely Crowd: A Study of the Changing American Character*, abbreviated edition with a new preface, New Haven: Yale University Press.

Ritzer, G. (1999) *Enchanting a Disenchanted World: Revolutionizing the Means of Consumption*, Thousand Oaks, CA: Pine Forge Press.

Robins, K. (2003) "Beyond Imagined Community? Transnational Media and Turkish Migrants in Europe," in Hjarvard, S. (ed.) *Media in a Globalized Society*, Copenhagen: Museum Tusculanum Press, pp. 187–205.

Rödder, S. and Schäfer, M. S. (2010) "Repercussions and Resistance, an Empirical Study of the Interrelation Between Science and Mass Media," *Communications* 35(3): 249–67.

Rogers, E. M. and Dearing, J. W. (1987) "Agenda-setting Research: Where Has It Been, Where is it Going?", in Anderson, J. A. (ed.) *Communication Yearbook* 11, Newbury Park, CA: Sage, pp. 555–94.

Rosenfeldt, M. P. (2007) "Hvor meget fylder religion?" ("How Much Space does Religion Take Up?"), *Kritisk Forum for Praktisk Teologi* 109 (October), Copenhagen: Anis, pp. 31–47.

Rothenbuhler, E. (1998) *Ritual Communication: From Everyday Conversation to Mediated Ceremony*, London: Sage.

Rothstein, M. (2000) *UFOer og rumvæsener: Myten om de flyvende tallerkener (UFOs and Aliens: The Myth of the Flying Saucers)*, Copenhagen: Gyldendal.

Roux, B. L., Rouanet, H., Savage, M., and Warde, A. (2007) *Class and Cultural Division in the UK*, CRESC Working Paper Series, no. 40. Manchester: University of Manchester.

Ryfe, D. and Ørsten, M. (2011) "Introduction, Special Issue: Journalism as an Institution, *Journalism* 12(1): 3–9.

Scannell, P. (1988) "Radio Times: The Temporal Arrangements of Broadcasting in the Modern World," in Drummond P. and Paterson, R. (eds) *Television and its Audience*, London: BFI, pp. 15–31.

Scannell, P. (1996) *Radio, Television and Modern Life*, Oxford: Blackwell.
——(2000) "For-Anyone-As-Someone Structures," *Media, Culture & Society* 22(1): 5–24.
Schlesinger, P. (1978) *Putting "Reality" Together*, BBC News, London: Constable.
Schudson, M. (1978) *Discovering the News: A Social History of American Newspapers*, New York: Basic Books.
——(1997) "Why Democracy is Not the Soul of Democracy," *Critical Studies in Mass Communication* 14(4): 297–309.
Schultz, I. (2006) *Bagom nyhederne – værdier, idealer og praksis (Behind the News: Values, Ideals and Practice)*, Frederiksberg: Samfundslitteratur.
Schulz, W. (2004) "Reconstructing Mediatization as an Analytical Concept," *European Journal of Communication* 19(1): 87–101.
Searle, J. R. (1969) *Speech Acts: An Essay in the Philosophy of Language*, Cambridge: Cambridge University Press.
Sennett, R. (1998) *The Corrosion of Character. The Personal Consequences of Work in the New Capitalism*, New York: W. W. Norton & Company.
Silverstone, R. (2007) *Media and Morality: On the Rise of the Mediapolis*, Cambridge: Polity.
Simmel, G. (1971) "Sociability," in Levine, D. N. (ed.) *On Individuality and Social Forms*, Chicago: The University of Chicago Press.
Sky, J. (2006) "Harry Potter and Religious Mediatization," in Sumiala-Seppänen, J., Lundby, K., and Salokangas, R. (eds) *Implications of the Sacred in (Post)Modern Media*, Gothenburg: Nordicom, pp. 235–54.
Stern, S. L. and Schoenhaus, T. (1990) *Toyland. The High-Stakes Game of the Toy Industry*, Chicago: Contemporary Books.
Storsul, T. (2011) "Deliberation or Self-Presentation? – Young People, Politics and Social Media". Paper presented to the Media, Culture, Society Division, Nordic Conference on Media and Communication Research, Nordmedia 2011.
Strömbäck, J. (2008) "Four Phases of Mediatization: An Analysis of the Mediatization of Politics," *International Journal of Press/Politics* 13(3): 228–46.
——(2011) "Mediatization and Perceptions of the Media's Political Influence," *Journalism Studies* 12(4): 423–39.
Sutton-Smith, B. (1986) *Toys as Culture*, New York: Gardner Press.
Taylor, C. (2007) *A Secular Age*, Cambridge: Belknap Press of Harvard University Press.
Thompson, J. B. (1990) *Ideology and Modern Culture*, Cambridge: Polity Press.
——(1995) *The Media and Modernity: A Social Theory of the Media*, Cambridge: Polity Press.
——(2000) *Political Scandal. Power and Visibility in the Media Age*, Cambridge: Polity Press.
Tomlinson, J. (1999) *Globalization and Culture*, Cambridge: Polity Press.
Tuchman, G. (1972) "Objectivity as Strategic Ritual: An Examination of Newsmen's Notion of Objectivity," *American Journal of Sociology* 77(4): 660–79.
Tunstall, J. (2007) *The Media were American: U.S. Mass Media in Decline*, Oxford: Oxford University Press.
Väliverronen, E. (2001) "From Mediation to Mediatization: The New Politics of Communicating Science and Biotechnology," in Kivikuru, U. and Savolainen, T. (eds) *The Politics of Public Issues*, Helsinki: Department of Communication, University of Helsinki, pp. 132–56.
Wahl-Jorgensen, K. (2008) "Op-ed pages," in Franklin, B. (ed.) *Pulling Newspapers Apart, Analyzing Print Journalism*, London: Routledge, pp. 70–79.
Wasko, J. (2001) *Understanding Disney, The Manufacture of Fantasy*, Cambridge: Polity Press.
——(2008) "The Commodification of Youth Culture," in Drotner, K. and Livingstone, S. (eds) *The International Handbook of Children, Media and Culture*, London: Sage, pp. 460–75.
——(2010) "Children's Virtual Worlds: The Latest Commercialization of Children's Culture," in Buckingham, D. and Tingstad, V. (eds) *Childhood and Consumer Culture*, Basingstoke: Palgrave Macmillan, pp. 113–29.
Weber, M. (1904; 2001) *The Protestant Ethic and the Spirit of Capitalism*, London: Routledge.
Weingart, P. (1998) "Science and the Media," *Research Policy* 27(8): 869–79.

Welch, B. (2008) *State of Confusion, Political Manipulation and the Assault on the American Mind*, New York: Thomas Dunne Books.

Willig, I. (2010) "Constructing the Audience: A Study of the Segmentation of the Danish Press," *Northern Lights* 8(1): 93–114.

Wolf, M. J. (1999) *The Entertainment Economy*, London: Penguin.

Wouters, C. (2011) "How Civilizing Processes Continued: Towards an Informalization of Manners and a Third Nature Personality," in Gabriel, N. and Mennell, S. (eds) *Norbert Elias and Figurational Research: Processual Thinking in Sociology*, Oxford: Blackwell, pp. 140–59.

Ziehe, T. (1989) *Ambivalenser og mangfoldighed* (*Ambivalences and Diversity*), Copenhagen: Politisk Revy.

Website

www.lego.com

INDEX

www.routledge.com/media

Related titles from Routledge

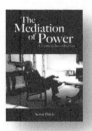

The Mediation of Power

By **Aeron Davis**, Goldsmiths,
University of London, UK

The Mediation of Power investigates how those in positions of power
use and are influenced by media in their everyday activities. Each
chapter examines this theme through an exploration of some of the
key topics and debates in the field, including:

- theories of media and power
- media policy and the economics of information
- news production and journalistic practice
- public relations and media management
- culture and power
- political communication and mediated politics
- new and alternative media
- interest group communications
- media audiences and effects.

The debates are enlivened by first-hand accounts taken from over
200 high-profile interviews with politicians, journalists, public
officials, spin doctors, campaigners and captains of industry. Tim Bell,
David Blunkett, Iain Duncan Smith, Simon Heffer, David Hill,
Simon Hughes, Trevor Kavanagh, Neil Kinnock, Peter Riddell,
Polly Toynbee, Michael White and Ann Widdecombe are some of
those cited.

232pp
Hb: 978-0-415-40490-7
Pb: 978-0-415-40491-4